CLIMB MARYLAND!

Mark "Indy" Kochte

DogDays
Graphics

PUBLISHING DIVISION
Washington Grove, Maryland

CLIMB MARYLAND!

Published by Dog Days Graphics, LLC.
P.O. Box 1353
Washington Grove MD 20880 USA

ISBN: 0-9663431-3-1

Book Design by Marida Hines

Copy editing, photoretouching, and book production by Dog Days Graphics, L.L.C.

Printed in Canada

Front Cover Photo: Scott Haines on Hard Up (5.8) at Maryland Heights
Back Cover Photo: The author on Dreaming Real (5.7) at Annapolis Rocks

This book is dedicated to all climbers in search of

adventure, discovery, and rock to climb.

Remember: live the journey. For each destination

is merely a doorway to the next journey.

Crag Map of Maryland

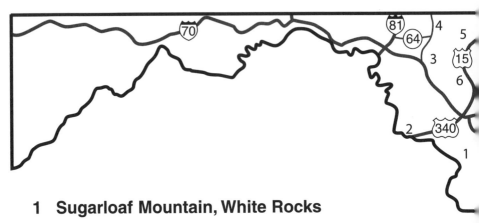

1 Sugarloaf Mountain, White Rocks

2 Weverton Overlook, Maryland Heights

3 Annapolis Rocks, Black Rock

4 Raven Rock Hollow

5 Wolf Rock

6 Right Fork Rock, Left Fork Rock, White Rock

7 The Fin, Bunker Hill

8 Raven Rocks

9 Rocks State Park

10 Route 1 Rock

11 Leakin Park

12 Ilchester, Friction Wall

13 Alberton Rock, Woodstock Rock

14 Carderock & Great Falls, Maryland

Contents

Why This Guide?

"It's about time somebody made a guide to this place."
—**Anonymous climber at Rocks State Park**

T here exists very little historically documented information on climbing in central Maryland—at least for the current generations of climbers.

Prior to 1990 there were only a few guidebooks available to local climbers. In the early '70s a D.C. climbing group put out a small publication of climbing around the Susquehanna River. A homegrown guide to Rocks State Park was distributed between local climbers of that area in the '70s to '80s (an online guide to Rocks State Park—as well as some other areas along the Susquehanna in Pennsylvania and Maryland—appeared in the mid '90s, put up by Ed Mistarka).

In the early to mid 80s several guidebooks to the area appeared. John Gregory published a small guide to Carderock (later supplanted by a more encompassing guide by PATC in 1990). PATC published a guide to the Great Falls of Virginia and Maryland (the guide to Great Falls by Marida Hines published in the late 90s covered only the Virginia side of life and therefore is out of the scope of this guide). And Rob & Kathy Canter put out several editions of *"Nearby Climbing Areas,"* a multi-state mini-guide with little or no real route descriptions (their third edition covered Maryland, Virginia, Pennsylvania, and a little of West virginia, and was eight pages long). This guide utterly vanished after only a few years.

Rob Savoye, one of several people who did a lot to help in the development of local crags near Baltimore, put together a photocopied guide to Maryland Heights, last updated in 1985. This rag guide was handed out to visiting climbers by the Park Service at the Harpers Ferry ranger station. Until recently they didn't keep a permanent copy in their archive, though Rob did make the same information available on the Internet by the late '80s/early '90s (where the Park Service picked up their new copies). He also put online a sketchy guide—ten routes and bad ASCII art (as if most ASCII art is good!)—to Annapolis Rocks. At the same time George King and members of the Open Sky Adventurers group were working on a home-grown guide to the Frederick Watershed area. But alas, it never made it out to the climbing community.

In 1990 a sparse guide (with almost no route info) to the rock and ice climbs of the D.C. area was apparently put out by Hukum & Skruum Publishers (but I never saw hide nor hair of the existence of this guide in final form, only a draft manuscript). In the early '90s John Kelbel put out a one-page guide to Leakin Park, as well as a small guide to Woodstock Rock. Other guidebooks that covered larger areas (such as *"The Climbers Guide To North America (East)"* by John Harlin III in 1986 and Tim Tuola's *"Rock 'n' Road"* climbing atlas for North America in 1995) touched on Maryland climbing, but rarely did more than mention some areas, or concentrated specifically on the fact that Great Falls/Carderock existed.

And finally, in the summer of 2001, a flurry of guidebooks for Maryland climbing hit the stands. First off, PATC's second edition of their *"Climbers' Guide to the Great Falls of the Potomac"* made it out on the market. Then Eric Hörst's long awaited guide, *"Rock*

Climbing: Virginia, West Virginia, Maryland" hit the stores, covering Maryland climbing in more detail (amusingly enough, it was available in Colorado long before many of the Maryland retailers got ahold of it). However, it didn't cover **everything**; it was a "best of," after all. Eric's book was followed closely by Robert Borotkanics' guide *"Carderock Big Wall: The Ultimate Guide to Rock Climbing at Carderock."* However, of these new guides, only Eric's covered more than the Carderock/Great Falls area.

When I first moved to Baltimore in 1988 I scoured the area looking for the local climbing areas and guidebooks. The two Carderock books and the PATC Great Falls book were the only ones available in stores, Rob Savoye's two guides were available online, and John Kelbel's two rags were being passed between other local climbers of the Baltimore area. The Rocks State Park rag guide had vanished, as well as most all the other earlier-mentioned guides. Thus most any place that did not have a published guide, route and climbing information was handed down from one generation of climbers to the next by word of mouth. Sometimes route information was lost in the transition, but for the most part, especially in areas with a high population density of climbers (such as Ilchester), the information remained relatively intact (although in researching the route information for this guide it became clear that there were growing discrepancies between what different people knew or thought about some routes—a consequence of the "word of mouth" method of passing information along). However, in areas with smaller or looser-knit climbing communities, much if not all of the historical climbing information was lost in obscurity. Newer generations of climbers in those areas did not get the information on routes previously established by earlier generations, so had to go it alone.

So, why this guide? The reasons are twofold. To begin with, it is meant to compile as much of the central Maryland climbing information as possible into one volume. Every effort has been made to verify the accuracy of routes and ratings, but as noted above, with some areas having never documented the historical information, route names will very likely have changed between the original pioneers and successive generations of climbers. It is hoped this guide will get out as much historical information to the regional climbers as possible. With luck it may even draw out some of the lost historical information from days gone by.

Secondly, it is meant to bring you on a journey. There is a lot of climbing in Maryland, far more than you might expect. Use this as an opportunity to travel away from your backyard crag and explore other areas in Maryland.

Mark Kochte

..

Acknowledgements

"Trailhead, man, I ain't no alpine climber!"—Chris 'Dr. ASCII' Weaver

The list of people who have helped in the ultimate creation of this guidebook, from the online guide in the early '90s to present, is too vast to keep complete track of. I have tried to maintain that list, but names have fallen through the cracks. For that I do apologize. The following are some of the key players who contributed to the guide in ways small and large. None of this would have been possible without their help and input.

Chris Anderson, Jon Aurnou, Chris Bender, Eddie Bergeron, Heather Bradbury, Bob Brundige, Sharon Busching, Lee & Jason Carpenter, George "Mosca Man" Chapman, Vanessa Char, Melanie Chang & members of The Betty Alliance, Jen Christensen, Chris Claytor, Eric Cook, Pat Cowen, Nick Crowhurst, Dave Crowther, George "Geode" Cummings, Anna Custo, Charles Danforth, Corinne Derderian, Pierre Dery, Pat Dingle, Ronald Drimmel, Ayris Falasca, Dave Fay, Robert Fenichel, George Fischer, Jef Franchere, Leslie Goldberg, Scott Haines, Margy Horan, Eric Hörst, Marian Iannuzzi, Noam Izenberg, Sharon Jacob, Bill Januszweski, Larry Johnson, Christian Kammer, Kristen Keefe, Mark Kenney, Nichole King, Krista Klapp, Mike Klein, Lisa Kreppel, Cat Lazaroff, Gary Lay, Jackie Lockhart, Dave Mackintosh, Toby Marchand, Scott McClurg, Clark Merrill, Pete Moisiuk, Don Mullis, Greg Nerses, Mark "Aqua" Neubauer, Andy Nichols, David Nugent, Stephanie Owings, Bob Ozgar, Brian Poore, Jody "Diesel" Powell, Heather Preston, Gabriele Rechbauer, Jim Reger, Merle Reinhart, Rafi Reyes, Lee Roderiguez, Jim Rose, Peter "Guns" Salon, Eileen Schjelderup, Dan Schmidt, Bob Scott, Robert Scumaci, Wynn & Anna Segal, Mike Seyedin, Ilana Stern, Daniela Stricklin, Karl Sumwalt, Ellen Swartz, Aaron Teske, Ashton Treadway, Alex Uy, Brian Walker, and Chris "Dr. ASCII" Weaver.

A special thanks to Donna Childress for her extensive help and sacrifice in editing nearly every chapter of this book. You have no idea how much work she did. And major thanks to Anne "Deimos" Gonnella for helping me out a lot with the road maps. That was a headache she thoroughly enjoyed.

Thanks to Rob Savoye, Joe McManus, Mike Carroll, and John Kelbel for providing a wealth of information of the climbing history in Baltimore.

I'd also like to thank Marida Hines of Dog Days Graphics for suggesting the idea of taking the website and turning it into a Real Book.

And thanks to my love, Fabrizia Guglielmetti, for her patience, understanding and support when we **didn't** take road trips so I could work on this guide.

Finally, I want to thank Ken Jacquot and Ed Van Otteren, who, back in the spring of 1983 dragged me kicking and screaming into the world of rock climbing. If they hadn't, who knows what different sort of trouble I'd be in, or causing.

Warning!

"See you guys at the bottom!"—Unknown partyer at the top of the West View Rocks of Sugarloaf Mountain just before leaping off; he somehow managed to survive.

T his is the part I hate to write, as most people **should** have enough common sense to **know** this stuff already. However, there are more examples than I care to think about out there on the rocks of people who are…well, in a word, stupid.

CAUTION

CLIMBERS HAVE BEEN SERIOUSLY INJURED WHILE ATTEMPTING TO FREE CLIMB IN THIS AREA

Hey! Hello! Yes, You! *Rock climbing is a dangerous activity!*

You do it, you take full responsibility for any consequences that happen, like falling, hitting the ground, abrasions, rope entanglements, injuries and stuff, even death. This guide will not help you climb any better, or safer. This is not an instruction in how to climb. This book is merely a resource for locating areas where climbing is **possible**. It is for reading purposes only. Any use beyond that means you have unconditionally agreed to accept full responsibility for whatever results from your actions. Any use of this guide for climbing means you, the reader (no matter what your skill level may be), release the author, the publisher, the seller, and any other providers of this information from any and all liability, including death, that may result. Gravity sucks. Learn it, live it, love it. You have been warned.

Ayris Falasca and Phil Hodge practicing counterweight rappel rescue technique at Boy Scout Ledges, Sugarloaf Mountain.

How To Use This Guide

"If climbing is not a spectator sport, what is the belayer supposed to do?"—**Scott 'No-Chalk' McClurg after an afternoon of aiding.**

The routes in this guide are described using a combination of text and (in most cases) topo photos and maps. There are topo photos for 90 percent of the routes, and most of these photos will be found close to the route description, usually either on the same page or on the facing page. Routes will be described either left to right or right to left as seems most logical when you approach the rocks for a given chapter. The direction of the descriptions will be noted at the start of the "Routes" section. Use of overview maps and topo photos should help the process. You will find on pages *iv* and *v* in the front of this book a state map indicating the relative locations of the climbing areas covered herein.

The area chapters will be in the following format:

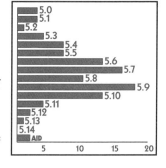

■ A **ratings breakdown graph**, indicating the number of routes and variations of a given rating in this area (so you can quickly decide if the area might be of interest to you if you are looking for a specific level of climbs to play on—and won't waste your time by going someplace that has nothing for you!)

■ A **set of icons** to quickly describe some aspects of the area. The icons include:

   Boot, shoe, teva—indicate how rough, moderate, or easy the trails are to the rocks. Also an arbitrary indicator of how long the trail(s) might be. You will need to use your own judgement for what footwear **you** will wear, though!

 Canoe—you will need some sort of water transportation to access some of the routes in this area.

 Helmet—usually recommended if there is considerable danger of rockfall in the area.

 Nut—there is multi-pitch climbing here; also, this will indicate if there are good single-pitch routes to lead as well (check the route details for further information).

 Bolt—notes that there is at least one bolted route in this area.

 Etrier—indicates that there are some aid routes to play on here.

 Binoculars—scenic views or overlooks (not that you **need** binoculars, mind you!)

■ An **introduction**, containing a brief bit of information on the area.

■ **Location and directions**, describing how to get to the crag in question—but not necessarily each and every way possible. Some of the directions are somewhat Baltimore-centric. But that's what the maps are for. There generally will be two to three maps for each area, showing you how to get to the crags. Each area will have a large-scale road map. After this will be a "close-in" scale map showing the parking and the trailhead (if applicable); these will be in the directions section. Finally, some areas will have a detailed overview map of the rocks themselves (notably places like Sugarloaf Mountain and Annapolis Rocks). These maps will be in with the route descriptions (kinda silly to put them elsewhere, no?)

■ Some **geology of the crag.** Maryland is an extremely geologically diverse state! If this sort of thing interests you and you thirst for more, I suggest paying a visit to the Maryland Geologic Survey on St. Paul Street in Baltimore and excavating the dusty tomes in their library. The toll free number is 1-877-620-8DNR (8367). I could have gone into dissertations for each area, but this is a climbing book, not a geology book.

■ **An equipment section** to discuss what you would generally need for setting up top-rope systems in this area. Occasionally there will be notes about other equipment (such as lead gear).

■ A note about whether or not there is **camping allowed** at this crag, or in the immediate area.

■ A brief comment about any **potential restrictions and access issues** you may have to deal with.

■ Where the (relatively close) **local places to get food** are (I don't know about you, but I get hungry after a long day of climbing!)

■ Another section that forms a "catch-all" for any further information you may need or want to know about an area, including **history, local flora/fauna, etc.**

■ **The routes themselves!** Here's the meat of it all, and the reason you bought this book…right?

The route descriptions contain the route name, the grade, a subjective quality rating denoted by one or more asterisks ("*"), the height (usually within 6 inches; if the exact height is not known, it will be noted as an approximation), and the information about the route itself. Subjective quality ratings are broken down as follows:

No asterisk means the route can be poor, average, or pretty good; no differentiation was made in this category (at this time).

One asterisk (*) means this route is pretty excellent or especially nice; definitely climb it if you get the chance.

Two asterisks (**) means don't miss this one! Beg, borrow, or steal a belay if you have to!

Variations to main routes are noted with a (**V#**). Some routes, particularly if they are leadable or have been led, will have a "protection grade" along with the difficulty grade. This will be in the form of "G," "PG," "R," "X," or a combination of two (e.g., "G/PG"). This simply means that for climbing the route on lead, the protection gear is either Good (you can find bomber placements everywhere you look), Pretty Good (protection is adequate, but you could face going up to 10 feet between placements, or have some placements that just aren't that ideal), Run-out (you are looking at a 20-foot-plus whipper if you come off and serious injuries could result; sometimes the protection is scanty or psychological), and "X Marks The Spot" (you are bringing the rope **only** to safely belay anyone coming up behind you; if you blunder, think 6 feet under).

As you can see by leafing through this book, there is a lot of climbing here. Every effort has been made to verify the accuracy of the routes and ratings, but errors do crop up, and information gets out of date. I have tried to climb as many of the routes as possible, but, ya know, it is impossible to climb them all. Ratings, in general, were derived from a consensus of climbers. But even that doesn't always work (e.g., *Renaissance* at Ilchester has a controversial rating history). Use this book as a **guide**, not the "final word." This book cannot substitute for your own experience, skills, and judgement in matters when climbing.

Also, climbs may change over time—rock does break! Weathering happens. Access to areas may change at a moment's notice—be aware of potential issues when you go visiting a crag. What was once open may no longer be—or what was once closed might have been opened! You never know….

SAMPLE ROUTE DESCRIPTIONS

7. Lord of the Misfit (5.5)—47 ft. Climb the blocky slab to the top, passing by an overhanging left-facing wall near the top (**V1**).

V1: Lord Of The Missed Fit (5.4+*) Scamper up the slab, then turn right to traverse up the overhanging left-facing wall.

18. Demonic Tutor (5.10a* R)—15 ft. Hope you learn something from this! Climb the center of the overhanging wall by following the larger right-rising hand crack with several bucket holds. Halfway up the crack aim for the finger ledge up left. Finish by pulling on round holds onto the ledge above. The rest of the rock above is 4th class.

Bob Ozgar deciding whether To Fin Or Not To Fin (5.10d), Sugarloaf Mountain

Climbing Ethics In Maryland

"Are you guys on Faint's Roof?"—Indy to an eco-challenge-like race class that had no less than seven rappel stations established, mostly unused.

"No, you're at Annapolis Rocks. "—One of the rappel instructors.

Editor's note: The vast majority of climbers in our area are respectful of the climbing environment and of other climbers. We provide the following 'rules of the road' as a service to them. If you run into one of the few who make climbing difficult for the rest of us, feel free to show them this section. Maybe it will make a difference.

L ike the WARNING disclaimer earlier, this is another one of those things that should go without being specifically mentioned but, unfortunately, there are some people who think certain things don't apply to them, even in the Maryland climbing community, and that they are above everyone else in these matters. Thus this rant ensues.

HOGGING ROUTES

Occasionally some areas will be overtaken by classes of various sorts (climbing classes, rappelling classes for eco-race events, rescue technique classes, etc.). This is prevalent at Carderock, but also happens at Sugarloaf, Annapolis Rocks, and Rocks State Park, among other places. Some groups are friendly and will happily share the rock with you. Other groups get an attitude and will tell you they "reserved" this area for their classes, and will insist you climb elsewhere because they cannot be bothered to share the rocks— even if they aren't using them for extended periods of time. With the exception of Wolf Rock and possibly Rocks State Park, this is hogwash, pure and simple. The rocks cannot be reserved, and these groups or schools that rope off and hoard the cliffs are doing a disservice to everyone—especially if the ropes are not being used for hours on end! Come on, share the rock, okay?

And if you can't (and don't have a damn good and legitimate reason for it), may you forever always find the routes **you** want to climb being "reserved" by others just as unwilling to share as you were.

BOLTING

Bolting. What a volatile topic. With over 95 percent of the routes in Maryland being **top-ropeable**, or able to be led on trad gear, there is little reason to be punching bolts in the rocks. At most of the state and national parks, bolting is **not** permitted. This includes Woodstock Rock. And at Sugarloaf Mountain, which is privately owned, don't even **think** about bolting! (Would **you** like it if your neighbors decided that they didn't like the color of your car or something and took it upon themselves to redecorate it for you?)

That said, there **are** some cases where bolts are justified, even in Maryland. These just happen to be very very few and far between.

The bolt belays at Maryland Heights are one instance where the bolting issue might be addressed (the belay stations, mind you, not the random bolt or two up on the wall). The Park Service has not yet banned bolting on the cliff, primarily because people aren't bolting the hell of out it. However, they are aware of the bolting issue and it is something they are thinking about. The current belay/rap bolts are 1/4-inch bolts and were put in without the blessing of the Park Service a long time ago. They are not very safe. They should be replaced with 3/8-inch bolts, **but only with the blessing of the Park Service!** If you want to discuss the bolting situation at Maryland Heights, contact Larry Johnson, head ranger at Harpers Ferry. He can be reached at 304-535-6232. Be polite; he is very helpful. Carderock is also undergoing an examination to install bolt anchors on the main cliffs (i.e. JUNGLE CLIFFS and HADES HEIGHTS). This is primarily due to the amount of traffic the area sees and the potential damage being done to the trees in the area from repeated use as top-rope anchors. You may want to contact the Potomac Appalachian Trail Club as to the status of this project (similar projects were successfully done at John Bryan State Park in Ohio and Pilot Mountain in North Carolina). In any event, remember: never top-rope **directly** through bolts or cold shuts! 'Less ya wanna die or get hurt real bad, that is.

GARDENING

Gardening is a touchy subject for some places in the country. Maryland is no exception. In some climbing areas it is okay to "garden" (removing flora from a route), but in other areas it is discouraged or outright illegal. This should not be much of an issue, as most places in this book are well established. However, check with the local climbers. Mostly gardening is discouraged. In the Frederick Watershed, it is a cardinal sin. Don't do it!

GLUING HOLDS

Fortunately, the gluing on of holds in Maryland is not something that is very prevalent. It shouldn't even be an issue, but as someone somewhere may decide that hey, this doesn't apply to **them**, it's being stated. You should not be gluing on holds. Look, rock breaks. It is not permanent; that's part of the geologic cycle. Deal with it. Rock changes over time. Usually this is over a period longer than the lifespan of the average person, but with climbers, this evolution takes place under the impact of use. And some rock in the state is brittle (especially at some of the more obscure crags listed herein). Once a hold's broken, leave it be. The nature of the route has now changed. This happened, for example, at Sugarloaf in the mid-'90s when a key hold on *Time of the Prophets* in the crack busted off, changing the crack/flake move to an offwidth move. Accept this, adapt to the changes, and climb on.

Oh, and gluing additional holds on a climb? No, you should not be doing that, either. Look, if you can't climb a route under its own terms, go away and get better, or go climb something else. Don't pull this "well, I can't get up that 5.11 over there because I can't make this one move, but since no one else can climb this route the way it is, then it's okay if I put a couple of extra holds on because, like, everyone will thank me!" crap. That don't wash, either. Lots of people can climb the route. Just because **you** can't doesn't mean someone else can't (either). And unless you personally own the rock in question, any glued on holds will be detected quickly. There are enough members of the Maryland climbing community who climb all over, and word will get out. And your holds will disappear. Climb the rock on its own terms.

Speaking of which…

CHIPPING HOLDS

Chipping holds (always save the best for last!)—why in the hell would you chip holds in the rocks? What, are you too **lame** and **weak** to get up a route on the rocks' own terms? Is your ego so delicate that, since you couldn't make the 5.10b/c move and since you're a "5.11 climber," you decided to doctor up the route so you could actually get up the thing (and say you did something you really didn't do?) Or were you not able to make the route as is because you aren't that good yet, but your own self-centered self-importance in the universe decided that you had to climb this, and instead of **you** getting better, you opted to bring the rock down to your level? So what if it's an old quarry, or if " no one climbs there." How do you know no one else climbs there? (Not everyone who climbs uses chalk, ya know!) What difference does it make if it's an old quarry? Do you **own** the rocks? Why did you chip holds? What is your **problem?** Can we, the rest of the climbing community, chip some holds in your head? Volunteers are standing by…

Okay, I'm done. I think the message is clear. Most of the Maryland climbing community feels pretty much the same way. Now on to better topics…

The Ratings Game— Climbing By Numbers

"...for I have known the fear of 5.3."—Mosca Man

Ratings are a highly subjective measure of the relative difficulty of one route as compared to another. There is no specific governing body in the climbing community that goes around rating each and every route. Instead, it is generally done by the first ascensionists and then possibly re-rated by those who follow. Usually, especially in popular areas, ratings become a general consensus of a route's difficulty level.

Due to a number of individual factors, the rating of a given route will vary from person to person, hence the subjective nature of ratings. A given route may feel to one person as being 5.7, whereas for someone else it feels 5.5, or even 5.9. The type of rock, your height, skill, experience, and where your strengths are in climbing (face, crack, slab, overhang, etc.) will all dictate how hard a specific route is for you. The ratings in this book are mostly a consensus of a number of climbers in a given area, and ratings between areas are generally set relatively equal to each other (thus a 5.9 at Rocks State Park should feel fairly close to a 5.9 at Annapolis Rocks). Use these as a guideline to judge relative difficulties, but also be aware that a given route may feel easier or harder to you than the indicated rating (this does not mean the rating is necessarily right or wrong—but if you feel it's badly off, tell me!)

When a route is referred to as "stiff," this means that the route is somewhat harder than what the rating reflects it as being. On the flip side, a route that is considered "soft" means that the climb is actually a bit easier than what the rating would lead you to believe. A "+" or "–" is sometimes added to ratings to indicate if a route is "stiff" or "soft" for a given grade. This generally holds true for routes of 5.9 difficulty and easier. A route's

Fabrizia Guglielmetti pays a visit to the excellent **Reprise de la Bastille (5.4), Sugarloaf Mountain**

"stiffness" doesn't necessarily mean the same thing as "sandbag," however. A "sandbag" route is one that is far more difficult than its rating suggests. A prime example is *Blue Rose* at Ilchester. It has "always been rated 5.8," and at one time in the past it was. But it is by far the hardest 5.8 route you'll climb today!

There are different ways people judge the difficulty of a route. Typically, a route's rating is set by either the single hardest move(s), or if there is a continuous 20-plus foot section of a given difficulty, the rating is bumped up by one level (to reflect the sustained endurance needed to pull the moves off; e.g. , a route that has as its hardest part a 25 foot section of 5.6 moves would be considered 5.7 by this philosophy). Ratings can also be judged through lead climbing or top-roping (or in some cases, soloing). In general, a route done on lead is going to be harder than the same route done using a top-rope. Some people feel that routes should be rated only by their lead difficulty. Others disagree. In this book, since the **bulk** of the routes are primarily top-rope routes (though many can be led), the ratings are given as if you were top-rope climbing.

This book follows the U.S. "standard" by using the Yosemite Decimal System (YDS). This system has its roots in the modified Welzenbach system (originally used by the British and Germans) introduced to the U.S. in the late '30s. In the 1950s, this system was modified to more accurately describe the climbing at Tahquitz Rock in California, and thereafter became known as the Yosemite Decimal System. This system is organized by terrain type and how you have to deal with it. The decimal rating of the 5th class terrain was originally meant to be a "closed" system, and by the 1960s ranged 5.0 to 5.9. However, people were climbing routes and finding that one 5.9 was much harder than another 5.9, and after a **lot** of discussion in the relatively small climbing community (at the time), the YDS was "opened" to include 5.10—but nothing was harder! However, climbers continued to get better, equipment (especially sticky rubber) improved, and one 5.10 had nowhere near the same difficulty as another 5.10. After much consternation, the "closed" philosophy for the system was abandoned, and 5.11 and 5.12 ratings appeared.

In short order, climbers realized that one 5.11 was not of the same difficulty as another 5.11 (likewise for other 5.10s, 5.12s), and in order to differentiate between harder and easier 5.10 and higher grades, they added the "a–d" system, hence 5.10b, 5.11a, 5.12c. Each letter grade represents approximately one full level increase over the previous (e.g. , the relative increase from 5.10c to 5.10d is essentially equivalent to that of 5.7 to 5.8). The split letter grades (5.10c/d) are more or less equivalent to the "+" and "–" noted earlier.

Now, what does each level (and terrain class) **mean?** Terrain is broken down into five "classes," and they can be roughly described as follows:

Class 1: Sidewalk, trails with little/no elevation change. Highways, roads, and the like fall in this range.

Class 2: Off-trail hiking, steep on-trail paths, and 4-wheel drive terrain.

Class 3: Scrambling up steep, possibly exposed areas, easily scrambling up boulders, sometimes using hands for upward progress. A fall here could hurt, but likely won't be severe or fatal. You might use a rope for extended lengths of 3rd class terrain. Or not.

Class 4: Borderline for climbing. You are likely scrambling up areas that are steep and/or exposed, and a fall could be severe or even fatal, depending on the area, but many people won't necessarily rope up. Very good climbers push this definition to include the easier to moderate end of the 5th class terrain.

Class 5: Now you're climbing! A rope is useful in case you fall, 'cause if you do, the landing is gonna hurt!

Class 6: Aid climbing; see page 12.

INTERNATIONAL RATINGS COMPARED

YDS	UIAA	French	Australian	British
5.2	I/1	1	<11	3a
5.3	II/2	2	11	3b · VD
5.4	III/3	3	12	3c · HVD
5.5	IV/4	4	12	4a · MS
5.6	V–/5–		13	HS · S
5.7	V/5		14	4b
	V+/5+	5	15	VS · 4c
5.8	VI–/6–		16	
5.9	VI/6		17	HVS
		6a	18	5a
5.10a	VI+/6+	6a+	19	E1 · 5b
5.10b	VII–/7–	6b	20	E2
5.10c			21	
5.10d	VII/7	6b+	22	5c · E3
5.11a	VII+/7+	6c	22	
5.11b		6c+	23	6a
5.11c	VIII–/8–	7a	24	E4
5.11d	VIII/8	7a+	25	
5.12a		7b		6b · E5
5.12b	VIII+/8+	7b+	26	6c
5.12c	IX–/9–	7c	27	E6
5.12d				
5.13a	IX/9	7c+	28	
5.13b	IX+/9+	8a	29	
5.13c			30	7a · E7
	X–/10–	8a+	31	
5.13d	X/10	8b		
		8b+	32	
5.14a	X+/10+	8c	33	
5.14b				
5.14c				
5.14d				
5.15a				

Climbing routes are generally considered 5th class terrain through and through. To differentiate the different levels in 5th class terrain, the YDS uses the decimal system (as outlined earlier).

5.0–5.4: Realm of the beginner.

5.5–5.6: Obvious for the experienced, but a challenge for the beginner.

5.7: Where most people are comfortable climbing for a gentle workout, and the beginner level for the French.

5.8: A challenge for the occasional climber, a warm-up for the God Climbers.

5.9: A confusing level. If it's harder than 5.8, but easier than 5.10, you've got it!

5.10: Usually about the upper range of the weekend warrior; the good holds are scattered few and far between.

5.11: There might be some reasonable holds on this route. Maybe. Somewhere up there. No more than two, in any event.

5.12: Smooth and vertical, or worse. Since it is obviously impossible, pretend there are holds or go home.

5.13: Pretend? Bah. There are **no** hand/footholds, so use both of them.

5.14: Think overhanging glass wall. This is considered theoretical, as no one has ever made these moves. However, in the '90s a small number of people have claimed to have done so.

5.15: Overhanging glass wall covered with Vasoline. Go talk to Chris Sharma....

5.16: If you're climbing at or familiar with this level, **why** are you even bothering with this chapter, or book?

Expanding on this a bit is the bouldering rating system, of which there are several. Bouldering is basically soloing at low heights above the ground (although there are those who will "boulder" what your average climber would not hesitate to put a top-rope on; this is referred to as "high ball bouldering" or, out West, "bluffing"—this is really solo climbing with (hopefully) crash pads below). Bouldering has its roots in climbing and mountaineering, but in the past decade or so has taken on a life of its own. Two popular methods to rate the difficulty of boulder problems are John Gill's "B" system and John Sherman's "V" system. Gill's "B" system ("B" for "boulder") is a sliding yet closed system, which goes from B1 (just shy of the hardest moves done on the hardest routes to date) to B3 (a not-yet repeated boulder problem). Sherman's scale is open-ended, does not slide, and

Yosemite Decimal System	Sherman Bouldering V-Scale
5.8	V0–
5.9	V0
5.10a/b	V0+
5.10c/d	V1
5.11a/b	V2
5.11c/d	V3
5.12a	V4
5.12b/c	V5
5.12d	V6
5.13a	V7
5.13b/c	V8
5.13d	V9
5.14a	V10
5.14b/c	V11
5.14d	V12
5.15	V13
and harder	V14
	V15

is comparable to the YDS ratings (starting with V0– being equivalent to 5.8). Neither system concerns itself with ground fall potential, only with the hardest moves on the problem.

Now, just to make matters slightly more complicated, there is the whole "aiding" thing (also known to some as "Class 6 terrain"). Aid routes are generally (but not always) routes that cannot be climbed free (at that time). Aiding involves using things other than the rock to get you up the cliff—other things such as pulling on gear, stepping up on etriers, etc. Aiding has its own rating system, with its own +/– tweaks to the ratings. Aid route ratings are generally prefixed with the letter "A" (for "aid"), but more recently "clean aid" routes (where the gear used can be removed without causing damage to the rock, i.e., not pounding in pitons and the like) use the prefix "C". In the chart below, you can replace A with C for "clean aid. "

A0: Bolt ladders. Fixed gear (i.e., it ain't pulling out!)

A1: Solid but removable pro. Easy placements. "French Free" climbing (simply grabbing the pro and pulling on it to get past a difficult section) falls in this level.

A2: Good but tricky placements. Requires a little "out of the box" thinking in order to get gear in. There is potential for a fall, but most of your gear should hold.

A3: Delicate placements that you should test very well; some will only hold body weight. If you fall, you could go as far as 60 to 80 feet, but without ground fall potential.

A4: Many placements hold **only** body weight. Falls of 80 to 100 feet are not unrealistic. Potential for ground fall exists. Suck it up!

A5: Placements hold body weight for entire **pitch**. No solid protection whatsoever. Pretend it's there and climb on. Leader falls can be up to twice your rope-length (and that usually is a Bad Thing). If the falls are longer, you have other problems.

A5+: Mental psych. Your belay anchors suck, your gear sucks, and if you fall, you **and** your belayer are going down! You can find routes like this on the chalk cliffs in England.

A6: Theoretical. Use anti-gravity boots.

There are other rating systems for different aspects of climbing (mountaineering, ice climbing), but they will not be covered here, as they are a bit outside the scope of this book. If you really want to know about them, check out some of the books in the "Further Reading" section (page 333).

Where To Get It

"These are toys. They help me play on the big stone things."
—Jackie Lockhart

So, you're looking for a new rope, additional webbing, or maybe a replacement 'biner for the one you dropped from the top of Annapolis Rocks? There is a bevy of sources in and around the central Maryland region to supply your every need. Don't know where they are? Then scan the list below and go explore! This is not the end-all, be-all list of stores (there are others, such as Sunny's Surplus, which sometimes carry an extremely limited amount of climbing gear), but it does contain all the major distributors of gear locally for your climbing needs.

Potomac Outdoors, Ltd.

www.adventureschool.com/potomac.html • potomaco@aol.com
7687 MacArthur Blvd., Cabin John MD 20818-1701 • 301-320-1544

Located maybe 5 to 10 minutes (by car!) from Carderock, this gem of a shop appears at first glance to cater primarily to the paddling community. But once you walk inside, you'll see they have a diverse array of equipment for a number of different activities, such as hiking, backpacking, cross-country skiing, and climbing. They are well-stocked. They rent cross-country skis and canoes/kayaks. The staff is very friendly and enthusiastic. If you need help, they'll go out of their way to do what they can for you (hell, they'll even draw you a map if you need one!)

The Trailhouse

www.trailhouse.com
17 South Market St., Frederick MD 21701-5524 • 301-694-8448

They have the outdoor market in the Frederick area. While it's not a huge store, it's packed with a lot of stuff. You may have to spend a bit of time hunting through the store for what you want. And if they don't have it, they can likely find a way to get it for you. Their website does not have a lot of product information—mostly reviews of select gear, rental information, and a trail-of-the-month section. You can contact their staff online with gear and equipment questions.

EarthTreks Climbing Gym

www.earthtreksclimbing.com • info@earthtreksclimbing.com
7125-C Columbia Gateway Dr., Columbia MD 21046-2101

1930 Greenspring Drive, Timonium MD 21093
800-CLIMB-UP or 410-872-0060

More than just a climbing gym and mountaineering guide service, EarthTreks also offers a surprisingly nice assortment of gear and equipment in its pro shop, located by the front door as you first walk in. Check it out! Then crank indoors on those rainy days.

Sportrock Climbing Gyms

www.sportrock.com
Sportrock II
5308 Eisenhower Ave., Alexandria VA 22304 • 703-212-ROCK (translates as 212-7625)

Sportrock III
45935 Maries Rd., Sterling VA 20166 • 571-434-ROCK (translates as 434-7625)

Two of the three Sportrock gyms in the D.C. Metro region carry a selection of climbing gear. Primarily stuff you'd need in a gym, but just as useable outdoors as well. You can find harnesses, quickdraws, 'biners, tape, and chalk, plus some clothing, in their pro shops. They are a gym, after all, not a retail business.

REI (Recreation Equipment, Inc.)

www.rei.com
63 W. Aylesbury Rd., Timonium MD 21093-4102 • 410-252-5920

9801 Rhode Island Ave., College Park MD 20740-1423 • 301-982-9681

3509 Carlin Springs Rd., Bailey's Crossroads VA 22041 • 703-379-9400

Your "standard" outdoor chain store, and the one that practically everyone recognizes across the country. Different stores will offer slightly different gear and equipment. Most of what they carry is selected for the region, so if you're looking for a variety of mountain or ice climbing gear, very likely they will not have it in these stores as there is little call for it here. However, on the flip side, if you want it and cannot find it at one store, they will gladly call another and see if they can have it shipped over to them, or directly to you. REI offers clinics on mountaineering, backpacking, cycling, kayaking, and a host of other activities at their stores. Usually the clinics are different for each store. The Timonium store in Baltimore has a small climbing wall that one can stop in and play on during Wednesday evenings and Saturday during the day. The Bailey's Crossroads store also has a small climbing wall. Staff expertise varies tremendously, but they are usually candid about that fact and will try to find someone who is knowledgeable to help you.

Eastern Mountain Sports (EMS)

www.ems.com
Towson Town Center, 825 Dulaney Valley Rd., Towson MD 21204-1010
410-296-1780

Annapolis Harbour Center, 2554 Solomon's Island Rd., Annapolis MD 21401
410-573-1240

The Market Common, 2800 Clarendon Blvd., St. R550, Arlington VA 22201
703-248-8310

Tyson's Corner Center, 7954 Tyson's Corner Center, Mclean VA 22102-4500
703-506-1470

Park City Center, 541 Park City Center, Lancaster PA 17601   •   717-397-8120

Maybe the second largest outdoor chain store on the East Coast? The regional stores here carry primarily outdoor activity clothing, but also have a decent supply of climbing and backpacking gear. Their New Hampshire store offers a mountaineering school if you want to check out that aspect of climbing. Staff expertise varies with respect to the different outdoor activities.

Hudson Trail Outfitters (HTO)

424 York Rd., Towson MD 21204   •   410-583-0494

Annapolis Mall, Annapolis MD 21401   •   410-266-8390

401 N Frederick Ave., Gaithersburg MD 20879   •   301-948-2474

12085 Rockville Pike, Rockville MD 20852-1603   •   301-881-2474

Tenley Circle, 4530 Wisconsin Ave, NW, Washington DC 20016-4627   •   202-363-9810

Pentagon Row, 1101 South Joyce St., Suite B29, Arlington VA 22202   •   703-415-4861

9488 Arlington Blvd., Fairfax VA 22031   •   703-591-2950

Fair Oaks Mall, Fairfax VA   •   703-385-3907

Springfield Mall, Springfield VA 22150   •   703-922-0050

An outdoor chain store, though not as extensive as EMS or REI outside of Maryland. While primarily an outdoor enthusiast's clothing store, HTOs do carry a sampling of a wide array of equipment for a variety of sports—including rock climbing, canoeing, bicycling, and backpacking/camping. Some of the stores also rent canoes at a reasonable rate. HTOs do offer a special order service, so if they do not have something in their stores, they will special order it for you. There are more HTOs in the Baltimore/D.C. Metro region than any other outdoor recreational chain store. HTOs hold a massive warehouse sale every spring at their Rockville and Fairfax stores. Their Pentagon City store planned to begin doing this in 2002. Staff experience with respect to climbing can be limited, depending on which store you happen to hit.

The Outfitter At Harpers Ferry
www.outfitterharpersferry.com • hikersgear@aol.com
111 High Street, Harpers Ferry WVA 25425 • 888-535-2087 (toll free)

Primarily a supplier of hiking, backpacking, and camping equipment, this store targets Appalachian Trail hikers. However, they do carry a minimum of climbing gear (webbing, 'biners, chalk, etc.), and would carry more if all of you climbers out there were to support them in this. The website is pretty sparse, containing only their contact information and hours.

Adventure Bound Outfitters
3803 Norrisville Road Jarrettsville MD 21084 • 410-557-7116

Mainly a canoe/camping/backpacking supply shop, they carry a very limited amount of climbing gear. They are conveniently located about a 10-minute drive from Rocks State Park, and would carry more climbing gear if the local climbing community were calling for it. The store is located behind the Ace Hardware Store. Hours vary, so call ahead first.

Galyan's Trading Company
www.galyans.com
2 Grand Corner Ave., Gaithersburg MD 20878 • 301-947-0200

This store is large. It's colossal, it's massive, it's enormous, it's huuuuuuge—ahh, dammit, Jim, I need a drink! The building Galyans is in would pretty much dwarf any of the other suppliers noted here, and they fill this incredible space with a **vast** array of sporting and outdoor gear and apparel. Think of it as a cross between EMS, HTO, and Dick's Sporting Goods. The outdoor recreation stuff is located on the second floor. Now, given just how extravagantly voluminous this store is, the climbing section is all but lost. You'll find it in an area equivalent to two four-by-eight tables next to the camping section. While compared to the rest of the store this isn't much, they do carry a surprisingly sizeable selection of 'biners, nuts and hexes, and various rope ascending/descending gear. They have a few harnesses, ropes, and climbing shoes, as well as a few helmets and an ice axe or two (mountaineering, not ice climbing). However, most of their staff is not very climbing-savvy, so if you have technical questions you will be better served by asking elsewhere. The store also has a 50-foot climbing wall, but the hours are fairly restricted. Call ahead, as hours change from season to season.

Sun & Ski Sports

www.sunandski.com
Arundel Mills Mall, 7000 Arundel Mills Circle, Hanover MD 21076 • 410-799-2800

This large Texas-based chain opened a store in Maryland back in November 2000, one of 19 located around the U.S. The store is extremely spacious, holding a **lot** of stuff. They have large sections devoted to skiing, bicycling, in-line skating, and camping. In addition, they have a small but well-stocked climbing section near their climbing wall (call the store for times it is open; they charge each person $3 per climb, however). The Sun & Ski Sports here in Maryland works closely with Earth Treks Climbing Gym, and if you have an Earth Treks membership, you can get a modest discount on gear (a nice perk). The store does have a very small selection of books. And finally, Sun & Ski Sports also carries, of all things, a few small 2- to 3-inch astronomical Celestron telescopes.

Bass Pro Shops Outdoor World

www.basspro.com
Arundel Mills Mall, 7000 Arundel Mills Circle, Hanover MD 21076 • 410-689-2500

Certainly not a place you'd expect to find climbing gear! They actually have some, but very little. A few 'biners, some figure-8s, a little webbing, a handful of chalk bags, and a few ropes, including some static ropes. The climbing gear is pretty lost in the camping section (the rest of the store is pretty exclusively hunting and fishing). There is a tall climbing wall near the center of the store (look for the stuffed moose display). The hours of operation are somewhat variable, and they charge each person $3 per climb, with a time limit of 5 minutes per climb. It is located in the same mall as Sun & Ski Sports, so you can visit both in one shot.

When It Rains

"Baltimore weather. Do you see outside? It's going to be like that for the next three days."—Weatherman on a local radio station

O kay, it's mid-September, and you wake up to not just a pitter-patter on your window, but a veritable deluge. It's raining cats and dogs (so to speak). You and a couple of your friends had planned to head to Rocks State Park or Sugarloaf and crank on a bunch of your favorite routes. You **still** need to get some climbing in (man, have you been a gumby climber-wannabe all year, or what?) but with water washing off the rocks like waves under the Ark of Noah, what do you do?

You hit a gym! But…where are they? Well, if you don't already know, that's what this chapter is for—to tell you were to go! (To climb indoors, that is.)

EarthTreks

www.earthtreksclimbing.com
info@earthtreksclimbing.com
7125-C Columbia Gateway Drive,
Columbia MD 21046
800-CLIMB-UP or 410-872-0060

1930 Greenspring Drive
Timonium, MD 21093

With over 15,000 square feet of climbing surface, this is one of the largest, if not **the** largest, climbing gym on the East Coast. Rough textured walls allow incredible frictioning. In two floors of climbing (one for short climbs, one for tall) they boast a wide variety of features—including several jam cracks of varying sizes! (Tape up unless you're collecting 'strawberries.') Gotta love it. They host routes ranging from 5.3 to 5.14 in difficulty. **And** if you're without a partner—you can rent a belayer! Now, this is more than just a climbing gym. They offer a variety of classes for all levels of climbing (as well as self-rescue courses—a must for anyone who plans to spend any time outdoors climbing!), host expedition mountaineering trips around the world, and have an **extremely** well-stocked "pro shop" for you gearheads. Their hours are posted on their website, as are their prices. Call to

Climbing at EarthTreks gym, Columbia.
Photo courtesy of Chris Warner

find out this info if you don't have access to the web.

Late in 2002 EarthTreks opened a second climbing gym, just north of Baltimore in Timonium. This much larger gym boasts 18,000 square feet climbing walls, topping out at 50-plus feet for the tallest routes, and offers more bouldering than you can shake a chalk bag at. It also has a very extensive gear shop, a coffee and juice bar, and a fully stocked fitness center. Everything a growing climber needs.

Sportrock
www.sportrock.com

Sportrock I
14708 Southlawn Lane, Rockville MD 20850 • 301-ROCK-111 (translates as 762-5111)

Sportrock II
5308 Eisenhower Ave., Alexandria VA 22304 • 703-212-ROCK (translates as 212-7625)

Sportrock III
45935 Maries Rd., Sterling VA 20166 • 571-434-ROCK (translates as 434-7625)

There are three Sportrock climbing centers around the D.C. Metro region. The first, and smallest, of the three with 6,000 square feet of climbing surface, is Sportrock I in Rockville. They sell no gear there, but it's not meant for that: it's a climbing **gym**. Come equipped (like you need much!) They cater to family and kid events a lot, so be warned if you go, you might have a bunch of your future peers around (all the Sportrock gyms offer strong kid-oriented programs). Sportrock II in Alexandria, Virginia, is the main gym for this series of climbing centers, and is very popular with the D.C. Metro climbing community. It has 12,000 square feet of nicely textured walls and a variety of features to play on. Sportrock III, having just opened in July of 2001 in Sterling, Virginia, is the newest addition to the Sportrock series. It boasts 10,000 square feet of climbing surface on a wide range of features, including a 30 foot long lead cave. Both Sportrock II and Sportrock III have well-stocked pro shops for gym attendees, offering harnesses, quickdraws, 'biners, tape, chalk, magazines (to read in the lounge), and some climbing clothes. All three gyms offer the same series of courses and programs for climbers of all abilities. Details can be found at the website or by calling the gyms directly. The same goes for admission fees, memberships, and gym hours.

* * *

There are small climbing walls at Galyan's, Sun & Ski Sports, a couple of the REI shops, and Bass Pro Shops Outdoor World, as well as a number of other climbing walls scattered among the various universities and colleges in the region. However, most of the university/college walls are not accessible to the general public, so aren't going to be covered in here in any detail. Information on the sports shops and REIs mentioned above is detailed in the "Where To Get It" chapter.

What's Next?
New Route Information
And Future Editions

"I'm writing the book I was looking for when I first moved here."
—Indy to local climbers looking for a guidebook to Maryland climbing.

There are still uncharted crags scattered about Maryland. There are still new routes awaiting the intrepid explorer who can find them. And there are a number of unknown/unnamed routes listed herein that may indeed actually have names. Any and all new route information, and any addendum, errata, or corrections you feel should be addressed in this guide, should be sent to:

> **Mark "Indy" Kochte**
> **c/o Dog Days Publishing**
> **P.O. Box 1353**
> **Washington Grove MD 20880**

Email of the same information may be sent to: **indy@bcpl.net**

The website, http //www.bcpl. net/~indy/climbing/guide.html will be kept up-to-date with this information. Check there periodically for updates. Ultimately, the information that is collected will find its way into a future edition of this guide, but you can at least see it ahead of time (and know if something was already done before you did it!)

One note: any new route information in the Great Falls/Carderock area should **also** be sent to those people who wrote the more comprehensive guidebooks to these areas. If you send the information to me, it will at the very least get on the web—and sooner than you'd see it if you waited for the next area book to be published. But I'm sure they'd like to have the information, too (this is supposed to be a cooperative effort amongst climbers, not a competitive enterprise).

Geode does a little bouldering exploration in The Uncharted Territories

CLIMBING AREAS

SUGARLOAF
MOUNTAIN

Brian Walker misses the lesson of the Demonic Tutor (5.10a)

SUGARLOAF
MOUNTAIN

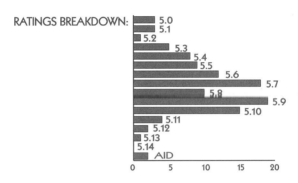

RATINGS BREAKDOWN:

NUMBER OF CLIMBS: 100 plus variations

SPECIAL NOTE:

"Yeah, there are some rocks up at Sugarloaf, but they're all small and not worth climbing on. Only for beginners and bouldering."—Anonymous **Carderock climber**

S ugarloaf Mountain is a privately owned and managed conservation/recreation area. It is open 365 days a year from sunrise to sunset (though very few people tend to visit during Thanksgiving and Christmas), and offers spectacular views of the surrounding countryside from several overlooks.

There are a wide variety of activities that you can pursue at Sugarloaf Mountain: hiking, horseback riding, and nature study. In addition to this, the people of Stronghold, Inc. permit climbing—as long as you are careful, don't go messing with the wildlife (i.e., leave the damned raven's nest alone when it's up on *Butterfingers*, okay?), and don't disturb others (this is rarely a problem; most times it's the tourist/hiker types who are stopped to watch you climb, especially if you're at BOY SCOUT LEDGES). Also, please, please be off the rocks and down to the parking lot by the closing time. This is private property, after all. None of this "well, the place closes at 7:30 p.m., so we can climb 'til then, then take down the ropes, then hike out...." The landowners are not hostile to climbers, but it seems that more and more they are waiting on climbers to vacate the premises so they can lock up.

If this keeps up, they may close or seriously restrict climbing here. Please be out on time.

Oh yeah, climbing is at your own risk (but you knew that already, didn't you?)

LOCATION/DIRECTIONS

From Baltimore: Get on I–70 West. Go approximately 30 miles to Exit 62 for Hyattstown. Turn left onto Md. 75. After approximately 3 miles Md. 75 will jog left onto Md. 80 for about 0.2 miles. At the light turn right, continuing to follow Md. 75. After another 5 miles, Md. 75 will end on the outskirts of Hyattstown at Md. 355. Turn left onto Md. 355 and follow that for 0.5 miles to a light in the booming downtown of Hyattstown. Turn right at the light onto Md. 109. After 3.5 miles, turn right onto Comus Road (the Comus Inn will be on the corner on your right). Another 2.5 miles later you will arrive in Stronghold, at the base and entrance of Sugarloaf Mountain.

From Washington: Head north on I–270 to Exit 22 (Barnesville/Hyattstown). Turn right onto Md. 109. It'll be about 3 miles to the Comus Inn from here. Follow the rest of the directions above.

From Frederick: Go south on I–270 to Exit 22 (Barnesville/Hyattstown, also Poolesville/Sugarloaf Mountain). Turn left onto Md. 109 and follow the signs to Sugarloaf

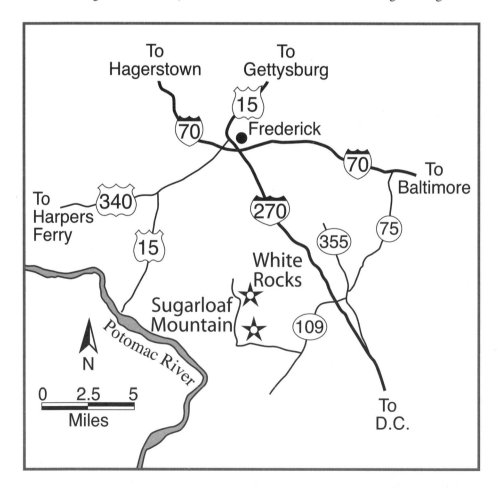

Mountain. It'll be about 3 miles from here until you reach the Comus Inn. Follow the rest of the directions above.

Once you are at the base and entrance to Sugarloaf Mountain, take the one-way road up the mountain. Just past the East View overlook is the DEVIL'S KITCHEN climbing area on the right side of the road. All other climbing areas on the mountain are reached by continuing up the road to the West View parking area and taking the A. M. Thomas Trail (marked by green blazes). After about 6 to 8 minutes (your mileage may vary) of average hiking, you will come to a set of stairs. The MIDDLE EARTH cliffs are in the woods to your right. To the left before you reach the stairs is a large talus field not covered by tree growth. The WEST VIEW ROCKS are over there. Continuing up the stairs, you will come to THE PILLAR and BOY SCOUT LEDGES.

GEOLOGY

Sugarloaf Mountain is what is known as a monadnock: a lone hill or mountain that rises relatively high above the surrounding terrain (which is in general relatively flat). This sentinel towers nearly 800 feet over the surrounding farmlands, its summit almost 1,300 feet above sea level, and is quite visible from great distances (from 10 and more miles away you can see the mountain rising up from the horizon). The term "monadnock" comes from Mount Monadnock in southern New Hampshire, and refers to areas of land that are more resistant to erosion than the bedrock that once surrounded them.

The upper slopes and summit area of Sugarloaf Mountain are made up of highly resistant white quartzite interleaved with softer sericitic quartzite, slate, and phyllite. This unique composite is known as Sugarloaf Mountain Quartzite, and is pervasive throughout the entire monadnock region (including White Rocks). Sugarloaf Mountain Quartzite has strong similarities in structure with the Weverton Formation, named after the rocks found near Weverton, Maryland. These rocks also make up the main ridge of South Mountain, including places like Annapolis Rocks and Black Rock. The surrounding lands are made up of softer phyllites, which weather far more readily than the Sugarloaf Mountain Quartzite, and thus explains why Sugarloaf Mountain stands alone.

EQUIPMENT

In general, there are plenty of natural features (trees, boulders) available for you to tie off anchor lines, although some spots will take gear for your anchor system. Sometimes this is preferable to potentially blocking paths of non-climbers who may be walking through— no fun having them trip over your lines while you're climbing on a route, ya know? The average lengths of slings for anchors range from 20 to 40 feet, though having one or two slings a bit longer can be helpful at times.

CAMPING

There is **no** camping here! Plan on this being a day trip or secure sleeping arrangements elsewhere. There is camping at Gambrill State Park, just west of Frederick off of Route 40. There is also camping at Greenbrier State Park, 10 miles west of Gambrill State Park, also on Route 40. Gathland State Park, off of Route 67 along the Appalachian Trail, also has camping facilities, but is meant for AT hikers rather than your average car camper.

RESTRICTIONS AND ACCESS

There aren't many access issues here—as long as you take care and obey the rules. This is private land, and the landowners are gracious to allow climbing on the mountain. They can easily say "no" to climbing. So, be out on time, don't get hurt, and have fun!

Pete "Guns" Salon pulls his way up the Road To Redemption (5.7)

Note: some of the areas here may be closed off periodically from year to year for raven nesting. Please heed the signs and respect the area closures when this occurs! The raven nesting period is from early to mid-May until late June/early July. The MIDDLE EARTH area is particularly susceptible to this, as the ravens like to nest right on *Butterfingers* (and they don't fall off, like so many climbers do). When the areas are closed…go visit another section of the mountain. There is **plenty** of rock to climb on!

LOCAL EATS

Every weekend from the end of July to the end of October the snack shack at the start of the West View parking area is open (used to be, anyway). The food offered is pretty basic: soft drinks, candies, chips, and hot dogs. Not a gourmet place, but if you're hungry and can stomach hot dogs and chips, here you go! Otherwise, you're on your own for food and drinks on the mountain.

Off the mountain you have some other choices, but most of these require a bit of a drive. Staub's Country Inn is in a nondescript building 6 miles south on Md. 109 (turn right at the intersection of Comus Road and Md. 109 when coming from Sugarloaf), on the corner of Md. 109 and Md. 28 (also the first light you come to heading south on Md. 109). They offer good home-style cooking with generous portions at a moderate price (in the summer, they have an outside ice cream window). They are open 7 days a week, from 11 a.m. to 9 p.m. all days except Sunday, when they are open 9 a.m. to 9 p.m. Alternatively, turning left on Md. 109 and heading back towards Hyattstown 3.5 miles, you will find the Hyattstown Deli and Restaurant at the junction of Md. 355 and Md. 109 (only half a mile east of I–270). They are open Monday through Saturday from 5 a.m. to 8 p.m. or 9 p.m. (depending on the day), serving breakfast, lunch, and dinner.

Going north to Frederick, there are a bevy of places to eat on Market Street (exit 31), both fast-food and sit-down restaurants. Down toward D.C. off of I–270 the options are a bit scarce until you get to the Rockville region, but it's not very obvious where the eateries are tucked away. You will still have to get off the highway and hunt around.

OTHER INFO

Sugarloaf Mountain was contested by the Confederate and Union troops who used the mountain as a signal station and observation point in order to maintain a watch on enemy troop movements in the region during the Civil War. Control of the mountain alternated several times during the War. The building at the West View picnic area is a remnant from that time. At the base of the mountain stands a log cabin that used to serve as a hospital during the War.

Many of the trees in the area are red and white oaks, but these are being severely impacted by the presence of gypsy moths. You can see signs of this blight around the mountain. In addition to these trees, there are a large number of other trees, plants, and wildflowers scattered around the mountain. Mid to late spring is a very pretty time to drive up the mountain when the mountain laurels are blooming.

There are many types of animals that live on and around the mountain. If you're lucky, you might catch sight of a flying squirrel flitting from tree to tree, or a red fox darting through the underbrush. There are plenty of deer around, so it isn't uncommon on days with small crowds to catch sight of these creatures. Bird lovers will no doubt recognize the pileated woodpecker (heard often, rarely seen) as it calls out in the woods, and everyone will recognize ravens and the common turkey vultures (who have this uncanny and almost disturbing habit of circling above climbers). Note: there is a difference between the "common crow" and ravens. For starters, crows don't live around mountainsides; ravens do. The sharp-eyed climber may also catch glimpses of the occasional red-shouldered hawk in the area.

Please be aware that the mountain is also the habitat of the timber rattlesnake and copperhead! Your author has not run across either of these yet, but do be aware that these creatures reside here, too. Somewhere....

Note that occasionally climbing schools will come to the mountain for their climbing classes (particularly to the BOY SCOUT LEDGES area). With few exceptions, unlike elsewhere in the region, these schools are amenable to neighboring climbers and will share the rock with you. Just be friendly and courteous and they'll very likely respond in kind.

To assist relations between the landowners and climbers, volunteer to help out with trail maintenance if possible. They have ongoing trail work days throughout the spring/summer/fall season (as of 2001, the contact person was Russ Thompson, land manager of Stronghold, Inc., at 301-874-2024 or 301-869-7846). Also, help do your part to keep the cliffs free of trash. You know all those extra blue grocery bags you've been collecting since time eternal? Bring a few with you whenever you go and take a few minutes at the end of your day (or start of it) to pick up the broken glass, cans, cig butts, and whatnot you find lying around. The landowners are quite grateful when you do this (hell, you prolly should do this wherever you go), and this will help solidify landowner/climber relations. This problem is especially prevalent out at White Rocks (the author and friends have pulled more than a few bags of glass and trash out of there over the years).

The Routes

The climbing potential at Sugarloaf Mountain is vast. It has one of the largest extents of climbable rock in all of Maryland. These areas are not contiguous, however, though most are no more than a 2-minute walk apart, if that. The outcrops have been divided into three main areas (comprising seven different sections), starting with DEVIL'S KITCHEN. White Rocks is part of Sugarloaf Mountain, but separated by a couple of miles from the summit area, so it has its own chapter.

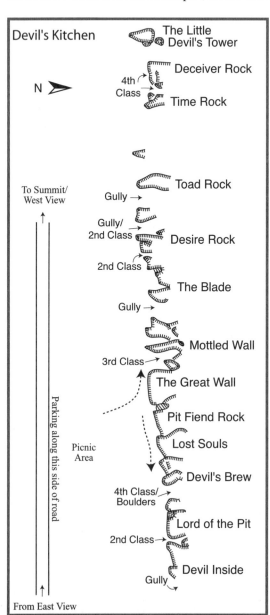

Devil's Kitchen

What's cookin' in the Devil's Kitchen? Quite a bit, actually! This area is the first climbing spot you encounter on your way up Sugarloaf Mountain, a few hundred feet west of the East View parking and overlook area. Parallel park on the right side of the road and head a couple hundred feet into the woods past a picnic area to find a broken line of rock, cut by gullies and breakdown boulders. From end to end the outcropping of rock here is nearly 600 feet long. Between the gully cuts are a number of sections that offer routes for climbing, upwards of 50 feet. You will approach the rocks more or less from almost the center of the cliff line, near THE GREAT WALL. The routes are described from far right to far left.

The main ways to access the tops of the rock here are by scrambling up the 2nd to 4th class gullies between DEVIL INSIDE ROCK and LORD OF THE PIT, to either side of THE MOTTLED WALL, to either side of TOAD ROCK, and between

DECEIVER ROCK and LITTLE DEVIL'S TOWER. You'll need anchors upwards of 50 feet long for some of the routes. Overall, though, they average 20 to 30 feet in length. Access is easy to the top of some of the rocks, a little trickier for others. Be careful!

THE DEVIL INSIDE ROCK

Find the rock outcropping with the crooked Y-forked tree on a ledge two-thirds of the way up. This is the eastern-most outcropping of rock. Further to the right are just jumbles of rocks in the woods, nothing worth climbing on, and a hiking trail.

1. The Devlyn Syde (5.10b)—17 ft. Climb the
center of the overhang 5 feet left of the left facing corner. The crux is pulling the lip. A pretty short route; a boulder problem with a crash pad.

LORD OF THE PIT ROCK

Just 50 feet left of THE DEVIL INSIDE ROCK, this outcropping sports a short overhanging wall split by a thin right-rising crack on the right end, and a major square roof on the left end.

2. The Devil's Traverse (5.12c/d)—13 ft. Start at the lowest point where the right-
rising finger crack splits the short overhanging wall, to the right of an off-width. Traverse along the thin crack to its end, then mantle onto the slab above. Good holds fade to thin and awkward exit moves.

3. Torture Chamber (5.9)—22 ft. You will feel it! Grunt up the widening, flaring, overhanging (can there be any more horrifyingly descriptive adjectives combined together?) offwidth to the ledge above. End the madness here or continue to the top up the lichen-encrusted face for another 10 feet.

4. Lord of the Fit (5.11a)—22 ft. If you're not in shape, you're not gonna make it. Climb the short overhanging white face on thin holds to the left of *Torture Chamber*.

5. Lord of the Pit (project)—28 ft. Work through the huge, 7-foot by 10-foot roof, finishing on *Infernal Combustion*. This has yet to see a successful ascent., even an aided one.

6. Infernal Combustion (5.7* PG)—28 ft. Climb the first 10 to 15 feet of *Lord Of The Misfit*

slab until you pass the tree **(V1)**. Turn right and get onto the center of the large left-facing wall above the huge roof. Hit some underclings, traverse right **(V2)** and finish by climbing up past/through two parallel cracks to the ledge above.

> **V1: Infernal Combustion Direct (5.9–*)** A slightly contrived variation to *Infernal Combustion*. Stand on the root from the tree and high-step your way onto the face, aiming for the parallel cracks above. Finish on *Infernal Combustion*.

> **V2: Eternal Combustion (5.6*)** Instead of traversing right, keep going up the center of the face to the outer right corner of the roof overhead.

7. Lord of the Misfit (5.5)—47 ft. Climb the blocky slab to the top, passing by an overhanging left-facing wall near the top **(V1)**.

> **V1: Lord Of The Missed Fit (5.4+*)** Scamper up the slab, then turn right to traverse up the overhanging left-facing wall along the edge. Very nice, good holds.

DEVIL'S BREW ROCK

Located 40 feet left of LORD OF THE PIT ROCK there is a tall, severely left-leaning blocky "tower" to the right of a short slab, which together form a deep cavity.

8. Fire (5.9* G)—20 ft. Don't get burned! The crux is right off the ground. Start at the right outside corner of the deep chimney. Climb the overhanging face and transition right **(V1)** onto the left-leaning wall through major buckets; pull around the square roof to a ledge on the right with a tree.

> **V1: Brimstone (5.9+)**—40 ft. Instead of transitioning fully onto the left-leaning blocky face, continue up the corner, passing the first square roof on the left, and follow the severely overhanging face on excellent holds up to a left-leaning hand crack. Sustained, and not recommended if you think you might fall, as a fall **will** slam you into the slab that makes up *The Black Cauldron*. Be careful.

9. The Black Cauldron (5.1)—19 ft. Climb the slabby face opposite *Brimstone*, following the wide hand dike to the end. The crack will take a couple of jams, but is otherwise too shallow and dirty to be much use. You can finish by turning right at the end of this slab and climbing the left-leaning hand crack on the upper third of *Brimstone*.

10. Mantle Piece (5.7)—25 ft. Scamper up the face beneath the large rectangular overhang. Pull through the left side of the overhang with little or no holds (hint: the key move is a mantle; otherwise…) This really is a one-move wonder problem.

LOST SOULS ROCK

Twenty-five feet left of DEVIL'S BREW ROCK is an east-facing wall broken by numerous cracks, hosting a few south-facing overhangs down low.

11. All You Zombies (5.6)—45 ft. Slightly contrived. Start at a stance just inside the chimney. Lumber up the face following breaks in the rock—do **not** use the overhanging wall/blocks behind you! There are two cruxes, one near the start, and one at the end.

12. Beelzebub (5.7–* PG)—49 ft. Starting at the right side under the overhang 8 feet off the ground, climb up and pull around the overhang (crux) on the right, then follow cracks up to a blank-looking wall. Find key hidden footholds to make this easier than it looks. If you miss them, you are going to be **significantly** more challenged! Finish on easy ground.

13. Burning My Soul (5.9+)—50 ft. Feel it deep inside. Start several feet left of Beelzebub. Follow the crack by a right-facing corner to the overhang above. Cut left, pulling onto the face to the left (**V1**) beneath another overhang. There are two hidden side-pull pockets in the middle of this face; your belayer will see them, you will not. Move right

and up on slightly desperate moves, weaving between the two overhangs. Follow the easy arête to the top.

V1: Burning My Sole (5.10a) Instead of traversing left, pull the overhang directly, then finish on the arête.

14. Tortured Soul (5.10b/c)—50 ft. Start at the lowest point of the rock here and climb up to the overhang on extra-sharp holds. Struggle onto the deceptively featured face above (crux). Using the outside left edge may or may not help you. Continue up on easy ground, following the face immediately left of the arête to the top.

15. Devil's Delight (5.6*)—48 ft. Power through the overhang formed by two blocks, 9 feet left around the corner from *Tortured Soul*. The climbing really isn't technically that hard—the holds are all extremely rough and positive—but it can be an arm-pumper. Finish on easy and pleasant ground above.

PIT FIEND ROCK

This is a broad, slabby wall with a slightly overhanging wall at the base, 25 feet left of LOST SOULS ROCK and 20 feet right of THE GREAT WALL.

16. The Devil Made Me Choose It (5.3)—43 ft. A one-move wonder route. Your job is to find that move. Climb the slabby face, basically following just right of the main dike/crack to the top.

17. Succubus (5.9+)—15 ft. Short, powerful, sequency. Undercling through the overhang with the Z-slash crack and use almost great holds to pull onto the dirt-encrusted ledge above. The climb is over at this point, but you can keep going on the 5.1/5.2 slab above for another 25 feet if you want.

18. Demonic Tutor (5.10a* R)—15 ft. Hope you learn something from this! Climb the center of the overhanging wall by following the larger right-rising hand crack with several bucket holds. Halfway up the crack aim for the finger ledge up left. Finish by pulling on round holds onto the ledge above. The rest of the rock above is 4th class.

19. Pride Comes Before A Fall (5.5*)—20 ft. A somewhat dirty route with great holds. Climb the overhanging wall with buckets to the left and around the corner from *Demonic Tutor*. Finish on the ledge above.

20. Balrog (5.10a/b* G)—30 ft. An inviting climb that is very dirty, mostly due to
lack of people climbing it, but partly due to the fact that it is a seepage area for when it
rains here. Clamber up the blocks in the back of the wide chimney to the roof, then follow
the widening right crack/corner in the roof out to the end, pulling past the roof onto a ledge.

THE GREAT WALL

The center of this massive 35 foot wide 45-degree overhanging wall is 20 feet left of
PIT FIEND ROCK. The main anchor point is 34 feet down a 4th class/5.0 "slab" to a lone
pine tree. Take care when getting down to the tree.

21. The Lesser Of Two Evils (5.11c/d)—33 ft. Beginning next to a tree, 8 feet left
of *Pride Comes Before A Fall*, climb up the right side of the wall, following the arête up and

left to a small ledge with a pine tree. You can finish on
the super-easy ground above if you want (though if
you're climbing 5.11, the final 24 feet shouldn't pose
any excitement).

22. Project (5.13-ish)—31 ft. Has yet to see a suc-
cessful ascent. Start near the center of the wall at two
pockets, then follow the seam up and right using sloping holds and *mono-doigts*. Finish on the easy holds far
up and right, then angle left to the ledge with the tree.

23. Freak On A Leash (C1)—20 ft. Aid up the
thin, gritty, flaring, overhanging crack on the left side
of the wall to ledge above. There is a fixed nut three
quarters of the way up.

24. Okay, Johnny (5.8)—21 ft. To the left
around the corner from *Freak On A Leash* is a short
face dotted with *mono-doigt* solution pockets and laced

with thin quartz veins. Using pinch grips and sidepulls in the pockets, climb the face to the trees above. Did you make it? Okay, Johnny!

MOTTLED WALL

Twenty-five feet left of THE GREAT WALL. *Pacemaker*, *Slow And Easy*, and *Slippery Doo Dah!* are on the mottled west-facing side of the rock. The low-angled rock to the left of the west-facing rock offers some moderate to easy thin slab-like climbing.

25. Demon Breath (5.9*)—38 ft. Excellent practice for friction slab climbing! Follow the short offwidth crack until it ends, and continue up the center of the face above, staying right of *A Light Touch*.

26. A Light Touch (5.6* X)—38 ft. Delicately friction straight up the arête. The left edge is "on" (without it the climb becomes significantly more difficult—well, go ahead, challenge yourself!)

27. Pacemaker (5.8* X)—38 ft. Take it easy. Climb the face to the right of the hand crack that vertically splits the center of the wall. Climbing further to the right is about the same difficulty.

28. Slow And Easy (5.7** G)—38 ft. Excellent jams up the crooked crack in the center of the wall. The crack is very similar to *TAD* on Devil's Tower, Wyoming—only not quite so long.

29. Slippery Doo Dah! (5.10b)—27 ft. Climb the face left of the *Slow And Easy* crack. Use razor blade edges and slopers to go up the short face.

THE BLADE

Look for the obvious, tall, sharp arête to the right of a large open book, 75 feet left of MOTTLED WALL.

30. Kiss The Blade (5.9+)—46 ft. Start with the short but beautiful layback flake several feet right of *To Fin Or Not To Fin* on the east (right) face. Climb up the face (crux) along the arête, left of the large tree root. Using the arête on the left is considered "on." Smaller fingers are a plus on this route.

31. To Fin Or Not To Fin (5.10d*)—46 ft. Do you use it or not? That is the question. Climb the short flaring offwidth with a hand crack to its end (using the right fin is optional; it may look easier to use it, but actually is harder), then step left and follow the knife-edge arête up to the top along the west (left) face. Once past the offwidth the climbing does not let up.

32. Gunboat Diplomacy (5.4* G)—40 ft. Don't force the issue. Dash up the ramp to the base of the large open book, then blast up this corner to the top. Be sure to look around for holds, as everything is there, even at the top. Stay out of the corner in the last 5 feet or so to keep the climbing sane.

33. Appeal To Reason (5.10a)—40 ft. A bit more subtle. Start up the ramp of *Gunboat Diplomacy*, but instead of going up the inside corner, step left and climb through the overhanging wall split by cracks. Finish on this left arête to the top.

34. The Devil You Know (5.9* G)—24 ft. This route is very similar to *Balrog*, only much shorter and not quite as sustained. Starting from the back right corner of the "cave," work up to the roof, then layback and jam the wide crack forming the right corner of the roof all the way out to the end. Delicately turn the roof (crux) and continue up moderate blocks and flakes to a ledge. Down low, do not use the left wall as you face into the "cave." Note that occasionally there is a nest halfway up this route.

35. You Little Devil (5.7)—24 ft. Begin just under the roof on the left side. Climb the left wall up to the roof, and pull through it into the right-facing corner above (crux). Once you reach better holds, continue up following sharp flakes and blocks to a ledge.

DESIRE ROCK

Sixty-five feet left of THE BLADE is a west-facing white and green wall forming the right side of a broad gully.

36. Don't Start With Me (5.8)— 33 ft. Follow the flaring crack splitting the south-facing overhanging buttress in front of the tree. Don't fall here or you'll likely crater. Finish on the arête.

37. Good Intentions (5.7*)—26 ft. Climb pretty much anywhere on this west-facing green wall to the white rock above. The crux is in the first 8 feet or so off the ground. After that the climbing is significantly easier. The right-facing lay-back flake to the far left is easy and fun, although entirely too short.

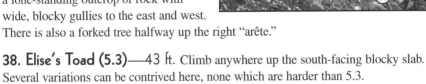

TOAD ROCK

Fifty feet left of DESIRE ROCK is a lone-standing outcrop of rock with wide, blocky gullies to the east and west. There is also a forked tree halfway up the right "arête."

38. Elise's Toad (5.3)—43 ft. Climb anywhere up the south-facing blocky slab. Several variations can be contrived here, none which are harder than 5.3.

TIME ROCK

Look for the second outcrop of rock 80 feet left of TOAD ROCK. The first outcrop has no real climbing on it.

39. Killing Time (5.4)—34 ft. If you're **bored**, mosey up the blocky face crossed by flakes and small overhangs. Start at the right side of the small roof 7 feet off the ground.

40. Serving Time (5.0)—34 ft. Around the corner to the left of *Killing Time*, wander up the wide, blocky chimney, passing by a tree, to the top.

DECEIVER ROCK

This is a large, west-facing wall 45 feet left of TIME ROCK, to the right of a broad gully. The wall here is similar to that of DESIRE ROCK 175 feet to the right.

41. How Low Can You Go? (5.9)—31 ft. Climb the arête, starting as low as you feel comfortable.

42. Deception Face (5.5)—28 ft. Don't be deceived, this is easier than it looks, and is a good wall for experienced beginners to practice climbing with small holds. Try it without climbing shoes. Climb up pretty much anywhere on the west-facing wall. When you think you've come to a blank section, look around for those small, unobvious holds. Moving left into the large crack makes the climbing easier.

THE LITTLE DEVIL'S TOWER

This "free-standing" pillar is 20 feet left of DECEIVER ROCK, and offers routes on all sides. Setting anchors is tricky, but you can get a medium hex and medium-sized nut in some of the shallow crevasse-like features at the top, in addition to wrapping the entire top of the rock with webbing.

43. Easy Up (5.0)—15 ft. Starting at the rightmost end of the east face, climb the short green slab to the top. Easiest and shortest route to the top of this rock.

Gabriele Rechbauer takes it easy on **Pacemaker (5.8)** Photo by Rafi Reyes

44. Shout At The Devil (5.7* PG)—43 ft. Start at the base of the long, south-facing slab arête with some overhangs and bulges down low. Climb through the square roof to the right of a crack down low (crux; **V1**) then up through an overhang (one committing move!) onto the slab arête above. Finish on 3rd class terrain to the top.

> **V1: Shout At The Devil Escape (5.5*)** It's much easier this way. Bypass the low, square roof by scampering up the face and corner to the right, then rejoin *Shout At The Devil* at the overhang above. Finish on *Shout At The Devil*.

45. Speak Of The Devil (5.5* PG)—43 ft. Paralleling *Shout At The Devil*, climb the bulges on the left half of the arête to the 3rd class terrain above. You have the same type of committing move at the same level as *Shout At The Devil*, although a couple of feet to the left.

46. Just Another Victim Of The Ambient (5.2)—37 ft. Starting on the lowest section of the west face, left around the corner from *Speak Of The Devil*, follow the left-rising wall with sharp holds and jugs to the top.

47. Quietly Confident (5.8*)—24 ft. Climb the left side of the west-facing wall past a short, right-facing corner (**V1**) to the overhang above. Follow the crack under the over-hang up and left to the top. Entirely too short.

> **V1: Flexible Demeanor (5.7*)**—24 ft. Instead of climbing the face right of the corner, go straight up the left-most part of the face, following the northwest arête/corner to the top. Using holds on the left corner is allowed (sure, contrive it and disallow them to make it harder for yourself!) Keep a sharp eye out for several hidden holds that are key to getting through this route. A worthy variation to play on.

48. Green With Envy (5.6)—15 ft. Don't be jealous, now! Climb the short, steep green north-facing wall on good, sharp holds.

The Upper Mountain

MIDDLE EARTH

This is the first rock outcropping you come to on the right a couple hundred feet into the woods as you are heading up the A. M. Thomas Trail (a.k.a. the Green Trail). It is a 120-foot length of broken cliff that has its highest point at about 50 feet up (averaging 30 to 40 feet overall). Since you are more than likely going to approach from the main hiking trail, the routes are listed from left to right.

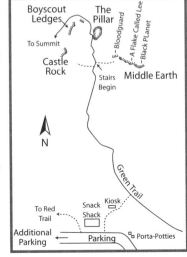

49. The Lemon Merchant (5.10a)—39 ft.

Climb the sometimes lichen-covered face left of *White Quartz Wielder (WQW)* to the top, using only the left edge of the *WQW* crack and any available face holds (fewer than there first appear to be). Going through the roof on the left of *WQW* is significantly harder.

50. White Quartz Wielder (5.8* PG)—39 ft.
This is the obvious, wide crack/chimney on the left side of the rock, to left of *Bloodguard*. Clamber up the crack (**V1**), then pull the roof to right of the small crack under roof. Avoiding the roof makes the route 5.5 or so.

V1: Keeper of the Cheese (5.9)
Climb the face in between *Bloodguard* and *WQW*, without using any *Bloodguard* holds, and only the right edge of the *WQW* crack, finishing on *WQW* through the roof. Contrived, but interesting to work out.

51. Bloodguard (5.9+** R)—37 ft.
Climb up basically the center of a smooth "blank" face with quartz veins, just below a small double roof. Starting in the center of the face, climb up a couple of moves to a quartz vein, then aim left on small holds until below a broken crack system (do not go to the left edge). Move up a move or two to the horizontal crack, then traverse right until below the double roof. Finish by pulling through the double roofs (a spot of friction here) and onto welcome jugs near the top. There are several different handhold options midway through the route for you to play with for variety. **Classic**.

52. Cording (5.3 G)—28 ft.
An excellent beginner route. Climb the wide crack and corner system 5 feet to the right of *Bloodguard*. Once up to the overhangs/roofs (**V1**), step right and follow the crack to the top. The climb can be made harder by initially avoiding the obvious crack and working the thinner crack and face below and right of the main crack system (5.5 at best).

V1: Cording Traverse (5.7* G)
Instead of stepping right or going straight up, make a rising traverse left under the roof then pull it at the left end, just before going around the corner. This makes an excellent lead climb.

Access Ramp (3rd)
Scramble (carefully) up the blocks right of *Cording* to access the top of the rock here. This is the easiest way to the top, though there is a steep gully to the right of *Black Planet* that you can also claw your way up.

53. Go Ballistic (5.10b)—37 ft.
Climb the shadowed face left around the corner of *Butterfingers*, right from the 3rd class scramble to the upper part of the crag. The direct start explodes past two dyno moves, the first to a great horizontal hand/finger lock, the second to a smaller fingerlock not quite so close (larger dyno). The first dyno is up an overhanging wall; the second starts from under an overhang and finishes on an almost pure vertical surface. After that, follow the rock to the top. Note: using flake or any handholds around the 4th class breakdown area, or any holds off the left of the main wall is considered "off-route," and "reduces" the grade to about 5.9+ or so.

54. Butterfingers (5.8 PG)—44 ft.

Don't slip! Climb the left-most line/crack through a series of multiple overhangs/roofs (**V1**) to the left of the large imposing roof immediately left of *Seven Wishes* (stand on "nothing" to get past the second overhang), and right around the corner from *Go Ballistic*. **Please do not climb here if the raven's nest is inhabited!** Even if there are no signs warning you at that moment, there will be soon enough.

V1: Butterfingers Right (5.10a)

Climb the initial part of *Butterfingers*. After surmounting the first awkward overhang, somehow get turned around and face the right corner. Follow this corner up and through another overhang, using a partial thin fingertip layback at one point. Continue either up right or straight up. The handholds get better the further up the route one goes.

55. Rhythm Roof (5.9**)—39 ft.

Keep the rhythm in your stride as you climb up under the huge roof (**V1**), pulling it by following the crack from the right side. Begin on the ledge 10 feet above and just left of *Seven Wishes*. Finish on buckets. **Classic.**

V1: Revenge of the Spider God (5.6)

Climb up the corner/right-leaning slab to huge the overhanging roof left of *Seven Wishes*. Traverse right over to finish on *Seven Wishes*. Watch for the spiders (they bite).

56. Seven Wishes (5.6** G)—51 ft.

Wish it were 5.7! Starting 50 feet to the right of *Bloodguard*, climb through an initial overhang/roof (**V1**) in a wide chimney to a platform 10 feet up, then follow the notch and crack to the right of the imposing *Rhythm Roof* to the top, trying not to step too far to the right (you can avoid the crux easily by doing this). A #3 or #4 tri-cam and/or a #7 hex are excellent anchor pieces if you have them. Note: this is a fairly popular route.

V1: Margy's Headcam Variation (5.7)

Work the short wall to the left side of the chimney to a blockage 7 feet up. Undercling/lieback to the left; it's delicate footwork for a move or two (it's possible and actually helps to headcam the corner above you). Swing around and pop onto the broad ledge several feet above. Finish on *Seven Wishes*.

57. I Am A Cam (a.k.a. Spring-Loaded Charles Device) (5.7)—51 ft.

Fun route. Climb the downward flaring chimney that forms the mouth of *Cave Route* (below), then ascend the face above to the right of *Seven Wishes*. It helps to pretend you are a camming device.

58. The Cave Route (5.1)—51 ft. A few feet to the right of *Seven Wishes* is a cave-like feature, wide at the bottom, constricting near the top. Climb out the constriction and up the steeper part of the gully. A very popular "adventure" for many non-climbing locals, and a diversion for climbers who wanna try caving.

59. 42 (5.8)—57 ft. The ultimate answer to the ultimate question—where to climb when all the other routes are taken? Start below the blocky overhang to the immediate right of the *Cave Route*. Climb up under the roof-like protrusion, stepping right at the block, sliding up the face for a few moves, then left over the roof (there are no useable holds to pull the roof directly). Finish on the face above. After 10 feet or so, the climbing essentially ends with 3rd and 4th class scrambling to the top. A nice route that is often overlooked, but not for any good reason.

    The next batch of climbs start around the corner, 30 feet right of Seven Wishes.

60. A Flake Called Lee (5.5 G)—**60 ft. Climb the finger/hand crack to the right of *42*, passing by huge right-facing flake. Begin below a left-facing corner 5 feet left of *For Short People Only*. Work up the corner and follow the finger crack system up (crux; note the broken pin in a crack here if you are comfortable). Past this the climbing eases off to about 5.1/5.2. A popular climb to challenge beginners, also an excellent route to practice lead climbing. Crying shame the bottom half of this route isn't three times longer. **Classic**.

61. Never Talk To Strangers (5.10b/c)—29 ft. Climb the face between *A Flake Called Lee* and *For Short People Only*, using neither crack of either route as a hand or foothold (can use thin crack partway up second half of climb just right of *A Flake Called Lee*). Delicately dance up the face, using small holds and technical skill. Exclude the obvious holds to the left and right and the route becomes a solid 5.11 (contrived, naturally). The route essentially ends after 30 feet. End it here or finish on *A Flake Called Lee*.

62. For Short People Only (5.5* G–PG)—60 ft. As the name implies. Climb the wide crack that spilts the lower middle section of the rock (crux), left of the prominent *Hyper-Gamma-Spaces* roof and layback flake dihedral. Climb as a chimney or offwidth when necessary. The climbing essentially ends after 20 feet (can finish off on 5.0 to 5.2 stuff). The crux is significantly harder if you stuff pro in the offwidth section before climbing through it—but to not do so invites the potential for cratering.

63. Nemesis (5.11b)—30 ft. Climb the thin face between *For Short People Only* and *Walk This Way*, without using the crack/flakes of either route, until you reach the block roofs. Come back down or finish on either *For Short People Only* or *Space Dwarves*. Short, pretty darn contrived, and fun if you like crimpy.

64. Walk This Way (5.5)—60 ft. Walk up the major left-facing crack/blocks beneath the *Hyper-Gamma-Spaces* roof, step left, joining *For Short People Only* (crux) onto much easier ground. A two-move wonder route.

65. Space Dwarves (5.6)—46 ft. Mine the rock for all it is worth. Start on *Walk This Way*, but instead of stepping left at the first block roof, pull over it and continue following the wide crack up left of the *Hyper-Gamma-Spaces* roof. Once through this and onto easier ground, walk toward the inside corner and climb the left-facing rose-colored blocks to the flat platform at the top. A nice climb with nice holds and some interesting problems.

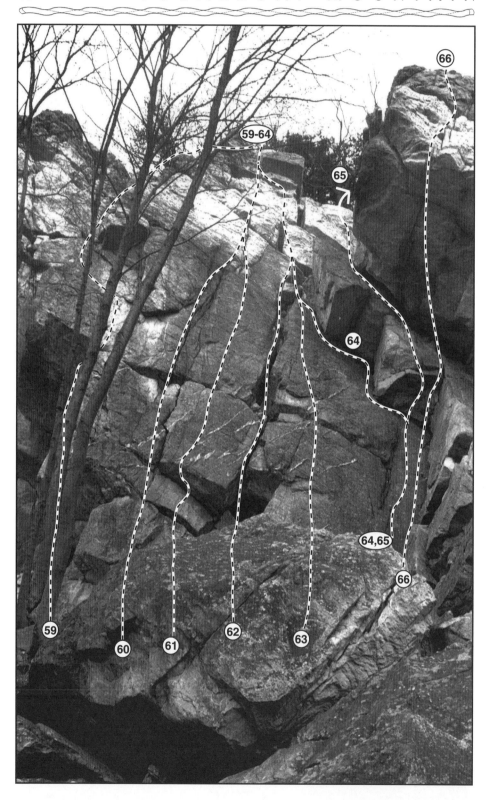

66. Hyper-Gamma-Spaces (5.12b)—46 ft. Prepare for a trans-dimensional experience. Climb the corner under the main blocky roof. Follow the thin cracks through the roof to easier ground above. Once you're through the roof the route is pretty much finished. Top off on blocks and ledges.

67. Shadow Warrior (5.9*)—42 ft. Stealthily slip up to the corner under the *Hyper-Gamma-Spaces* roof, then battle through the awkward and committing moves to traverse right on the face under the roof, pulling around the right end to easier ground to the top.

68. In Your Head (5.7*)—42 ft. Climb the center of the face to the right of the *Hyper-Gamma-Spaces* roof, surmounting the lower overhang. After a few difficult moves to get through the overhang/bulge, the climbing eases off dramatically. Remember, it's all in your head.

69. Sugarloaf Arête (5.7*)—43 ft. Climb the arête to the right of the *Hyper-Gamma-Spaces* roof. Work up the bulge in the face, traverse right to the arête, step right around the arête, up a move or two, then back onto the arête itself. Climbing eases off dramatically halfway up the arête. It is easiest to use the *Black Planet* anchors.

70. Black Planet (5.9*)—33 ft. Not quite out of this world, but still pretty sweet. Climb the face (**V1, V2**) around the corner of the *Sugarloaf Arête*, 35 feet right of *For Short People Only*. The face has a rose-colored discoloration in the center, below some slight overhangs. There are several different starts, easier to the far right, harder toward the left. Work your way up using hidden holds, flakes, and slight finger ledges. Surmount the final overhangs up top. Using the far left hold or two at the crux (near the rose-colored rock) keeps the climbing at about 5.9 or so—it's more serious without the arête holds. Working the blank section of the wall up and right of the rose-discolored rock is also about 5.9—**if** you find the hidden finger ledge. Working the right edge/arête on the easy ground is about 5.3. The gully to the far right of the rock allows access to the top for anchor setups.

V1: The Haines-Klein Arête Variation (5.3 PG–R) Climb up 10 feet to the horizontal crack line. Follow that left to the arête, move up and finish on *Sugarloaf Arête*. The moves get easier the higher you go. Pro is sparse around the arête, but good below and above.

V2: The Haines-Klein Head Variation (5.7* PG) Climb up 10 feet to the horizontal crack line. Traverse left to the arête, then keep going until partway under the overhang. Finish on *In Your Head* (crux). Pro is decent, but finicky at the overhang. Watch for rope drag around the corner.

THE PILLAR

Continue up the Green Trail past the MIDDLE EARTH area. As you go up the stairs, a house-sized boulder rises out of the ground before you. There is, unfortunately, spray paint on sections of it. The lower north (stair-side) section has a small overhang where *Little Herc* starts. *Pebbles And Bam-Bam* begins on the overly peb-bled main wall facing down the trail/stairs at the lowest section of the rock.

Anchors for this area are general-ly long (30 foot plus) webbing and/or medium-sized gear. Routes are described from right to left.

71. Pebbles And Bam-Bam (5.4)—48 ft. This route ascends pretty much anywhere up the pebbly-looking main slab face of THE PILLAR. Begin 4 feet right of the lowest point of the main wall, at a crack system. Climb up onto the main wall using said crack system, then bang your way up the nobs and nubbles any ol' way you want to the top. The cruxes are near the bottom and top. Climbing in the middle is fairly straightforward and easy. Variations can make the climbing somewhat more difficult (but not outrageous). A good route for beginners to try their luck.

72. Barney Rubble (5.6*)—48 ft. Really a start variation to *Pebbles And Bam-Bam*. Start 5 feet left of the lowest point of the main wall, 9 feet left of *Pebbles And Bam-Bam*. Climb up the slightly bulging bottom section to gain the slab above. If you find the hidden flake hold, you're golden. Finish on *Pebbles And Bam-Bam*. Somewhat of a reach problem.

73. The Thin Green Line (5.8)—44 ft. Somewhat contrived. Starting to the right of the tree, in a notch formed by a right-leaning left-facing corner below a crack, climb up the crack to the faint green lichen growth on the slab-side of the arête. Begin a rising traverse, working up the arête and steep face for as long as possible. Stepping right at any time will make things a lot easier (hence the contrived nature of the climb).

NOTE: These next four routes should be totally avoided during periods of high traffic on the stairs—unless you want to cause a nuisance of yourself and add to the list of reasons why people don't like climbers and try to shut places down. Please, if you do this, be sure to let the rest of the climbing community know who you are.

74. Project (unrated)—43 ft.
Begin left of the tree, on a small, flat "platform" at the base of the rock, just right of a large, overhanging crack system (*Darkness Imprisoning Me*). Climb the witheringly steep wall until a few feet from the apex, then step right onto the main slab and follow the arête to the top. It has not yet seen a successful ascent.

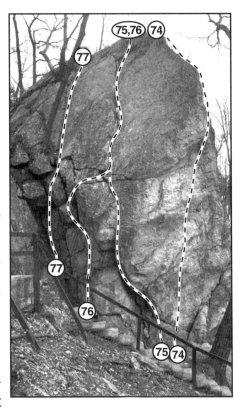

75. Darkness Imprisoning Me (5.10b*)
—40 ft. Begin at the large, overhanging crack system just left of *Project*. Work the crack up and left to the outside corner. You could head left around the corner and finish off on *Little Herc* (you get a little more climbing in this way), but the nominal route turns upward toward the daylight and follows the thin crack until you gain the horizontal on the slab above. After this the hard stuff is finished; scamper to the top.

76. Little Herc (5.9* G)—37 ft.
Start at the point of rock three steps down from the platform where the stairs turn 90 degrees to the left. Yard up the cracks trending left to a right-facing corner, then pull up onto the easy face at the horizontal above. Finish on the large vertical crack system. This is essentially a boulder problem. But please avoid it when there are a lot of people walking by.

77. Just Another Crack In The Wall
(5.0)—35 ft. From where the stairs suddenly turn left there is a blocky corner, left of the prominent crack that vertically splits THE PILLAR's face. Easily romp up the blocks, traverse right on easy ground and finish by following the crack up.

BOY SCOUT LEDGES

As you continue up, passing THE PILLAR, the stairs turn left 90 degrees for about 15 feet. Before you, about 50 feet away, is a short wall sliced by vertical and horizontal cracks with a prominent pointed roof sticking out on the right side. Follow a path from the top of the stairs left over to the wall. There is a short bouldering wall on the right as you walk toward the main section of BOY SCOUT LEDGES. This is a great area to practice technique or to take beginners (you will sometimes find classes here; unlike at Carderock, some groups will share the rock with you if asked politely). Or be filmed by the weekend city hikers as they walk by about 100 feet behind you. Sometimes you can encounter fire-fighting personnel here practicing rescue techniques (I myself have come here to practice self-rescue techniques on occasion), so don't be too surprised if you overhear any of the tourist hikers on the stairs telling others that you're a bunch of firefighters.

Anchors here generally utilize the nearby trees and boulders, although The Prow easi-ly takes medium-sized gear in its blocky top.

78. The Prow, Right Side (5.10c*)—28 ft.
Climb the right corner of the main Prow pillar, working to the right as necessary. Go up, then angle left through a thin face. Continuing out to the left edge of the Prow (above the roof) is about 5.10– or so. Continuing straight up from the corner after the jog right is hard 5.10.

79. Spiderman's Route (a.k.a. The Prow) (A5)—32 ft.
Climb the large, very prominent body-length roof sticking out from the right end of this wall. So far it's only been done using creative aid techniques. No one has freed this to your author's knowledge. There are teeny holds under the roof, and the lip is nowhere near as good as you'd want it to be. The moves above the roof are pretty straightforward. This route has been rated A5 by the first ascent party due to the technical difficulties to be overcome and innovative techniques that were required to get up this route.

80. The Prow, Left Side (5.7*)—31 ft.
Climb the left half of the main face directly under the major Prow roof. Once at the roof, step left, then angle right on the face above. Grasp up and right to gain a mostly horizontal crack with some flat and flaring holds (crux). Delicately step up to the top.

81. Cub Scout Cracks (a.k.a. Cakewalk Cracks) (5.3 G)—35 ft.
This face is to the left of the large prow-like roof and right of the low roofs, split with crisscross cracks. Pick a line and go up. The starts are generally the hardest parts. Good for pro-placements while doing lead practice and for beginners.

Just left of the *Cub Scout Cracks* are a few roofs of varying heights and sizes with cracks that run to the top. It's a good place to practice some roof and crack techniques.

82. Indiana Mark vs. The Weather God (5.4 G)—32 ft.
Climb the left-facing wall under the first roof left of *Cub Scout Cracks*. Climb up to roof, then step around right onto the face. Work the crack and face above at your leisure.

83. Road to Redemption (5.6* G)—34 ft. This is the same roof as *Time of the Prophets*, and basically a slightly contrived variant to get around the roof. Climb up to under the roof, reach way up and right for a sharp slotted handhold, then pull the roof—have fun with the feet! Using the left corner of the block that forms the roof for a left handhold to pull the roof makes it approximately 5.5+; it's harder if not used. After pulling the roof, stay right and make a few delicate moves up the face/crack until easier climbing is reached (about a body length and a half). Finish going up the crack (no fair "cheating" and using cracks to either right or left, either, after pulling roof). An interesting problem to work out, especially if eliminating the left balance handhold for pulling the roof. And yes, a somewhat contrived route.

84. Time of the Prophets (5.6 G)—34 ft. The "second" roof left of the large prow-like roof, smaller than the first roof left of the same large prow-like roof. Climb up until under the roof, then squirm up through the off-width crack to the left of the roof. There used to be a flake in here that one could reach up and pull on, but sometime during the late 1994/early 1995 season it broke off, changing the nature of the climb to be an off-width (rock is not permanent, you know). And now it's harder, less elegant, and more of a pain for shorter folk. Taller climbers will likely be able to reach through the offwidth section and make it easier. You can climb around/outside the offwidth section to make it easier by working the face on either side. Once past the roof, finish by following the cracks to the top (easy).

85. Dave's Route (5.9+)—34 ft. A bit awkward. Climb the narrow face between *Time of the Prophets* and *Wish You Were Here*, without using either crack (but the arête edges are on). Contrived. Make a tricky balance move onto the face itself, then mainly 5.4 to 5.6 moves the rest of the way.

86. Wish You Were Here (5.8* PG)—26 ft. Find the roof with a V-notch to the left of *Time of the Prophets*. Climb up the right crack and left-facing (**and** overhanging) wall through the V-notch, working the feet. Handholds are all there, and are great, but are reachy at times (especially in the beginning; short people will probably find this harder). Finish by going up the easy crack. Be sure to hang your anchors a little low if you don't want problems with the rope getting jammed in the crack.

87. Wish You Were Beautiful (5.8)—26 ft. Find the wide crack in

the roof to left of *Wish You Were Here*. Surmount the overhang, squeeze through the short wide crack, and finish off on easier ground. Watch that the rope doesn't get caught in a crack, which makes belaying a pain.

Uphill and to the right 30 feet from the BOY SCOUT LEDGES is a short, 15 foot high bouldering wall, facing downhill. Some people boulder the problems (the traverse problem is fun, but not very hard). Those more timid (i.e. those not into potentially breaking their ankles!) can either drop a short top-rope or use a crash pad. Medium to large pro can be useful in setting the anchors at the top. There are a number of variations that you can do. Most climbed is the right half of the wall, full of features and finger ledges. But don't be too fooled. Looks can be deceiving…

PS: If you want to boulder the wall, do one favor: be careful, don't fall, okay? And if you do fall, don't break an ankle.

CASTLE ROCK

This small outcropping is located downhill from BOY SCOUT LEDGES, and directly across the path from MIDDLE EARTH. To get to it, hike up the Green Trail from the parking lot until you reach the stairs, then turn left and scramble through the boulders and bushes (watch out for any poison ivy) to the crag. During the spring through autumn months, while the leaves are out, this rock is fairly hidden from the spying eyes of the tourists as they hike up and down the trail. If relative seclusion is your thing, and/or all the

Fabrizia Guglielmetti hanging out at Boy Scout Ledges

other routes in the area have been taken, this is a worthy stop. Be aware, however, of ignorant yahoos who periodically like to throw things (usually rocks) off from the summit down into the woods around you (the same danger applies at the WEST VIEW ROCKS).

There are plenty of trees to rig your anchors from. Just be sure that your anchors are in the 20 to 30 foot range. Routes are described from right to left.

88. Closet Love Harpy (5.7* PG)—46 ft. Start at the left end of the small overhang 2 feet off the ground. Pop up though the overhang with an amazingly great hold and head up the blackish face until you come to a bush underneath a rectangular overhang. Pull through the overhang at the shallow groove immediately left of the bush (crux). Finish on easier ground. You can avoid the crux by going to the right of the bush (but then the route is no longer 5.7).

89. Tender Feet (5.4* PG)—51 ft. Start 5 feet left of *Closet Love Harpy*. Climb the featured slab past the thin crack to the blocky overhangs. Finish by following the large crack to the top. A nice climb to teach beginners how to use small holds. Be aware of the tree branch that will catch you in the back when you lower off.

90. The Pin Route (5.5* PG)—51 ft. The original name of this climb is long lost in history, but the route itself has stood the test of time. Starting from the bottom of the arête that forms the center of this crag, 5 feet left of *Tender Feet*, follow the thin crack up and right until the crack levels out horizontally in the black-faced rock (note the old piton stem buried in the rock 1/3 of the way along the crack). At this point you can either keep traversing off to the right (and off the rock), or break left, heading up for the blocky overhangs and finishing on *Tender Feet*. If you want to lead this route, bring small wires for the first half of the climb.

91. Purple Spandex (5.4* PG)—56 ft. On the left side of this outcropping, start on
the broad ramp next to some large blocks. Follow the layback crack/flake up right to a shelf,
then continue straight up a short section with two parallel cracks to the blocks above.
Pull straight through the upper blocks (watch for loose holds!) or step left and go up.

92. Two-Faced (5.9* X)—62 ft. Starting immediately left of *Purple Spandex*, intri-
cately dance up the finger crack/flake arcing to left to the top of the short, 20 foot wall.
Pull past the boulder onto a broad but canted ledge, and scramble up to the light brown and
white wall. Without using the large flake system of *Purple Spandex*, step up onto the small
boulder and claw your way onto the white slab, following the thin crack and groove system
to the top. This route offers some nice moves.

West View Rocks

If you're looking for a little adventure in an out-of-the-way area, this section of Sugarloaf Mountain is for you. Climb the stairs past BOY SCOUT LEDGES to the summit area and work your way over to the West View overlook area. Keeping left as you approach the rocks (but right of the right "ridge" leading from BOY SCOUT LEDGES), work your way out to the furthest point of rocks that will suddenly drop precipitously beneath you to a talus field far below. The top of the rocks are covered with white stuff (warning: this is not chalk). Someone engraved into the rocks near the top here the word(s) "HE LAI" in 4 inch tall red letters to the right of a pine tree. You can get down to the base of the rocks via 4th class scrambling to the left (south side) or via a 2nd class scramble "trail" to the right (north) which starts out down a gully-ramp. The left end scramble directly accesses the Upper West View Rocks, whereas the right trail takes you down more than 100 feet to a flat area at the base of the Lower West View Slab.

UPPER WEST VIEW ROCKS

There are only a half dozen lines in this area, and half of them can be variants of each other. Most of these are basically stacked boulder problems (a lower and an upper). Most of the routes start off the top of the 13 foot friction slab that runs up to a short (10 foot) but severely steep wall with a vertical black streak. Routes are described from right to left (as if you were approaching from below) from the base of the slab. Above the first short wall is a ledge followed by another short and steep overhanging section where the different routes can cross each other.

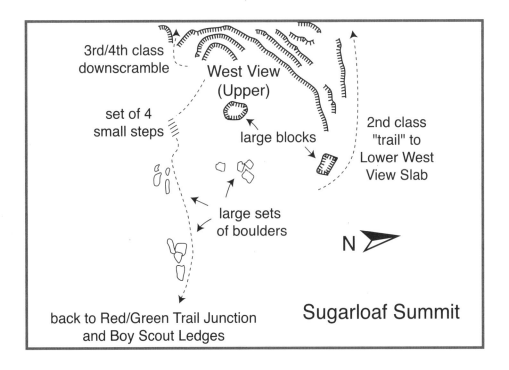

3rd/4th class downscramble

West View (Upper)

set of 4 small steps

large blocks

2nd class "trail" to Lower West View Slab

large sets of boulders

N

back to Red/Green Trail Junction and Boy Scout Ledges

Sugarloaf Summit

93. I May Look Like An Idiot, But I'm Kicking Ass (5.9*)—57 ft.

The name is almost longer than the climb itself. Step off the slab at the rightmost end of the short steep wall, and utilizing a few flake-like handholds, work your way up and left on the rising traverse ramp. Pulling onto the ledge above, work right and weave through the right-facing overhanging wall/blocks above with some awkward moves.

94. Black Crack (5.11d)—57 ft.

This route is seriously harder and the crux significantly shorter than its name-sake at Annapolis Rocks. Starting 10 feet left of *I May Look Like An Idiot…*, crank up the overhanging finger crack through the black streak to the sloping ledge above. There are no feet. For continued fun, ascend the right-facing overhanging wall directly above. Otherwise finish by weaving through the overhangs above.

95. Torqued Off (5.10b*)—57 ft.

Awkwardly climb the overhanging crack and left-facing corner with good holds to the ledge 10 feet up. Great holds, awkward moves. Finish as with *Black Crack*, weaving through the overhanging blocks above.

96. Geezer Face (5.6*)—61 ft.

On this old folks' variation to *Torqued Off*, work the cracks and face 4 feet left of *Torqued Off*. Finish on through easier ground up and right.

97. E Z (5.1*)—75 ft.

It cannot get much easier and still be called "climbing." Climb the narrow easy face 15 feet down and around the corner from *Geezer Face*. After about 30 feet, step left and continue up easy rock leading to even easier terrain. Be careful of the vulture's nest that is sometimes built here (especially after the increase in traffic around *Butterfingers*).

LOWER WEST VIEW SLAB

This is a tall slabby area about 70 feet down and 30 feet left (as if looking uphill) from the UPPER WEST VIEW ROCKS. It is predominantly easy 5th class climbing over blocks and slabs. Routes are described from right to left. To set up top-ropes, work your way up the gully/path on the left side of the rocks here, and after 20 to 25 feet find the 4th class "gully" that goes up and right past a short but steep washboard ribbed wall. Once there, find some blocks to wrap long (20 foot) slings or cracks to put pro in. There are some trees around in the jumble of rock here, but they are rather small. I would not recommend using them (though I have encountered people who use less; scary).

98. Gravity's Angel (5.7 PG)—67

ft. At the base of the rock, find the long, blocky roof 15 feet off the ground. Scramble up to the roof and pull it at the widest part on the right side. The route is over once you've moved a couple of body lengths past the roof; the rest is 5.0 scrambling to the pine tree above.

99. Reprise de la Bastille (5.4** G)—66 ft. Climb up astoundingly sharp holds

directly below a beautiful right-leaning, right-facing, flake-edge layback crack. Follow the crack up to easier terrain. An excellent route to practice lead climbing. **Classic**.

100. Rosemary (5.7* PG)—65 ft. If you have the thyme, garnish your climbing day

with this spicy little route. Starting on the stacked blocks 4 feet left of the tree directly below the *Reprise de la Bastille* flake, climb straight up to the blank face above, passing several feet left of the *Reprise…* flake (crux; much easier if you are several more feet further left). The technical climb pretty much ends after 45 feet ; the rest is 4th class to a good spot for belaying or setting anchors. If it's the afternoon and the sun is out, have your sunglasses handy when you climb out from the cover of the trees. Pleasant face climbing on sweet rock.

WHITE
ROCKS

Gary Lay makes **The Sherpa Connection** *(5.8)* Photo by Rafi Reyes

WHITE ROCKS

RATINGS BREAKDOWN:

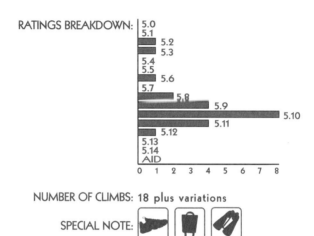

NUMBER OF CLIMBS: 18 plus variations

SPECIAL NOTE:

"That first part's a bitch."—**Anonymous climber**

White Rocks is a small west-facing wall tucked away on one of the peaks north of Sugarloaf Mountain, but is about 300 to 400 feet lower in elevation than the summit of Sugarloaf itself. A nice hike will bring you to this gem of a wall that offers some nice views of the sunset during the summer months. This is private land, part of the Sugarloaf Mountain Preserve.

LOCATION/DIRECTIONS

White Rocks is located roughly 2 to 3 miles away from Sugarloaf Mountain. From the West View Parking Lot atop Sugarloaf follow the blue-blazed Northern Peaks Trail (a 5 mile loop) in either direction (it is shorter to head down the western side of the loop). After a couple of miles you'll come to the White Rocks area.

An alternative approach would be to drive (probably faster this way, too, though not quite as scenic and you will have to deal with the rather limited parking options). From the base of Sugarloaf Mountain, continue west on Comus Road for half a mile to the T-intersection of Ephraim Road (Comus Road will turn from pavement to gravel halfway there). Turn right and continue up Ephraim Road (also a gravel road—it is also barely one lane wide, so **be careful** and watch for oncoming traffic behind blind hills and curves, especially in the

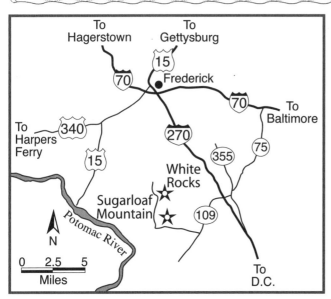

fall during leaf season!) After 2 miles, the road will suddenly take a sharp (90 degree) turn to the left and cross a small stream (passable by just about all makes and models of car unless it's flooding, which is rare). Barely 20 feet further on the right will be the trailhead from this area for the Northern Peaks Trail. Park somewhere on a nearby pull off (be warned: there is **not** a lot of parking here, so groups should attempt to carpool as much as possible). Hike up the fairly easy trail for nearly 20 minutes at a moderate pace to get to the rocks (the trail isn't flat; it goes up and down—mostly up—but it isn't terribly difficult, either).

As you approach the White Rocks area, the trail will climb somewhat steeply (note, there are a couple of uphill climbs on the trail, which drop down again). There will be a small sign near the top of this rise pointing to the rest of the loop trail and indicating that you are at the White Rocks area. You want to bear right, following the direction of the arrow for the White Rocks North View. It takes about 90 seconds to walk over to these rocks.

You will approach the rocks from the top. There are over a dozen and a half routes here ranging from relatively easy (5.2) to fairly difficult (5.12).

GEOLOGY

The rock here is of the same Sugarloaf Mountain Quartzite that you find on the summit of Sugarloaf Mountain itself. This allows for great climbing on some sharp holds.

EQUIPMENT

You will need long slings for the anchors here, approximately 20 to 40 feet in length. Gear really isn't very useful unless you plan on doing some lead climbing.

CAMPING

See the Sugarloaf Mountain section for camping information.

RESTRICTIONS AND ACCESS

There are no special access issues or restrictions at this time. That is, short of throwing people off the cliff who like to throw things down on you (naturally without their being aware that you are even down there; don't think for one minute that your anchors will clue them in!) Also, remember that while this area is open to the public, this is private land and the landowners would like you to be out by sunset.

LOCAL EATS

See the Sugarloaf Mountain section for food information.

OTHER INFO

Almost no historical information exists for White Rocks, but it is not inconceivable that troops from both the South and North used the overlook in addition to the summit of Sugarloaf to monitor enemy troop movements. The rocks furthest to the right, where the climbing is located, offer an excellent view to the northwest, where you can see Catoctin Mountain stretch toward the north, and the western portions of Frederick.

Be aware of glass at the bottom of the cliffs from bottles tossed off the top by uncaring people who think the world is their personal garbage disposal. For years, an effort has been made to clean up the area, but it is an ongoing process. Your help is greatly appreciated.

Also be aware that in the late summer to early fall the abundant Swamp White Oak trees rain acorns down all along the trail and around the rocks, causing some potentially treacherous footing (think ball bearings).

The Routes

There are a number of boulder problems strewn throughout the boulders below the overlook. Some of them are pretty short; others have rather nasty landings. Take care. The routes listed here pretty much cover the main climbing potential of White Rocks, and are described from right to left. Note that some of the routes have two listings for height/route lengths. This is because there is a 22 foot heavily featured slab one must scramble up from the optimal belay stance at the bottom in order to reach the main wall. The main wall height/route length is the first number; the second number is the length from the top of the rock to the optimal belay area.

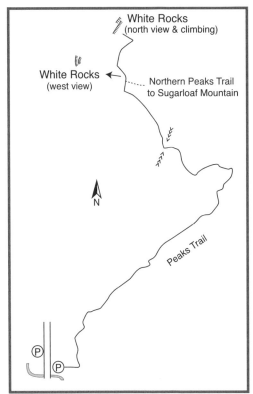

White Rocks
(north view & climbing)

White Rocks
(west view)

Northern Peaks Trail
to Sugarloaf Mountain

N

Peaks Trail

P
P

Catwalk (2nd) For wannabe cavers, there is a little hollow you can scurry through at the right end of the cliff face. It starts through a hole at the base of the large *Lucifer* roof, bends left, and pops out by the *Wynning Solution* boulder. It is all walking passage, so you won't be on your hands and knees much.

1. Green Thumb (5.8–*)—35 ft.

Steep and finger-pumpy. Climb the slightly overhanging greenish wall at the

far right end of the cliff, several feet right of a blocky and imposing roof. Trend left *(V1)* and step onto the blocks capping the roof. Finish up on the featured and ledgy face above. Good holds most of the way.

V1: Brown Thumb (5.9) For added fun, aim for the brown overhang above and pull it directly.

2. Lucifer (5.10a/b*)—33 ft.
Named for an Alan Parsons tune. Immediately to the left of *Green Thumb* is a wannabe-cave with a blocky roof. Climb the down-sloping shelves to the left of the roof, stretch, leap, or what-have-you to the top block in the roof itself (**V1**), and swing to the far right wall and pull the roof. Finish through another overhanging section to a lichen-coated ramp.

V1: Lucifer Direct (5.11c*) Instead of stretching right, use small and interesting holds to pass the roof on the left, following the shallow arête to the top.

3. Wynning Solution (5.9+*)—34 ft. Ascend face and blocks immediately left of the *Lucifer Direct* arête (**V1**). Finish on easier ground.

V1: Wynning Solution, Left (5.9) It is possible to make the start easier by beginning on *Tom Wanted It*, then moving right onto *Wynning Solution*.

4. Tom Wanted It (5.10b)—34 ft. But he never got it. Between *Lucifer* and *Sugar & Spice*, and above and a little to the left of the *Wynning Solution*, is an overhanging wall. Climb up between two boulders (**V1**) to the wall. Step left and follow the crack up until it is possible to reach a ramp to the right. Traverse right and up, using a heelhook if necessary, until above the gap between the two boulders. Continue to top.

V1: Tom Wanted It, Direct (5.11b) Same start as *Tom Wanted It*, but instead of moving left once through the gap between the two boulders, go straight up through the overhanging wall to the top.

5. Sugar & Spice (5.2*)—28 ft. And everything nice. On the right side of the main White Rock face is a blocky left-facing corner. Start on top of the large boulder just below the corner. Clamber up the shelves jutting out to the right of the corner. Feels harder because it overhangs.

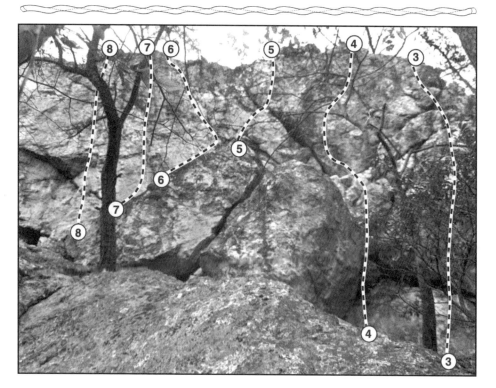

6. Phasers On Stun (5.3*)—28 ft. Start just left of *Sugar & Spice*, atop a large boulder directly below the corner. Follow the left-arching flake/crack system, finishing below a small pine tree.

7. Dogs Of War (5.12a*)—28 ft. Climb the wall just left of *Phasers On Stun*. A shorter and easier start begins at the start of *Phasers On Stun* and traverses up and left on the main wall along a leaning shelf/crack with good holds. When the good holds run out, go up. Enjoy the needle-sharp *mono-doigts* in the upper section. Even though the holds logically head right to the left edge of *Phasers On Stun*, using that edge drops the grade about a level (okay, so it's slightly contrived).

8. Hubble (5.11c/d*)—28 ft. In between *Dogs Of War* and *Force Ten*. Climb up on the right side of the mini-overhang by stepping off the pointed rose-colored quartz boulder. Follow sharp finger flakes/ledges to an undercling in the black area, then deal with the crux above. Try not to grab the right edge that is part of *The Sherpa Connection* (this drops the route to 5.11– or so). A stellar route.

9. Force Ten (5.10b/c**)—26 ft./48 ft. In the lower center of the main face is a small roof/overhang. Climb the left side of roof/overhang, then angle for blackened area halfway through *The Sherpa Connection*. Finish on *The Sherpa Connection*. **Classic**.

10. Force Ten Direct Finish (5.10c/d*)—26 ft./48 ft. Instead of finishing on *The Sherpa Connection* from *Force Ten*, continue on up the face on thin holds to the top.

11. The Sherpa Connection (5.8** G)—28 ft./50 ft. Find the obvious, diagonally right-leaning hand-crack that splits the main face. Start at the lower left and follow the crack to the top. Definitely **the** area classic.

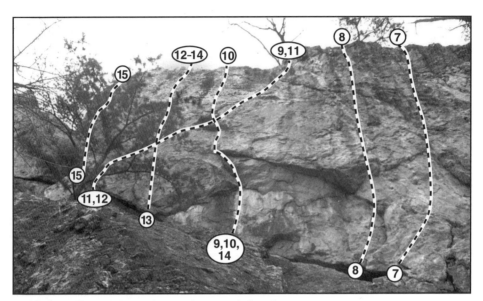

12. Where Eagles Dare (5.10c*)—26 ft./48 ft. Not quite halfway along *The Sherpa Connection* is a line that shoots straight up, following a thin finger crack through a slightly bulging face. Surmount the bulge and finish on easier ground.

13. Where Eagles Dare, Direct Start (5.10d)—26 ft./48 ft. Instead of beginning with *The Sherpa Connection*, start on the main wall directly below the thin finger crack of the upper part of *Where Eagles Dare*, to the left of the black area on *The Sherpa Connection*. Tricky feet at the start. Finish on *Where Eagles Dare*, or slip off onto *The Sherpa Connection*.

14. Guns Of Navarone (5.10d*)—26 ft./48 ft. Start on *Force Ten*, traverse left approximately 8 feet when you reach *The Sherpa Connection*, and then finish on *Where Eagles Dare*. Basically a variation linking two different routes.

15. Treat Me Like The Dog I Am (5.11c)—22 ft. A short climb with a long name. From the start of *The Sherpa Connection*, work up the arête by creative use of side-pulls, underclings, and a pinch-grip or two to the ledges above.

16. Climber Sensitivity Training Wall (5.5–5.10a*)—34 ft. An excellent place to train for climbing sensitivity. This wall is 25 feet down and left of the main White Rocks face, with a white vertical streak running down the center. Routes vary from 5.5 to 5.10. Generally the routes are harder on the left, easier to the right. Climbing the white streak itself is about 5.10a, using no holds far left or right. At the right end of *Climber Sensitivity Training Wall* is the start of *Gap Of Rohan*.

17. Gap Of Rohan (5.6 G)—49 ft. A Tolkien reference. To the left of the start for *The Sherpa Connection* is a wide gap with a tree growing out of it. Below this is a thin finger/hand crack at the right end of *Climber Sensitivity Training Wall*. Start in this finger/hand crack and work your way up through the wide awkward split. A good practice lead; accepts small pro lower down, large pro (up to #4 Camalot-sized) higher up.

18. Thumbthing Else (5.9)—15 ft. Above *Climber Sensitivity Training Wall* is an
overhanging pillar that most of the routes on *CST Wall* can finish on. This pillar can also be
climbed independently, as there is a large sloping ledge separating *CST Wall* and the pillar.
The pillar forms the left side/wall to the upper half of *Gap Of Rohan*. Pick the easiest way
up the face of the pillar and enjoy.

WEVERTON
OVERLOOK

GOODLOE E. BYRON
1929 — 1978

MARYLAND STATE LEGISLATOR 1963–1971
U.S. CONGRESSMAN 1971–1978

HIKER AND FRIEND OF THE APPALACHIAN TRAIL

LEADER IN THE MARYLAND STATE LEGISLATURE
AND U.S. CONGRESS, IN SEEKING PROTECTION OF
THE APPALACHIAN TRAIL FOR FUTURE GENERATIONS

WEVERTON
OVERLOOK

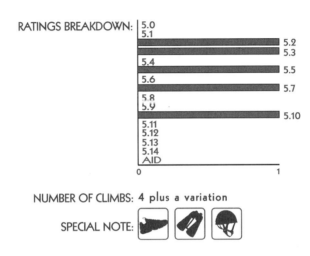

RATINGS BREAKDOWN:

NUMBER OF CLIMBS: 4 plus a variation

SPECIAL NOTE:

"Okay, this isn't a Disney ride, now."—Belayer to climber who was swinging and twirling about on the rope under an overhanging route.

Perched nearly 600 feet above the Potomac River on the south end of South Mountain, this little outcropping of rock offers some nice climbs and great views. While the cliff is not expansive, it does have a range of routes for climbers to play on—assuming one is feeling adventurous enough to run up here and dig them out. You see, getting to the base of the rock can be problematic (the easiest way is probably to follow the hillside down to the right of the rock from the top rather than the left), and due to the infrequent number of climbers these days, most of the routes are choked with vines or thorn bushes, either up on the wall or at the base of the rock. Be careful when moving around down below as a number of the trees down there were badly damaged from a fire some years ago, and may spontaneously fall (or be easily pushed over by you leaning on them). Those trees that have already fallen add to the excitement and challenge of walking around the base of this cliff. In order to enjoy this at its fullest potential, go in shorts.

If you decide that climbing here just isn't your thing, the view from the top of the rocks of the Potomac River does make the short hike up the hill worth a visit. It is one of the nicer overlooks along the Appalachian Trail in Maryland. The relatively short hike ensures that this feature of the cliffs will keep it quite popular. Expect crowds up there, especially during the fall foliage season.

LOCATION/DIRECTIONS

From Baltimore: head out towards Frederick on I–70. At Frederick, get off at Exit 52. Head west on Route 340 (towards Harpers Ferry) for approximately 14.5 miles until you come to an exit for Md. 67. Taking this exit, bear right when it forks, and continue for less than 1/4 mile, turning right at the first right you come to. There will be a sign pointing this way indicating 'Weverton.' Go down the road another 1/4 mile and pull off into the parking area on the right.

From Washington, D.C.: head up I–270 to Frederick, then skip over to Md. 340 via I–70 West, and follow the directions outlined above.

Once you've parked, follow the Appalachian Trail north along the road and guard rail until the road ends at a T-intersection, which is visible from the parking area. Cross the road and continue into the woods on the AT. Follow the sometimes rugged trail with numerous switchbacks up the steep hill for two-thirds of a mile (this should go without saying, but…please stick to the switchbacks; they make going up the steep hill easier, and it helps cut down on erosion). Once you reach what is essentially the top of the ridge (remember, this is the southern end of South Mountain), the trail splits left and right. There will be a small brown sign just before this split indi-

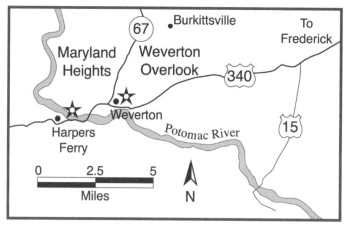

cating the overlook is 300 yards to the right. The AT heads left, uphill along the ridgeline. The trail to the right (blue-blazed) will take you to the cliffs.

GEOLOGY

The rock type here is known as Weverton Formation Quartzite, named after the nearby small town of Weverton. This is the southern-most end of the South Mountain ridge, which also includes Annapolis Rocks, Black Rock, and Raven Rock Hollow. Due to folding and faulting, the rock does not have the familiar horizontal strata that is characteristic of Annapolis Rocks and Black Rock, but if you look closely at the surrounding rock poking out of the ground, you can see the same strata layering—just at a highly inclined angle.

Note that in some places the rock contains somewhat rotten bands, prone to breaking. This is due to weathering and the interlayering of weaker rock formations in the harder stuff. Just keep your attention to it as you climb.

EQUIPMENT

For the most part, moderate to long slings (20 to 40 feet) for anchors will be all that you need to wrap rocks and sling trees, though there are a few places where you could throw in some gear. As for leading any of the routes here, most of these are primarily top-rope climbs. Consider the gear placements for leading to be in the R to X range. And due to the brittle nature of some sections of the rock, belayers may occasionally find a helmet prudent.

CAMPING

There is no camping permitted at the overlook, but there are designated camping areas further north and south on the Appalacian Trail. To the north approximately 6 miles is Gathland State Park. To the south, see the Maryland Heights chapter for additional camping details.

RESTRICTIONS AND ACCESS

There are no restrictions to climbing here. The only access issues are dealing with the overgrowth of thorn bushes at the base of some of the routes.

LOCAL EATS

The closest place to get food would be at The Restaurant (also known as "Cindy Dee Restaurant") a short piece down Md. 340. To get there get back on Md. 340 and head west for 0.9 miles until the divided highway aspect of 340 ends, and turn left onto Keep Tryst Road. Turn left again at the stop sign. The Restaurant will be on your left, next to the Hillside Station. They offer both sit down service and carry out, but no refills on drinks with carry out orders.

Other close by eats are located east on Md. 340. Head back towards Frederick and get off at the exit for Route 17 (Burkittsville/Brunswick—yes, that would be the same Burkittsville from the *Blair Witch Project* movie; please leave their street signs alone). Here you will find a couple of fast-food and sit-down restaurants.

OTHER INFO

This is the southern end of the South Mountain State Park, and nearly the southern end of the Appalachian Trail in Maryland. In the surrounding area there are a number of historical sites you can check out.

There is a dedication plaque to Goodloe E. Byron (1929–1978) here, on the right end of the main cliff. He was a congressman back in the '70s who fought to preserve the Appalachian Trail for you to enjoy.

The Routes

The few known, established routes are scattered along the cliff, not always close to one another, or easily accessed from one to the other (due to the choking overgrowth and steep terrain at the base of the rock). The first two routes, perhaps the most popular ones here, are easily accessed by downclimbing the notch just to the right of the dedication plaque, and then moving along the cliff base for about 25 feet. The fourth route is best

approached on rappel.
The last routes are best
approached on rappel, or
by scrambling down the
steep ground to the far left.
The routes are noted from
left to right, as if you are
looking at the rock.·

1. See Nick Overlook (5.7* PG/G)—32 ft.

Don't **you** overlook this
route! Begin 6 feet right of
the pine tree growing next
to the rock. Step up the
corner to a ledge, then continue up the face and over-

hanging corner past severely left-leaning cracks (toe/foot-jams are helpful) until you reach a
rotten band of rock (be careful, especially for your belayer!) Make a couple moves up the
overhanging left-facing corner and pull around to the right onto the outside face. Climb up
this face past a number of weird cracks to the point at the top. Jugs allow you to top off if
you'd like. Despite the rotten band of rock halfway up, this is a pretty nice climb.

2. See Nick View (5.5)—31 ft.

Start 8 feet right of *See Nick Overlook*.
Climb up somewhat awkward overhanging ledges next to the bush (get intimate
with it if it hasn't been pruned lately)
and gain the face cut by numerous weird
cracks. Climb the face to the roof at the
top. Using a sidepull undercling (**V1**),
make a blind, 4-foot reach to a decent
hold above the roof. Work your feet up
and haul yourself to the summit. If you
see Nick viewing, give him a wave.

V1: Nick's View Escape (5.3)

Instead of pulling through the roof,
traverse left under the roof and finish
on *Overlook*.

Much of the rock between the *See
Nick* routes and *Too Hard To Hannanow*
is mostly steep, ledgy 4th class scrambling, but towards the right end the wall
overhangs pretty severely and there are a
few harder lines at this point. They are

rarely climbed, however, as access to the base of the cliff here is difficult at best. No information on details of these routes currently exists.

3. Goonies Never Say Die (5.2)—45 ft.

This route is located approximately 60 feet right of the *See Nick* routes, below and to the right of a square notch with a pine tree, and just to the left of the large overhanging wall. It is mostly 4th class to 5.0 climbing. Clamber up blocks and ledges, aiming for the square notch at the top. Not the most exciting route around. You can spice up this climb with somewhat harder variations by heading straight up the steeper rock on the right to the top. Access this route by bushwhacking in from either side. Or rappel.

4. Too Hard To Hannanow (5.10b)—51 ft.

This route is approximately 100 feet to the right of the *See Nick* routes, to the right and around the corner of the large overhanging wall. It is best accessed from the top by working your way from the main overlook area downhill along the edge of the cliff for 100 feet until you come to a stack of pointed rocks near the end of the overlook. Climb the south-facing wall next to a large, somewhat overhanging left-facing corner, staying off of the left-facing corner rock, to a sloping ledge. Span the gap formed by the ledge and continue up the blank wall above, following the sharp arête on the left (crux; if this is too hard for you to handle now, climbing the ledges of the left-facing corner on the right keeps the climbing no harder than 5.3). Gain the right-sloping friction ramp, climb up to another, then weave quickly through the final blocks at the top.

There are a few additional routes to the right here that are uncharted at this time.

MARYLAND HEIGHTS

Scott Haines on Hard-Up *(5.8)*

MARYLAND HEIGHTS

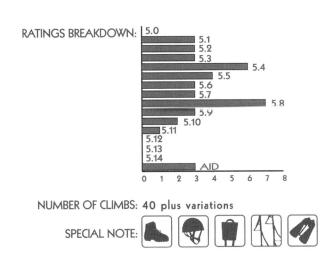

RATINGS BREAKDOWN:

5.0
5.1
5.2
5.3
5.4
5.5
5.6
5.7
5.8
5.9
5.10
5.11
5.12
5.13
5.14
AID

0 1 2 3 4 5 6 7 8

NUMBER OF CLIMBS: 40 plus variations

SPECIAL NOTE:

"Hey Climb-err! Whatcha climbinn?" —**Annoying kid down on the trail shouting up at Indy while on lead.**

This area isn't the best or prettiest place to climb, but for both multi-pitch and top-rope routes, it has some of the tallest stuff within a 90 minute drive of Baltimore. Many of the routes are not very heavily traveled, and there is probably good reason for this: the area has difficult access (many of the climbs are just physically difficult to get to; the "climbers' trail" is a bit arduous), much of the rock is very fractured and loose (it's akin to alpine-style climbing), you sometimes have tourons up on top throwing things down on you (not that they can see you, they just like to throw things; too bad for you if you're in the way—and good luck actually **catching** the ignorant morons who are throwing stuff down!), the cracks that are in the rock don't always take a lot of easy pro placements (this is **not** an area for beginners), and the only known copies of the original guidebook put together by Rob Savoye exist only on the web (any copies of the old guidebook the rangers have come from Rob's online guide). But even still, the online guide is sketchy and lacks helpful details in locating various routes. This chapter is an attempt to clear that up and clarify where the routes are for the intrepid adventurers who wish to pit themselves against this "wilderness next to civilization."

Climbing has been going on at Maryland Heights for many decades, mostly on the *A-D Climbs* and the area around the Sign. Most of the rest of the rock was pretty much ignored (it was more awe-inspiring to climb up beside the Sign where everyone in town could see than, say, play around on YELLOWJACKET WALL). Exploration of the rest of the rock came about in the late '70s to early '80s, when Rob Savoye, Scott McClurg, and Dru Marshall, plus a host of others, descended upon the area. But much of the rock was left untouched, and there are still first ascent opportunities available for the bold and adventurous.

Warning about some of the belay stations: a few stations have bolts set in at the belays (notably on *Hard Up*). While these bolts are less than 10 years old (as of 2000), they are **small**—quarter inch sized! Pay careful attention when using them for belays or rappels. Some of the belay stations on the main wall (around the Sign) have rap-links in the hangers.

LOCATION/DIRECTIONS

For most people in Maryland, the best (easiest, fastest) way to go is to work your way to Frederick, and then from I–70 take Exit 52 (Charles Town & Leesburg) for 340 West. After 16.5 miles, you'll come to a long bridge that spans the Potomac River. On the opposite end you enter Virginia. Continue going, passing a light, and after 0.75 miles you'll enter West Virginia (probably the fastest you'll have ever entered and left a state). Continue onward for another mile and reach another bridge, this one crossing the Shenandoah River. After the bridge, the road will turn and go uphill, and a passing lane will develop. Get in the left lane, as once you crest the hill, 1 mile after leaving the bridge, you'll come to another light. Turn left at this light and in about 0.1 mile you'll come to the Park entrance. Once you've parked you need to take the shuttle bus into town.

If you are coming from D.C. and do not wish to travel up 270 and swing around 340, your best option is to run up Route 7 to Leesburg, then hop on US 15 North. Take this to 340, then head south on 340 and follow the signs to Harpers Ferry.

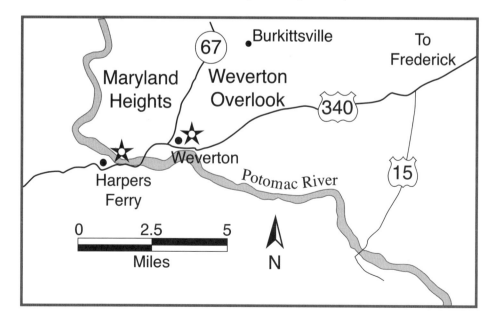

GEOLOGY

The rock of Maryland Heights is composed primarily of Weverton Formation Owens Creek Member rock. Underlying and forming the base of Maryland Heights is what is known as Harpers Formation rock.

Although fairly weather-resistant, the Owens Creek Member does weather easier than and differently from the Buzzard Knob Member that makes up Annapolis Rocks, Black Rock, and Raven Rock Hollow. The quartzites and greywacke also contain pebbly conglomerates, and the rock feels slick and smooth sometimes (doesn't always make for good friction climbing), though depending on the exact composition of a specific area, most of this crag still has good frictionable rock. The weathering effect on the rocks overall here means that there is a lot of loose rock around, particularly higher up, so pay attention and be careful.

The Harpers Formation rock is composed of shale, siltstone, sandstone and quartzite, and forms the base of most of the exposed climbable rock here. You can see massive exposures of this formation at the roadside if you hike north on the Canal Trail a short ways.

EQUIPMENT

For 90 percent of the routes here, you'll need to have a standard rack consisting of a set of nuts/stoppers, camming devices, and other odds and ends you may be partial to (such as tri-cams, hexes, etc.). This goes for both lead and top-rope routes in general. A few routes, such as those on the Yellowjacket Wall, can be rigged off of nearby trees. For this reason, among others, this area should be considered the realm of the experienced climber, not a beginner (unless you're heading out with experienced folk). For any routes you may intend to top-rope climb, also bring some medium to long anchors (in the 40 foot range for most top-rope routes).

The issue of helmets in the climbing world is controversial, although more people are coming around to the idea of when to wear them. In most of the areas in Maryland it is not necessary to wear a helmet (unless you're doing something that warrants it!), but here at Maryland Heights, wearing a helmet by **all** members of your party is **strongly recommended**. The climbing here is serious, even on the easy stuff. Loose rock is the norm, and there are always those people up top at the overlook who can't be bothered to think that **maybe** someone is below them when they start chucking things off.

CAMPING

The closest camping to Harpers Ferry is the Harpers Ferry KOA, located just outside of the Park entrance off of 340. If you feel up to a long walk and primitive camping, the Huckleberry Hill Hiker-Biker Overnighter Campground (cute name) is located 2 miles upriver along the Potomac from Harpers Ferry. You cannot drive to it; you have to hike or bike the towpath to get there. And there are an extremely limited number of sites. Another alternative is the Harpers Ferry Youth Hostel which offers tenting facilities as well as a single building with 40-some beds near the Appalachian Trail. Full details for these and other campgrounds within an hour's drive of Harpers Ferry can be obtained at the Ranger Station in Harpers Ferry.

RESTRICTIONS AND ACCESS

The Rangers request that you sign in (and out) at the Ranger Station in historic downtown Harpers Ferry. Please do this. If you do not, a Ranger or four will be sent out to "rescue" you (at a cost—currently $50). This is for your protection, and to dissuade those non-climbers who think it's no big deal to scramble around/up/down the cliffs (and then suddenly get a clue as to where they are and what could happen, and freeze up in fear).

Be aware of what time the Park closes, and what time the last shuttle leaves for the parking lot (assuming you parked in the National Park parking area). If you miss the shuttle due to coming down off the rocks too late, it's a 2-mile walk back to the cars.

Note that in 2001, the Park Service began a 2-year program to reintroduce Peregrine Falcons to the area. You can find out more information (and even see the tracking of a couple of the birds) on the extensive National Park home page for Harpers Ferry (http://www.nps.gov/hafe/home.htm). For this program, nesting boxes have been provided for the falcons, but in the future, should the falcon population expand, sections of the cliff may become off-limits during certain times of the year. And while many of you who would not climb here normally or regularly would not have a problem with this, you should be aware of this potential developing situation in case you do come down to climb one day and find that access to the cliff, or a section you were intending to climb, is closed. For now, this is a non-issue. But in the future…

LOCAL EATS

No climbing trip to Maryland Heights/Harpers Ferry would be complete if you didn't stop at Cindy Dee's, just off of 340 in Maryland. For that home-cooked meal, this is the place to go. To get there, take 340 back into Maryland and take the first right you come to after crossing the Potomac River. This is Keep Tryst Road. A short distance up the road on the left will be a gas station (with a convenience mart) and next to it to the right is the Cindy Dee Restaurant. And unless they repaint the building in the near future, it is a dark blue-gray color.

If you are down from the rocks in time and the historic section of Harpers Ferry is still active and open, there are a number of small eateries and ice cream shops scattered therein (though unless you're a whacked ice climber, you probably aren't going to be looking for ice cream in the dead of winter—but who knows!)

If you are not able to stop in town, and are not going back toward Maryland, there are a few restaurants scattered along 340 between Harpers Ferry and Charles Town. And once you hit the outskirts of Charles Town, you pick up a number of fast-food joints as well.

OTHER INFO

Harpers Ferry is rich in history, as a lot of activity occurred there around the outbreak of the American Civil War. If you just want a day off from climbing, check out the town. There are a number of museums to visit, pubs and restaurants to check out, trinket shops to browse, and Ranger-led history programs to participate in. Take advantage of these resources!

Many people wonder about the Sign on the rock over the railroad tunnel. It was put up near the turn of the 20th century, and it is accepted that it was painted on the rock in 1903,

Climbers on **Hard Up** *(5.8)* 1980; Rob Savoye Collection

by the Mennen corporation (the same Mennen's that is still around today). It was put up as a giant advertisement (think "billboard") for passengers to read on the train before entering the tunnel. What does the Sign say? In the square border, you can make out **"Mennen's Borated Talcum Toilet Powder."** In the white streak below are the following obliterated words, in smaller scale lettering: **"B C Maxwell Co Trenton N J."**

Oh, and about people throwing rocks off of the top? If you can catch them, or provide the Park Service with a good description of them, the testers of gravity will suffer a $75 fine (as per 36 CFR 2.1(c)(3)).

The Routes:

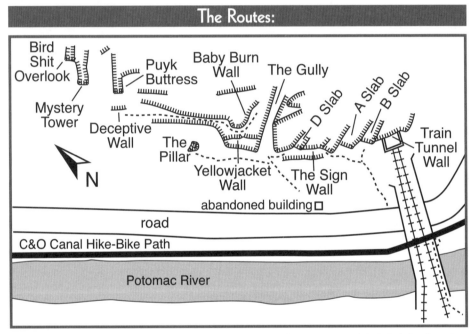

The routes are basically described from right to left. Many route/pitch heights/lengths are close approximations, not always exact. Use your own judgment in these matters.

The rock here is not exactly pristine (think "alpine quality"—what some might call "chossy"—mixed with train soot from the past century and a half), and the cracks do not easily take gear (often they are shallow or flare). Or the lead routes are fairly run-out. All these things considered, not many routes here get a "G" protection rating.

Just accessing the rock can be a small adventure in and of itself. You'll understand why when you visit this place.

TRAIN TUNNEL WALL

The first set of routes are located on the wall directly over the train tunnel, to the right of the first major ramp system. This wall is **not** Park property! It falls in the realm of CSX and Amtrak. Be warned that if you climb here, you could be charged with trespassing (the train police will come for you). These routes are noted for historical purposes only. The pitch lengths are guesses or unknown. Most of the wall overhangs severely, especially down low. This is most pronounced if you were to drop a top-rope or rappel line down it.

This wall is probably the highest free rappel in Maryland: you are away from the rock for more than 120 feet.

If you are climbing on this wall, unless you are **climbing**, you should probably keep a low profile and not hang out on the concrete wall above the railroad tracks. Currently the railroads are tolerant of climbers up on the wall itself, but if you start hanging over the edge of the pit, you're begging for problems.

1. Unnamed (5.4)—? ft. There is a free climb that goes up the right corner of the wall in the pit to a flat area just right of the tunnel. There is an old ladder wedged in the offwidth crack in this corner (but you can climb around it easily enough on the face). Nothing much more is known about this route.

2. Unknown Aid Route (A3?)—approx. 180 ft. This is one of several aid lines that adorn the wall over the train tunnel. As so little is known about the line (somebody **has** been working on it!), the rating is in question. Be prepared for worse.

Pitch 1: Beginning 6 feet left of the corner of the wall, aid up the crack past a pin 10 feet up to a ledge (this could be free-climbed). Continue up from the ledge to the left side of the huge ceiling directly overhead. Follow the seam to the left of the ceiling and work up the blocky wall until another ledge system is attained.

Pitch 2: Free-climb up left to another ledge (top of *Center Stage And All Alone*).

Pitch 3: Finish on the final pitch of *Center Stage*.

3. Air Show (A4)—approx.180 ft. This is a delicate route. Take care climbing the first pitch. Pitch two is more solid, but more exciting.

Pitch 1: (A4) Beginning 25 feet left of the far right corner of the wall, 19 feet left of *Unknown Aid Route*, where the graffiti "Outrage" is painted on the wall, work up past a

small left-facing corner and some bars in the wall wrapped with duct tape until you gain the ledge with a tree. Follow the second seam/crack to the left up and left for approximately 12 feet or so, then cut right and diagonal across the face, crossing a blackened inset corner to another thin (finger) crack. Work up this crack to a good ledge with a fixed gear anchor on the right (warning: if still there, the faded green and yellow webbing should **not** be trusted!)

Pitch 2: (C1+) Aid up the corner to a roof above. Setting a solid piece in the corner of the roof, s-t-r-e-t-c-h out right to a vertical crack on the wall past the roof and desperately plug a piece. Very airy, very scary, solid gear. Turn the roof and pass a few more overhangs and left-facing corners to reach a ledge. Easy climbing off to the left finishes this route.

4. Tomentosa Torment (project)—approx. 40 ft. The tree is not the most traumatic part of the route. The torment will be on the final moves to the belay. This mostly free line crosses the first pitch of *Air Show*. Climb up the left-facing corner to the left of the graffiti "Outrage" and gain the small ledge with the Paulownia tree (warning: the concrete "popcorn" on the lower part of the wall easily shears off). Follow ramps up right until the wall starts to push out (warning: there is a rather large loose rock up there!), some 15 feet below and right of the ledge that marks the end of the first pitch of *Air Show*. Stiff moves up the flared corner may allow these final 15 feet to go free.

5. Center Stage And All Alone (5.4 R*, A3+)—approx. 60 ft. This route starts in the center of the wall, at an obvious and flaring crack just left of the circled "A" graffiti, left of a 12-foot tall left-facing corner with partially concrete-covered rods. Allow a long day to climb it. You may find it handy to have two full sets of TCUs as well as a handful of birdbeaks on your rack for this route. Work the variable-sized crack up the severely overhanging wall. Once past the blocky section above, step out of your aiders and make a run-out 5.4 scramble to a ledge where you will find a fixed nut with slings and rap rings. Rappel from here or finish the final two pitches of *Long And Hard*. A beautiful line that is seeing repeated ascents, and because of this, may one day go free.

6. Long And Hard (5.9*)—approx. 200 ft. Don't let the name fool you. While definitely one of the longest in the area, there are only a few hard crux moves. Can be top-roped from trees above the B SLAB, but a fall will swing you **far** out into space; you won't be able to get back on the rock again. Otherwise you can lead it (probably a better option).

Pitch 1: Start on the block 28 feet left of *Center Stage*. Climb up and right to a tree on an outside corner. Move up and past a large steel rod (first crux) to climb the larger inside corner to a ledge with two quarter-inch bolts (both hangerless). Continue up until you gain a second ramp/ledge at the base of a left-facing corner that has an offwidth part way up.

Pitch 2: Climb up the left-facing corner to a short, awkward offwidth (exciting 5.8), gaining another ledge. Keep going a bit further, over 5.3/5.4 rock until you reach a spacious belay ledge.

Pitch 3: While mostly 4th class to the top from here, it is possible to climb the face to the left of the left-facing corner behind the ledge and finish on more esthetic and challenging ground.

The routes from here on out are all on Park property, public land, and you are permitted full access to the rock here (note the possible restriction earlier re: Peregrine Falcons).

7. Rainbow Warrior (5.8 PG)—36 ft.

A nod to Rob Savoye. This short, often overlooked route is worthy of jumping on, especially after you've come down from either *A* or *B Climb*. Work the shallow chimney-crack that splits the face of the rock, 20 feet up from the fence next to the railroad tracks. Be aware of the ledge above that is full of loose stones and is the start of the *B Climb* slab.

THE SLABS

The next five routes ascend the long, broad slabs that rise over the train tunnel. The origin of the rather unimaginative names? Well, before climbers came here, the Park Service referred to the most prominent of the ramps by letter: A, B, C, and D. Thus the names. Why they did this? No one knows. Another one of those "lost to history" mysteries. In any event, the "main" routes on A and B ramps are to the left, the "variants" are generally to the right. The base of A SLAB is approximately 80 feet to the left and uphill of B SLAB, and C SLAB is approximately 50 feet to the left and uphill of A SLAB. *A Climb* is probably the most popular route here at the Heights due to ease of access and the low difficulty rating.

8. B–1 Climb (5.3* G)—165 ft. Two pitches.

This is considered a variant to *B Climb* below, but it is a completely separate line for the first pitch. Also it is far cleaner and has more opportunities for pro placements than *B Climb*, which is a plus!

Pitch 1: 100 ft. Starting on the lowest section of the slab, follow the broken crack system and fractured rock up to a good ledge with some trees.

Pitch 2: 65 ft. Do a rising traverse to the left and hook up with *B Climb* in the center of the slab at the left-facing corner. Finish on *B Climb*.

9. B Climb (5.3 PG/G)—165 ft. Two pitches.

From the road, scramble up the ravine to the left of the railroad tracks until you can look up and right to the first broad ramp that rises over the tunnel. Scramble up steep terrain to a small, loose stone covered ledge at the base of this ramp. The left end is fairly choked with thorn bushes. Belay at one of the two trees.

Pitch 1: 100 ft. Picking your way past the thorn bushes, follow the left side of the slab up along the large right-facing corner to a small grove of trees (half of which are dead—beware!) at a good ledge.

Pitch 2: 65 ft. Continue up the slab to the steep "headwall." Follow the small left-facing corner in the center of the wall past some small trees to a rock-covered ledge. Finish up the crack past another tree to the top.

10. B Real (5.4* PG)—195 ft.

Get real! This route "variation" is often over-looked by people climbing up the B SLAB.

Pitch 1: 100 ft. Climb the first pitch of *B–1 Climb*.

Pitch 2: 95 ft. Follow a rising traverse left to the tall right-facing wall on the left. Work up the corner there until it is possible to get off the slab and start heading up the vertical wall. Make more than a few exciting moves up past leftward-sloping holds and a few left-facing corners. Exposed. Near the top, you will be able to step left onto the *A Climb* slab. Finish the last 30 or so feet up this slab on easy ground, passing through a few trees, to the spacious top.

11. A–1 Climb (5.1* G)—190 ft.

Instead of climbing the corner and chimney, just work your way pretty much anywhere up the wide ramp. Much of it is 4th class, anyway. But don't let that fool you into climbing without a rope if you are not comfortable with it. There are still some technical climbing sections to be negotiated.

12. A Climb (5.1 PG)—190 ft.

This route climbs the wide, large ramp to the right of the main wall (and the Sign), up and left from the train tunnel, left of the *B Route* ramp.

Pitch 1: 120 ft. Follow the corner up until you reach a good tree on a ledge.

Pitch 2: 70 ft. Continue up the corner and through a chimney (a better option is to turn right just before the chimney and climb up the left-facing corner). After the chimney, work right on easy ground a few moves to the top. The main way off of this half of the Heights is to rappel back down this route from the pine tree. Climbers who put rap slings on this tree to protect the tree will likely find their rap anchors gone the next visit. You can assume someone is stealing these (they are non-climbers) and apparently they want to encourage you to damage the tree by running your rope around it (very considerate of them, no?). Two 60 meter ropes will reach the ground in one shot. Otherwise you may be in for some downclimbing…

13. Not To B (5.5 PG)—160 ft.

If you are looking to access the B SLAB from A SLAB, this is not the way to go. And from mid-spring until late autumn this climb is not to be (unless you have a flame thrower or machete).

Pitch 1: 100 ft. Climb the first pitch of *A Climb,* but stop about 20 feet or so shy of the belay tree (optionally, stop at the belay tree, but you'll have to downclimb a bit to do pitch 2).

Pitch 2: 60 ft. Climb up into and through the "break" in the left wall. You will need to charge through a barrier of thorn bushes and rampant poison ivy. The crux is getting up the first 15 feet or so, and that is where the foliage bars you. Once past the formidable plant life, continue up on better holds (and places for pro) until you reach a ledge. Head up left along a ramp until it is possible to climb straight up the easy corner to the top.

THE SIGN WALL

The next five routes climb up, through, and/or around the wall sporting the Sign.

14. C Climb (5.4 PG)—approx. 100 ft. This two-pitch route is sometimes overlooked in favor of the more obvious routes in the area. Begin below a thorn bush choked corner to the right of the base of a slab that leads up to the start of *Hard-Up Direct Start,* 50 feet up from where *A Route* begins.

Pitch 1: Climb the somewhat awkward corner (only 5.4) to an easy ramp. Continue up the ramp to a stance.

Pitch 2: Climb up the corner above (5.4) to a "cave" and scramble off to the right.

To get to the next set of routes, scramble up the gully and the rocky ramp to the left for about 20 to 25 feet up from the bottom of *C Climb.* Here starts *Hard-Up Direct Start.* At the top of the ramp, do a 4th class scramble left through a narrow but exposed constriction (horizontal chimney; you may want to rope up for this) to a rock and grass ledge on the far side. Here are the starts to *Hard-Up* and *D Climb. Hard-Up* starts behind the first grove of trees after the horizontal chimney constriction.

15. Hard-Up Direct Start (5.8* PG)—30 ft. This route starts directly below the Sign (and a white streak directly below the center of it) at a dihedral in the rock. Climb up the awkward left-facing corner past an overhang until you reach a ledge (where the white streak is). Step left to the belay bolts. Finish pitches 2 to 4 of *Hard-Up.*

16. Hard-Up (5.8 PG)—140 ft. Three to four pitches. Many parties combine the first and second pitches together into one. This route goes right up the left side of the Sign.

Pitch 1: approx. 45 ft. Climb up the wall behind the trees until a) the rock gets steep and b) you can step off around the corner to the right. Continue right until you are directly below the Sign and at a set of belay bolts.

Pitch 2: approx. 25 ft. Turn left and climb up the right-facing corner to a major overhang. Either delicately slip around to the left or flop through the overhanging wall and onto a block slab with a set of rappel/belay bolts.

Pitch 3: approx. 35 ft. Work your way up the left side of the Sign on the main wall, following a shallow right-facing corner and somewhat flared crack system until you can step left onto the arête. Keep going up on easier ground to a large boulder-covered ledge.

Pitch 4: 35 ft. Finish on *D Route* (**V1**). Rappelling down requires two ropes to reach the bottom.

V1: Hard-On (5.8+* PG)—35 ft. At the end of the third pitch of *Hard-Up,* right of the last pitch of the *D* route, climb up to the roof split by a clean hand-crack. Pull the roof, finishing on easier ground above to the trees. Rappel.

17. The Sign Route (5.10a/b PG/R)—approx. 50 ft. Climb the first two pitches of *Hard-Up*. Work a short ways up the third pitch until it is possible to follow the right-leaning cracks that split the face/sign on the main wall. Cut across the Sign until you come to a small cave at the top right corner of the Sign. To finish, scramble off to the right.

18. D Climb (5.4 PG)—2 pitches, 140 ft. Perhaps the second-most popular route here, due to its ease and the fun rappel back down. Start 40 feet left of *Hard-Up*. There is a white spot at the base of the slab/ramp, above the boulder.

Pitch 1: 105 ft. Scramble up the boulder to the white spot and then proceed up the wide ramp, climbing the face on the center or to the right (sporting), or staying more in the corner (better pro), until you come to a large rock-covered ledge with some trees atop the Sign (be careful—the rocks here are loose!) The overhang halfway up can be pulled on the right, near the left end where it is broken, or bypassed by heading up the corner.

Pitch 2: 35 ft. Climb the squeeze chimney (easier facing to the right) to the two trees above. Rappel either from the trees at the top of the chimney (rap slings; you'll need two ropes to rap down *Hard-Up*) or work your way up the 3rd class scramble, then move over to the right and downhill until you are over *A Climb* (rappel). Be aware of loose rock on this route, particularly immediately below the chimney.

THE GULLY ROUTES

The next three routes start off a ledge partway up The Gully. Access The Gully either by scrambling up from the bottom near the Park Service sign left of the abandoned white building, or traversing left 80 feet from the start of *D Route* (note: the entire gully is **full** of loose rocks—**take care in this area!**) At this latter point, 4th class it up The Gully for about 50 feet until you reach a large tree on the right. Step right out of The Gully and around the corner past the tree to a reasonable but sloped belay ledge.

19. Dee's Rival (5.4* R/PG)—110 ft. This is a two-pitch route that climbs the large ramp above and to the left of *D Climb*. Warning: Protection is almost nonexistent on the first pitch.

Pitch 1: 40 ft. From the middle of the slab, climb up a couple body lengths to a narrow but broad ledge system. Traverse right 25 feet or so to a right-facing corner (you also can get your

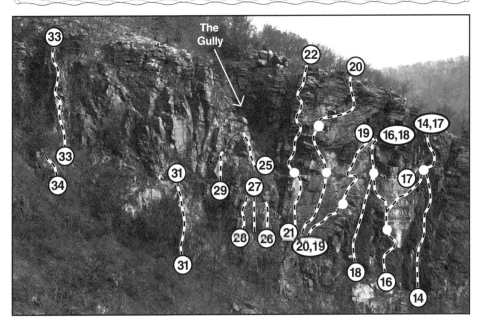

first good—but small!—piece of gear in at this point). Climb up the corner for 15 feet, wading through a few trees, and belay either off of the largest of the three trees, or on a small ledge just up and right of the uppermost tree. There is good gear all around the trees here.

Pitch 2: 70 ft. Follow the shallow right-facing corner with a crack system (beware that some of the rock up here is dangerously loose and **large!**) until the slab before you…ends! (don't fall off the other side). Turn left and step around the right-facing corner onto the friction slab. Climb up the friction wall past a series of ledges for about 30 feet. Trend right away from the overhanging corner above and find a beautiful splitter finger crack. Climb up this for 10 feet until it ends, then traverse right and up to reach the trees at the end of *D Climb*. Walk off or rappel (two ropes reach the ground).

20. Hairy (5.6 R)—approx. 150 ft. So named for the lack of gear in the overhang. This multi-pitch route begins just to the left of *Dee's Rival*. If you wander about the face of the first pitch, you can find some neat little bouldering moves in the blank areas along the way.

Pitch 1: approx. 80 ft. Climb straight up the face, staying a few feet right of the right-facing flake/corner system, until you reach a spacious ledge with several trees (one beefy enough to belay from), 15 feet below a large overhang.

Pitch 2: approx. 35 ft. Step left around the right-facing corner and work up to the brown and black overhang. Pull through this on the right side through a cleft in the overhang, and climb up to a ledge and a tree.

Pitch 3: Climb up and angle right (**V1**) to a pine tree near the top of the rock. Scramble up and off.

V1: Hairy Escape Variations (5.6—5.9) Instead of taking the easy third pitch, it is possible to continue up the corner. Pull any of the overhangs anywhere for a much nicer finish.

21. Cakewalk (5.2 PG/R)—approx. 150 ft. This is a pretty easy route that kinda wanders up the easiest way to the top. There is a fair bit of loose rock on this route, so be careful, especially higher up.

Pitch 1: approx. 80 ft. The start is the same place as *Hairy*, but stay left. Climb up the easy right-facing flake and corner to a large ledge next to The Gully, 25 feet left of the *Hairy* belay station.

Pitch 2: approx. 70 ft. Work up and left, taking the path of least resistance. Traverse left to the next buttress and climb straight up that to the top (you could scramble up The Gully a bit first instead of doing the rising traverse climb).

22. Boob Killer (5.5 PG)—approx. 150 ft. So named after Joanna M., a 4 ft. 11 in. climber, who accompanied Rob Savoye and Scott McClurg on this route during the first ascent. Suffice it to say, she never wore a bikini top climbing again. Either climb the first pitch of *Cakewalk* or scramble up The Gully approximately 80 feet and step right onto the ledge at the end of the first pitch of *Cakewalk*. From there, follow the seam up to the brown and black overhang. Slip around to the left and continue up, weaving through the overhangs as you encounter them (or pulling through them when you can't weave). In the immortal words of Rob Savoye, "the most rotten, miserable climb at Maryland Heights."

BABY BURN WALL

Instead of turning off to the right in The Gully to access *Dee's Rival*, et al., continue up 15 feet and scramble through the ramp on the left to reach another platform at the base

of a short friction wall. You can scramble further up The Gully to gain access to the ledge above for setting up top-rope anchors. Gear is desirable, but there are boulders you can sling as well.

23. The Other One (5.7)—40 ft.
Starting immediately left of the 6-inch wide ledge 4 feet off the ground, friction straight up the middle of the wall. Near the top where the wall steepens, you'll find a nice horizontal handjam.

24. Baby Burn (5.8 R/X)—40 ft.
Begin at the right side of a small, 1 foot wide ledge 5–1/2 feet off the ground on the left side of the wall. Follow the most obvious of the thin, right-rising cracks until you reach a large vertical crack. Go straight up from there. This was first climbed chalkless in full sun on a 100 degree day in July of 1983 by Rob Savoye and Mike Carroll, hence the name.

25. Bacon And Egg (5.7 PG/R)—40 ft. This route was put up a month after *Baby Burn* when it was still hot enough to fry bacon and eggs on the rock. Starting at *Baby Burn*, climb straight up the left side of this wall to the top. There is a small overlap just before the end that you'll need to negotiate.

YELLOWJACKET WALL

Just 45 feet to the left of BABY BURN WALL is a large ledge with a few trees and boulders. Below this is a short and steep wall. The easiest way to get to the climbs is to rappel down to the ledge that has a cedar tree. These routes are usually top-roped nowadays.

26. Yellowjacket (5.6)—27 ft. Named for the active hornet's nest that the belayer (Scott McClurg) of the first ascent team (Rob Savoye, Scott, and Paul Clancy) was sweating next to back in 1983. Begin 9 feet right of the cedar tree on the ledge. Climb up the broken section of the wall here, following a crack. Many of the holds are flat or sloping in nature. Beware of loose shards of rock near the top of this route, and especially beware of the loose rock and boulders at the top of this route! You want to keep your belayer and ropes intact, right?

27. Black Anorexia (5.9+)—32 ft. This route starts at the cavity at the base of the wall a couple feet left of the cedar tree. Follow the thin zigzag crack up the black wall, using nearly anorexic holds. At the roof near the top, you may or may not find the small vertical finger crack to be helpful. Pull past the roof and reach up to the big ledge to end the route.

28. Good Guess (5.8)—32 ft. This route ascends the obvious crack (flaring) 14 feet left of and around the corner from the cedar tree. Climb up the left-facing corner until it ends, and continue up, following the right-leaning crack to and through the roof to gain the top.

To get to the next route, start from the broad ledge atop YELLOWJACKET WALL. Head to the left about 40 feet on the narrow grassy ledge with some small trees, until you come to a short but steep wall split by a thin vertical crack next to a corner on the right. THE PILLAR will be evident off to your left. If you want to set this up on top-rope, follow the direction above for BABY BURN WALL but continue along the ledges upstream (with respect to the river below) until they end. You'll definitely need gear for anchors here.

29. Cracking Up (5.10b* G)—21 ft.
Without using the right wall or the corner (yes, somewhat contrived), climb the thin finger crack to the top. Although it's nice looking, the lack of traffic ensures this route stays dirty.

THE PILLAR

The next three routes are located on the freestanding column of rock known as THE PILLAR, which is located below the "trail" that connects DECEPTIVE WALL to the BABY BURN area. These are usually led, and the easiest way off of THE PILLAR is to rappel down *Frenzy*. The easiest way to access THE PILLAR is to start from the base of The Gully (approximately 250 feet up from the road) and traverse left along the base of the rock for approximately 100 feet. The only way to set a top-rope anchor on THE PILLAR is to lead up one of the routes. To get off THE PILLAR again, you'll need to either downclimb one of the routes or work out a creative rappel option (without leaving behind any anchors).

30. Bullshit Five-One (5.1 PG)—approx. 40 ft.
As you approach THE PILLAR, scramble up right through the foliage to the "backside" (downstream end) of THE PILLAR. Climb the crack and left arête to the top, passing through a small overhang near the top.

31. Sunshine Daydream (5.2 PG)—approx. 70 ft.
This route ascends the face oriented toward historic downtown Harpers Ferry. Climb up the center of the face, following a small right-facing flake system as far as it goes. After it ends, continue straight up to the top. Enjoy!

32. Frenzy (5.4 R)—approx. 70 ft.
Start on the upriver side of THE PILLAR. Climb up the steep wall to a thin vertical crack. Follow the crack to the top.

PUYK WALL

From *Cracking Up*, follow the narrow and sometimes exposed ledge left for 200 feet. This will put you at the base of the short wall below *Puyk*.

33. Puyk (5.5)—approx. 60 ft.
Pronounced "puke," this route ascends the tall southwest-facing wall near the far left end of the Maryland Heights area. It is better to lead this climb than try and set up a top-rope on it from above (try it and you'll see why). Follow the prominent left-rising crack system to a small block ledge. Aim straight up for the roof

capping the top of the brown wall. Pull around the left side of the roof and finish at an exposed ledge. From this point, 4th class it up and off.

V1: Puyk Direct (5.6) Instead of going around left at the roof high up, pull it directly by following the crack.

DECEPTIVE WALL

These next three routes are on the short wall in front of and below *Puyk*. They are typically top-roped. You'll need some gear for anchors.

34. Deceptive (5.8)—28 ft. Start in the center of the wall at the right end of the ramp that forms a ledge 6 feet off the ground, beneath where two cracks merge 10 feet up. Climb up to just left of the two cracks, then follow the left crack until you can gain the main crack to the right, and follow that to the top.

35. Surprise! (5.7)—28 ft. Starting at the left half of the ledge 5 feet off the ground, climb the reverse-C shaped crack a few feet right of *Wasted*. When the crack curves left toward the tree, continue straight up the face to the top.

36. Wasted (5.5)—20 ft. Ascend the shallow left-facing corner on the left side of the wall below a curved forked tree. Finish when you get to the tree.

MYSTERY TOWER

The MYSTERY TOWER is a wall located about 60 feet left of PUYK WALL. It sports a small handful of potential lines all over it, some easy, some not so. There are currently two recorded routes. You'll need medium gear and 20-foot or so long slings to set the anchors.

37. Rafi's Route (5.3)—51 ft. Begin at the right end of the wall, just left of a tree. Climb up (try not to chimney off the tree) and move a little right, ending up to the right

A young Scott McClurg on Hard Up *(5.8)*
1983; Rob Savoye collection

of the tree. Continue up the face next to the arête, without reaching around the arête for better holds (otherwise you'll make this ridiculously easy). Once you get to a broad ledge (careful of loose blocks!), finish the last 20 feet on *Blackwinter*.

38. Blackwinter (5.8)—
51 ft. Climb up the left-facing overhanging corner until it turns sharply enough to become a small roof. Pull through this roof and follow the broken line of rock to the left of the sheer face. As you come to the ledge 30 feet up, step right around the blocky arête and climb the somewhat overhanging right face on good holds to the top (good holds, not great or bomber holds). A fun route, and a little pumpy as you figure out the sequence along the way.

BIRD SHIT OVERLOOK
This is the left-most overlook at Maryland Heights, and is infrequently visited by humans (as they say, the white stuff is **not** chalk!) Forty foot anchors will easily reach the beefy tree set back 30 feet from the rock edge.

39. Whole Lotta Lichen (5.2 PG)—24 ft. You'll get a whole lotta lovin' from the
dusty lichen that coats this wall. Begin on a small platform a few feet below the main ledge 20 feet down from the top of the rock (said ledge has a young pine tree on it). Climb up the steep and horizontal crack-sliced face to the top, staying left of the squeeze chimney. While most of the handholds are slopers, you should be able to find decent holds throughout, and even some finger dishes. Barring that, there are plenty of pinch holds to go around. There is even a spot down low for you to practice kneebars. Have fun!

JEFFERSON ROCK
Jefferson Rock is located on the Appalachian Trail, a few minutes' walk south of downtown Harpers Ferry. The lone recorded route here is most easily accessed by working around the far right end of the chain-link fence, scrambling down the gully and around to the left until you are at the east-facing downstream side of the rock. Splitting the center of the wall will be a sick-looking wide crack. This rock is technically in West Virginia, **not** Maryland, but it was part of Rob Savoye's original guide to Harpers Ferry/Maryland Heights, and it just wouldn't do to lose this information.

40. Sick Pursuit (5.11b/c*)—approx. 30 ft. You'll have to be a little sick to pursue
this route. Climb the obvious wide crack up through the overhanging wall to the top.

There are a number of other routes on the rocks around and below Jefferson Rock near where the buses turnaround that people do climb on and rappel down. The Park Service does **not** require climbers (or rappellers) to register when climbing in this area. You are free to play here without hassle (but try not to get in the way of traffic, okay?) There is currently no recorded route information for these walls.

A more mature Scott McClurg scampers up Baby Burn *(5.8)*

ANNAPOLIS
ROCKS

Mark "Aqua" Neubauer beginning the long traverse on Nixon's Nose (A1)

ANNAPOLIS
ROCKS

RATINGS BREAKDOWN:

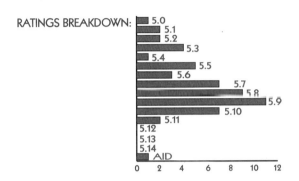

NUMBER OF CLIMBS: 43 plus variations

SPECIAL NOTE:

"How is this route?"—**Climber Bill**

"It gets a little pumpy as soon as you get off the ground...and tapers off when you reach the end."—**Aqua**

Being nowhere near the capital of Maryland, Annapolis Rocks is located off of the Appalachian Trail, (AT) approximately a 2.25 mile hike north from Route 40. It is one of the more remote places to go climbing in central Maryland, so in effect gives you a wilderness experience (assuming, that is, you can ignore the drone of traffic from I–70 hidden in the trees below, or the Mason-Dixon Dragway off in the distance).

Surrounded by woods, the southwest views are pretty nice, especially in the fall when the leaves are changing color. And as a side benefit of this west-southwest facing area, you can witness some very nice sunsets...or watch as storms roar toward you across the flat valley between here and the next line of mountains to the west!

Annapolis Rocks, as well as Black Rock, is part of the extended South Mountain State Park, a park that not very many people are aware exists. The park is long and narrow, covering the entire length of South Mountain. Nearly 40 miles long, it stretches from near the Pennsylvania border all the way down to just outside of Harpers Ferry, encompassing the bulk of the Appalachian Trail as it winds its way through Maryland.

LOCATION/DIRECTIONS

From Baltimore: Take I–70 to the Myersville exit (42 for you Douglas Adams fans). Turn toward Myersville. You will pass a McDonald's and a couple of gas stations as you head into town. From here, there are several options available. The easiest is to turn right in

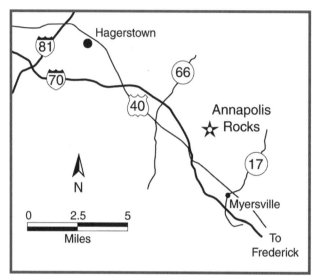

the middle of town, following Route 17. Take this maybe half a mile until you reach Route 40. Turn left onto Route 40 and zip on down the road. After 3 miles of steep hills (both up and down) you will come to a parking area on the left, near the top of yet another steep hill. If you go over the hill and then cross a bridge, you've gone too far. Turn around and try again.

From Hagerstown or points west: Take I–70 to exit 35, heading right (south) on Md. 66 for approximately 1 mile or so. At the intersection with Route 40, turn left and go uphill for 3 miles. Just after you go over a bridge and crest the hill, you will come to a parking area on the right. This is it—park the car!

Across the street from the parking area is an access trail that parallels the road for about 100 feet or so before turning and hooking up with the Appalachian Trail. Once you reach the AT, continue straight, heading north.

Alternatively, if that trail is inaccessible for some reason, follow the barricaded off and unused road immediately south from the kiosk to the end, where you will come upon an access trail on the left. This will take you down to the AT itself—directly above I–70. Turn right and head north.

Follow the Appalachian Trail northward 2 miles until you come to a major side trail leading off to the left. There is a small brown sign with "Annapolis Rocks" in blue lettering on a tree to the left here. This trail will bring you 1,000 feet to a spacious camping area (to the left), and a nice view from the rocks of the west-southwest. The south-end climbs are far to the left. ARGO ROCK is at the right extreme end. The path dumps you out between ARGO ROCK and FAINT'S ROOF. Bear left to the main overlook, and you will be over the FAINT'S ROOF section. The spring is located about 500 feet to the left, along a small path back from and above the cliffs (look for a pipe that feeds into a shallow pool from which some people wash their dishes, bathe, and even drink!) Note that the water is very cold, coming from deep inside the mountain. Some people drink the water straight from the pipe, some boil it (the water, that is), and some use filters. **Use your own judgment when drinking from this water source.**

Rob Savoye gets In Your Face *(5.3)* 1978; Rob Savoye collection

Gary Lay slips in a little late-season climbing on Black Crack (5.9)

GEOLOGY

Characterized by numerous horizontal cracks and round, bulging walls, Annapolis Rocks (and Black Rock) hosts routes that either overhang at various degrees or are blocky slabs and almost too easy to climb. Annapolis Rocks and Black Rock are basically the same type of rock: a Weverton Formation quartzite—a metamorphic rock composed primarily of, you guessed it, quartz! This sedimentary rock is **very** weather resistant and outcroppings of it exist almost continuously the entire length of South Mountain (for the most part these outcroppings aren't tall enough or in any significant shape to climb). Weverton Formation quartzite comes in several flavors. The particular flavor of this is referred to as Buzzard Knob Member.

EQUIPMENT

You will do well to have long slings (upwards of 40 or so feet) as well as some gear (medium to large pieces) for setting anchors in this area. While the main rocks are at the edge of the woods, many good, beefy anchor trees are set far back from the edges, thus the need for carrying extra pro. Some spots require you to either wrap boulders and/or use gear exclusively (notably FIN ROCK, ARGO ROCK, and NIXON'S OTHER NOSE).

CAMPING

While most places in this guide do **not** allow or offer camping in their immediate vicinity, there is actually camping **right here!** In the cleared and flat areas above the rocks that are in the woods, you can pitch a tent pretty much anywhere. These camping spots will be fairly obvious, as numbers of large and small groups come here on the weekends. Water is readily available from the aforementioned spring in the woods 100 yards to the south of the camping area.

RESTRICTIONS AND ACCESS

There are no real restrictions or access issues. But please don't bolt anything here. It is not necessary or needed (see also Equipment, above).

LOCAL EATS

There really isn't much of anything "local" to Annapolis Rocks itself, but Frederick and Hagerstown both offer opportunities to eat. Frederick has a fast-food/sit-down strip of restaurants along Route 40 just outside of town. Head east on I–70 from Myersville until you come to the exit for Route 40 East. Take 40 for a few miles, and you'll be in food heaven.

Hagerstown has its own strip of fast-food and sit-down restaurants. From the parking lot at Annapolis Rocks, head west on Route 40 for approximately 7 miles (within the first 3 you'll come to a Sheetz gas station) and you'll come to a broken line of gas stations, car dealerships, hotels/motels, and food joints, all starting after you pass the I–70 interchange.

OTHER INFO

This is not an area where your average beginner climbers should venture alone. Be proficient in setting anchors for top-ropes, and be prepared for self-rescue in the event of an emergency. Should something happen, help is a long way off.

This remoteness also allows for more chances for encounters with creatures of the wild—such as timber rattlesnakes or copperheads. While such encounters are rare, just be aware that they could happen. This ain't the city, ya know!

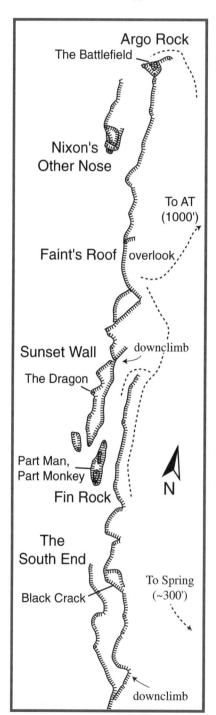

The southern section of South Mountain Environmental Area bore witness to a significant battle from the Civil War: namely, the Battle of South Mountain. In mid-September of 1862, shortly after the Union army suffered yet another serious defeat (the Second Battle of Bull Run), the Yanks had an opportunity to deliver a retaliatory blow to the widely dispersed Confederate army. The Rebs were in the process of gearing up for the "Maryland Campaign," in which the South would take the war to the North. The Union armies attempted to break through several passes between Harpers Ferry and Annapolis Rocks in order to decimate the Confederates, but the South held on to the gaps and blunted the Union assault.

Be aware that, in the autumn, large sections of South Mountain Environmental Area permit hunting, so don't be too surprised if you hear gunfire in late October through December. Fortunately, the Appalachian Trail (as well as the Annapolis Rocks/Black Rock overlooks and immediate areas) is in the "safety zone," though the same cannot necessarily be said for a number of the side trails off of the Appalachian Trail.

Of all the mysteries in Maryland, perhaps the biggest (at least in the climbing and hiking community) concerns Annapolis Rocks. Namely, where did it get its name? Well, one story says that just after the Revolutionary War, people were trying to decide where to put the Maryland state capitol. The name of Annapolis was agreed upon, but there were bitter disputes on where to locate the city. The bickering continued for many years until Jonathan Hager decided to take the matter into his own hands. You see, Mr. Hager lived out toward the western part of central Maryland and thought that where he lived was the best candidate. Rather than decree that his locale was to be called "Annapolis," he named a narrow band of exposed rock "Annapolis Rocks." He figured, incorrectly as it turned out, that since there were rocks nearby called "Annapolis Rocks," that his town would simply have to be called Annapolis. The other legislature folks of the day (actually they were not legislators because they didn't yet have a state capitol) didn't think very much of Mr. Hager. To spite him and his arrogance, they agreed to locate Annapolis as far away as possible—on the banks of the Chesapeake Bay. They felt, however, many years after his death that they were too mean to him, so decided to name a town after him; thus Hagerstown was born.

And that, my friend, is how Annapolis Rocks got its name.

However, the **real** answer is that no one seems to know. Perhaps this will fall into the mystery category of "lost to history."

The Routes

Climbs are listed from left to right (from north to south) as if you were facing the rock from below (reverse the order if you came from the trail and are trying to figure out which way to go). Be sure not to miss *Black Crack* and *Faint's Roof* while visiting here.

ARGO ROCK

This outcropping is located at the far north end of the Annapolis Rocks group. Medium to large pro and medium length webbing are good for anchors.

1. The Battlefield (5.10a* PG)—30 ft. Climb the center of the north-facing wall of the northernmost rock in the area. Charge up the center of the "blank" wavy face, following a thin seam, to good horizontal crack immediately below the roof high overhead (**V1**). Pull through the tiered roof system at the triangular shaped rock under the main roof. Reach a good bucket at the edge of the roof, mantle up, and enjoy victory in the final easy moves to the top.

V1: Exit Field Right (5.9) From the crack turn and head up and right, passing around the roof on the right. Finish to the right of the large, protruding flake to gain the large ledge at the top.

2. Argonaut (5.11c* R)—45 ft. Climb directly up the overhanging arête, sailing through the bouldery moves of the arête's roof (crux). Higher up, the climbing tapers off to about 5.5 or so, but the rock is still steep.

3. Keelhaul Traverse (5.1) Start left of *Argonaut* and traverse right under the Argonaut roof to the broken face right of the Argonaut arête.

4. Wall Of Wander (5.5–5.9* PG)—45 ft./26 ft. (depending where you start). A variety of lines go up this south-facing wall to the right of *Argonaut*. Start either at the very bottom and climb the corner to the wall above, or start on the ledge system halfway up (which basically avoids the lower corner and puts you right on the wall immediately).

V1 (5.9*) Climb the corner to the bottom center of the face, then traverse left until just right of *Argonaut*. Climb the face next to the arête to the top.

V2 (5.5*) Start as for **V1**, but continue the traverse onto the *Argonaut* arête itself. Finish along the arête to the top.

V3 (5.5*) Instead of traversing left toward the *Argonaut* arête, follow the broken line of weakness and left-facing corner to the top.

V4 (5.7*) Climb the face between **V2** and **V3**.

5. Dare To Be Dull (5.7 PG)—26 ft. Start at the base of the left-facing corner below the square, stepped roof system. Pull through the lower roofs onto the steep, broad, lichen covered face and scramble for the top.

NIXON'S OTHER NOSE

Approximately 50 feet south of ARGO ROCK lies the next outcropping of rock. This outcrop, when seen from the overlook above *Ounce Of Perception* (when there are no leaves covering it) has, with a little imagination, an uncanny visage of ex-President Richard Nixon. The main climbing starts on the platform/ledge approximately 20 feet below the square ledge/roof halfway up the cliff. There has been some confusion, depending on whom one talks to, as to exactly what route in this area is *Nixon's Nose*. Some have said it is *Ounce Of Perception*, others have indicated it's the aid route to the right of *Faint's Roof*, and others have thought that it was the rock outcropping approximately 130 feet north/left of *Faint's Roof*. According to information from some of the original climbers to the area (Rob Savoye, et al.), *Nixon's Nose* is the aid route to the right of *Faint's Roof*, making the pillar of rocks to the north/left NIXON'S OTHER NOSE. Anchors here are long runners and medium pro.

6. Cheeky (5.2 G)—20 ft. From the same shelf/platform as *Nixon's Other Nose*, climb up the ledgy face to the left of the large, square roof above. After turning the initial corner onto the west wall, the climbing, while steep, is quite easy and straightforward.

7. Nixon's Other Nose (5.9+*
PG)—20 ft. Work your way up the face directly below the large, square roof. Pull the roof using slightly lichen covered slopers. Not a bad climb, although short.

8. Turn The Other Cheek (5.7
PG)—20 ft. Ascend the face immediately right from directly below the square "nose" platform above. After about 12 feet, the climbing tapers off dramatically to a sloping staircase. It is basically a bouldering problem.

FAINT'S ROOF

Easily one of the most popular areas at Annapolis Rocks, it is relatively easy to find. Angle left at the end of the quarter mile trail off of the Appalachian Trail until you come to an obvious break in the trees/bushes that opens onto a broad area of flat rock—the main overlook area at Annapolis Rocks. To the north from the overlook about 130 feet, you can see the rock outcropping NIXON'S OTHER NOSE.

To get to the bottom, continue heading left (south) along the back edge of the rocks until you come to a chimney-like notch in the rocks. Take this 3rd class down scramble to the base and head right around the corner. In 30 feet or so you will see approximately 30 feet away a large roof to the left of a tall, bumpy face.

9. Bashin' The Boys (5.8)—35 ft. Named for a climber who crushed his, ah, family jewels against the rock when pulling through the final part of *Faint's Roof*. Ow. Beginning left of the tree immediately next to the rock, follow the brown and green water streaks up beside a blocky right-facing corner to some overhangs. At the top of the corner, move left and continue up the rounded walls to the substantial ledge above, ending up left of a large rhododendron bush. Watch the dusty lichen on the upper wall.

10. Cell Phones And Fast Food (5.9*)—38 ft. Begin at the tree growing immediately next to the cliff base. Staying right of the water streaks on *Bashin' The Boys*, climb up easy holds to the overhangs. Pull through four successive overhangs to reach a steep wall, and finally a large ledge with a large boulder to the right of a rhododendron bush.

11. Faint's Roof (5.10a G)**—46 ft. Find the large roof split by a wide crack approximately 130 feet right of NIXON'S OTHER NOSE. This is the most obvious roof in this section of the rock. Go up through easy moves (4th class) to the roof. Follow the wide fist/arm-sized crack through the roof. Climbing essentially ends after you surmount the roof (all easy ground for approximately 10 feet to a huge ledge). You'll want to set your anchors off some blocks on a lower ledge just north of the overlook (you'll need to do a 3rd/4th class downclimb to reach it). Look for the first finger-like projection of rock just north of the *Ounce Of Perception* overlook (as seen from above; can't see this as easily from below). Drop anchors on the north side of this projection. This is one of **the** area classics. But it's not climbed as much as it deserves due to the intimidating roofs.

12. Nixon's Nose (A1*)—50 ft. This is an old aid route that goes through the massive
FAINT'S ROOF to the right of the *Faint's Roof* route itself. Scramble up the first part of *Faint's Roof*, but at the roof angle out right to follow the line 25 feet to the lip of the roof. There is a piton at the start of this route with a cord on it. There are 4 more pitons and blades further out along the thin crack. The pitons are very old, so exercise your own judgement about using them. At the end of the roof (you are 35 feet above the ground at this point), head up on excellent holds (the horizontal cracks take medium to large gear at that point) to a small ledge. The climb is basically over at this point. Walk left 10 feet and scramble up the 3rd/4th class notch. A stellar climb.

13. Cracks In The Earth (5.9*)—70 ft. Terra breaks the stone it makes, leaving....
You'll find this is mostly face climbing, but plenty of cracks lace this route. Work up the shallow left-facing corner 20 feet right of *Faint's Roof* to the roof and traverse right, ending up at a stance below a small roof just left of *Ounce Of Perception*. Use an undercling to reach a finger ledge, then aim for good holds in the black rock up and left. From here romp up the steep rock on excellent holds to the top.

14. Blood And Pus (5.10d*)—66 ft. Start at the orange and black section of rock, 5 feet right of the shallow corner. Climb up and right, following the black and orange rock until you are at a stance below a small roof. Finish on *Cracks In The Earth*.

15. Ounce Of Perception (5.9** PG)—65 ft. Keeping a little insight will get you a long way on this triple overhang route. Climb up the corner/arête formed by the outside edge of the left-facing wall, 10 feet right of *Blood And Pus*. Pull the three successive overhangs then follow a line of weakness up the steep wall up to the final roofs (which are relatively easy to navigate through). It's more popular than *Faint's Roof*. The name comes from a line in a **Rush** song.

16. Pound Of Obscure (5.3 G)—40 ft. Holds are so available that even the most dense climber ought to be able to find the way. Scramble 15 feet up the 4th class terrain onto the large foliage covered ledge right of *Ounce Of Perception*. Weave through the easiest terrain on the wall just right of *Ounce Of Perception*, staying left of the bulge (**V1**) halfway up on the right.

V1: Pound Of Obscure Right (5.5) Stay to the right and pull the bulge directly.

17. Corner Crack (5.3 G)—36 ft. Scramble up the 4th class ledges as high as you can go, aiming for the corner with the wide chimney-like crack. Follow the off-widthy chimney crack to the top. You can skip part of the awkward (but educational) moves by slipping around to the left under the roof and finishing on the easy face above (the climbing is no harder than 5.2 in this instance).

18. Face The Roof (5.8* PG)—35 ft. Climb the face 20 feet right of *Corner Crack*, starting on a large block at the base of the northerly facing wall (optionally start 20 feet lower on the trail and scramble up easy rock to the ledge). Work your way up to the center section of the wall to the small, wide roof above. A tricky little move below the roof through the blank face gains a hand crack just under the roof. Hidden but welcome handholds are above the roof.

19. Face The Notch (5.4)—55 ft. Begin at the blocky arête 30 feet right of *Ounce Of Perception*, next to a beefy oak tree. Scramble up easy rock to the white face above, aiming for a notch on the right side of wide but shallow roof. Pull through the notch to gain the top.

20. Anticipation Of A New Lover's Arrival (5.8* PG)—46 ft.

Begin a few feet right of *Face The Notch*. Climb up easy moves to a large bulging section of rock. Pull through this bulge to easier ground. Traverse right until you are under the large, pointed roof, and pull it on the left side for a climactic finish. The holds are not as good as you'd like them to be in the roof.

21. In Your Face (5.3*)—46 ft.

Starting a few feet right of *Anticipation*, directly below the pointed roof high overhead, climb up easy rock through a wide "groove." Work your way past the roof on the left, maintaining the easy climbing as best as you can.

SUNSET WALL

This is the broken band of rock that extends south from just right of the buttress containing *In Your Face* and *Anticipation Of A New Lover's Arrival* until it ends at a corner that separates it from FIN ROCK. This stretch of rock does not see a lot of climber traffic, although there is no good reason for this. It is probably due to the fact that most people gravitate to either the FAINT'S ROOF area or the SOUTH END. But don't ignore this area; there are routes here well worth doing.

Descent Route (3rd) There is a notch in the rocks that allows the quickest and easiest access from/to bottom and top in this area. From below it is fairly obvious where it is. From up top, head south from the top of *The North Face*. When the rock cuts to the right, find the notch splitting the rock wall. Scramble through and down.

22. The Left Hand Of Darkness (5.8 PG)—34 ft. Begin 65 feet right of

Anticipation Of A New Lover's Arrival, below the south-facing wall with a crack going up the center, next to a large corner, to the right of a huge triangular roof right of the *Descent Route*. Either climb up the major corner to gain the crack and follow that to the top, or climb up the smaller inside corner capped by a roof, traversing right around the roof to gain the crack and white face above, and climb to the top. A bit of funky climbing on this one.

The Cave You won't get aphotic in here (according to conventions of true caving, this isn't a cave). Immediately right of *The Left Hand Of Darkness* is a crack that goes up the corner of the open book. Beneath the low roof, the crack cuts through the rock to the other side. Pretend to go caving and writhe through this narrow tunnel, chimneying as you need, until you are in the sun once again. The rock is fairly polished inside, evidence that it may have been heavily used at one point in time (more likely from weathering, though). This isn't a climbing route **per se**, but noted only as a feature in the area.

23. The Dragon (5.10a** PG)—
43 ft. Be sure your roof techniques are
down pat for this one. Starting to the left
of a tree at the base of the cliff 20 feet
right of *The Left Hand Of Darkness*,
climb through the steep rock directly
below the huge, fear inspiring roof above.
Long reaches allow you to claw through
the tiered roof on good holds. Reach high
with a low lockoff at the top. A most
excellent route.

24. Dreaming Real (5.7* G)—43
ft. You'll think you're dreaming when
you get to the jugs. Climb the shallow
chimney through some overhangs just
right of the tree directly below *The
Dragon*. Hit the steep wall, then pull on
large holds through the tiered sections of
the rock on the right side of the main
roof. Rough, rounded jugs finish the route
on a ledge. The route can be a little intimidating near the top. Try not to escape off
to the right.

25. Don't Fear The Reaper
(5.5*)—50 ft. Climb the face and
bulges 25 feet right of *Dreaming Real*,
10 feet left of the roof cut by two parallel
cracks. Avoid the huge walk-off ledge
15 feet up. The crux is pulling through
the small buttress-like projection of rock
just above the walk-off ledge. A fairly
steep route with nice exposure, but the
climbing is never outrageous. You can
make it a little harder by climbing the
steep wall to the left of the buttress.

26. Trantor (5.6** G/PG)—50 ft.
This route makes a good foundation for
learning some roof techniques. Beginning
10 feet right of *Don't Fear The Reaper*,
climb up the blocky wall, aiming for the
roof with the two more or less parallel
cracks. At the platform just below the
intimidatingly large roof, steel yourself,
then work out left along an excellent

finger crack in the upper corner of the roof (a reach problem; this is going to be a lot harder for shorter people). Heelhook the horn out left, rock over, and pull up past the roof. Continue up on easier rock to the top. The great moves out the roof make this a climb not to be missed.

27. Gully Dwarf (5.0)—50 ft. There is a steep, mostly 4th class south-facing fissure-chimney that cuts up halfway between *Trantor* and *The Little Climb That Wanted To Be*. It's tall, so don't fall! It's also full of lichen and other types of flora, so it isn't really traveled much. And there's probably a good reason for that, too.

28. The Little Climb That Wanted To Be (5.7)—31 ft. Begin 35 feet right of *Trantor*, near the right end of SUNSET WALL. Start the climb a few feet right of a two-trunked tree. Climb up approximately 15 feet (crux) and finish on *Gully Dwarf*. You can keep the real **climbing** going by aiming straight up the lichen covered face above the aforementioned corner, but it never really reaches 5.7 in difficulty at this point.

29. Grunts And Poses (5.6)—25 ft. Get into position and smile for the camera! Begin a few feet right of the start to *The Little Climb That Wanted To Be*, and haul your way up the blocky arête through the overhangs on lichen covered holds.

FIN ROCK

This lone fin of rock is located approximately 180 feet south of Faint's Roof, approximately 40 feet southeast of *The Little Climb*.... Easiest way to set up the routes is to 4th class it up *Access Arête* and place the anchors. Watch out for glass in the area. Lately broken shards of glass have been found near where some of the anchors would nominally be rigged. Bring some trash bags to help clean this area up if you would.

Access Arête is located at the north corner of the rock fin, by a tall tree. Lately some-

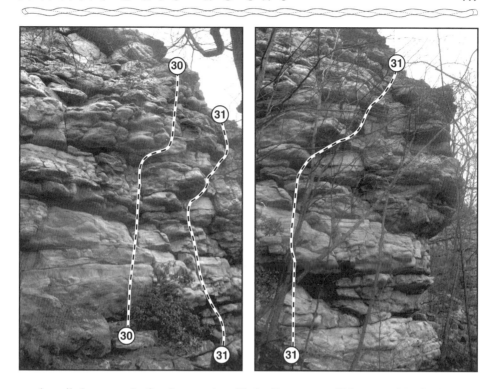

one has piled up a stack of rocks to assist with the first moves off the ground (or back down for the downclimb). The routes are described by starting on the northwest face and working one's way to the right around the arête to the southeast face.

Anchors here comprised medium to long webbing and medium to large pro.

Northwest Face:

30. Part Man, Part Monkey (5.7* G)—35 ft. You'll need to be a little of both. Approximately 10 feet to the left of the *Amazon From Ozegna* crack is a clean, likely look-ing face with bulges protruding out all around. Go straight up to a small shelf (**V1**), then angle right and up past a right-pointing horn (crux). Short but sweet climbing on good holds.

V1: Part Man, Part Monkey Left (5.3) Work your way left and weave around the overhangs on good holds.

31. Amazon From Ozegna (a.k.a., Short Italian Girls) (5.7* PG)—30 ft. On the flip side of *Blondes Just Wanna Have Fin* is an easy looking, short right-rising stepped crack that works its way around and through a couple of overhangs/bulges to some tiered ledges higher up (approximately 25 ft.). Follow the crack (**V1, V2**) to the top (note: the crux is the first half or so of the climb). The climb is a bit harder than it looks.

V1: Amazon Direct (5.8*) Instead of following the crack over from the left, start approximately 7 feet right beneath the overhanging bulges immediately off the ground. Go straight up, neither veering left nor right. Crux is pulling through the first bulge, but the upper half is not trivial, either.

V2: Aqua's Ascent (5.9*) Climb up the overhangs to the right of *Amazon Direct*, immediately left of the start to *A Call To Arms*. Pumpy and sustained, but a very keen variation.

32. A Call To Arms (5.9* PG)—32 ft. To the right of *Amazon From Ozegna* is a tiered roof arête. Wind your way up through the tiered roof system, heading left, then traversing right to the square "notch" in the upper roof halfway up the route. Getting to the traverse is definitely easier if you're taller. Pull through the notch and go up easier rock to the top. Being able to do a heelhook can be helpful. From the top, aim to drop the rope just right of where the arête seems to be.

Southeast Face:

33. Blondes Just Wanna Have Fin (5.5 R)—31 ft.
You can make it harder depending on where you start on this one, or on what holds you decide to ignore/avoid. All variants go up to the left of the leftmost crack-to-the-hole that splits the face of the southeast-facing wall (but not around the corner). Pick your route to go up to a wide platform/ledge (could park a motorcycle on this). The upper section bulges out and overhangs, but there are good holds that go up just right of center.

34. End Of The Day Wall (5.8–5.10c R)—26 ft. May be even harder than rated. Pick a start anywhere in the greyish quartzy bulging wall, right of the vertical cracks that split the face to a hole in the rock, and go up. It's easier if you stay to the left, harder if you go to the right, but particularly hard if you try straight up the middle through the main part of the bulge (let me know if you do this!) Basically any route between the tree on the right and the crack-to-the-hole in the left center of this fin of rock qualifies. Since this isn't climbed too often, you'll no doubt have to deal with the spiderwebs and their inhabitants—

try not to be too harsh on them (although traffic has been increasing lately; you may find chalk marks instead of spiders now).

35. Access Arête (5.1)
The kinda dicey first move off the deck is now easier since someone stacked a bunch of rocks to make that step off the ground; you still may want someone to spot you on it at first, though. Go up through the series of down-slanting steps in the

Scott Haines takes on **The Dragon** *(5.10a)*

northeast corner of FIN ROCK, to the right of
a tree growing right next to the rock. Once
you're up, be very careful when scrambling
around up top. There are a couple of exposed
moves, and a fall could be bad. For starters,
help is generally a long ways off....

THE SOUTH END

Approximately 90 feet south of *Blondes
Just Wanna Have Fin* is a short wall that rises
up out of the trees, containing a chimney-like
cavity. This starts the SOUTH END routes.

36. Black Hole Sun (5.6 G)—32 ft.

Fight through the bushes near the base of the
cliff to reach a wide ledge that forms the base
of the large cavity. Stem up through the cavity
to the overhang. Once past the cavity, go up
the short section to a ledge. Aim a little right
and continue up the last section to the top (relatively easy, but not entirely trivial). This interesting moderate level route is worthy of a visit.

Drop anchors off the slab approximately 20 feet to the right (as you face out) of where the *Black Crack* anchors rest. An alternative is to aim a little left once past the cavity and finish on the ground above.

37. High Hopes (5.9 PG)—32 ft. Another interesting route. Same start as *Black Hole Sun*, but move right and up to under the somewhat imposing roof rather than going into the cavity. Traverse right about 4 feet or so under the roof on good holds, then pull the right side of the overhang where it's shorter (you may have to "garden" the one good hand-hold above the roof to make it useable, as it occasionally becomes colonized with large lichen growth). A heelhook may or may not help. If you can pull the wide part of the roof, let me know!

38. White Arête (5.8*)—49 ft. Wind your way up the steep face immediately to the left of *Black Crack* and to the right of the rounded arête until you reach the lower angled ramp. Continue up to the roof above. Traverse left 5 feet (**V1**) or until you can reach the ledge above, then hand traverse back right until under the anchors (and you have good holds). Pull through the roof onto the ledge. Stand up and you're done.

> **V1: White Arête Direct Finish (5.10a)** Instead of traversing left then right, pull the roof directly, using a thin finger ledge under the roof and making a seriously long reach up and right to a bucket. Pull the roof and finish.

39. Black Crack (a.k.a., Pine Tree Route) (5.9** G)—49 ft. Located 20 feet south of *Black Hole Sun*, just to the right of *White Arête*, is a steep face with a broken crack

through a black section of rock. A good arm pumper—very sustained. There used to be a large pine tree leaning near or on the rock here decades ago; one day some local climbers went out and found the pine tree gone—whether it was cut or simply fell was not clear, but shortly thereafter the route became known as *Black Crack* by those who came after the pine tree incident. **Classic**.

40. Cynosure (5.10b/c** R)
—49 ft. This should keep your attention. It used to be a "project" between *Illusion* and *Black Crack*. Climb up the steep face 5 feet to the right of *Black Crack*, until you reach the major overhangs above. At that point aim right (**V1**) and climb up through the deep notch to the top. A wonderful route, it's a nice rival to its neighbor, *Black Crack*.

V1: Cynosure Direct (5.11a/b*) Instead of passing the overhangs on the right, pull directly through them to the top. Even more pumpy than the regular route.

41. Illusion (5.8* PG)—38 ft. Begin approximately 15 feet to the right of *Black Crack*, just left of "cave." Climb up into the cavelike maw, then up the left side to go around the cave. After getting above the opening, turn and traverse right 8 feet (**V1**) until under the overhangs above and to the right of the "cave." Then go up through a small notch. If you drop your anchors down this notch, your exit hold (ouch as it is) will be unusable.

V1: Illusion Direct Finish (5.8*) Instead of traversing right above the "cave," climb straight up through the large notch to the top.

42. Illusion Right (5.8+)—38 ft. Climb the face just to the right of the cavelike opening, finishing through the final overhangs of *Illusion*. It's a little harder than *Illusion*, but easier than *Black Crack*.

43. Beginner Wall (5.0–5.2)—25 ft. Climb anywhere up the short wall to the right of *Illusion Right*. The crux is pretty much within the first 8 feet of the rock; after that it's a staircase to the top.

The rest of the rock to the right of *Beginner Wall* is ideal for bouldering traverses.

BLACK ROCK

George "Mosca Man" Chapman high-steps to prevent
Falling Towards Apotheosis *(5.10a)*

BLACK ROCK

RATINGS BREAKDOWN:

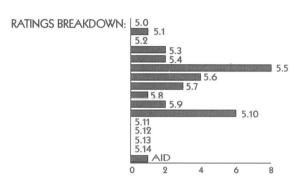

NUMBER OF CLIMBS: 29 plus variations

SPECIAL NOTE:

"You've got a really cool move up ahead…no, to the left…yeah, there, just out of reach."—Indy

"That 'out of reach' part wouldn't happen to have anything to do with how cool it is, would it?"—Seattle Bob on "No Surrender, No Retreat"

Is Annapolis Rocks getting too crowded for you? In the past few years, the traffic at Annapolis Rocks has increased by quite a bit as more and more people are braving the 2.25 mile hike to enjoy the fine quality rock that they've heretofore only heard about (plus it doubles as a really nice overnight/weekend adventure for some groups). When this happens and your favorite routes are taken, a viable option may be to continue north on the Appalachian Trail to Black Rock. Located a "mere" 1 mile further north along the trail past the turnoff to Annapolis Rocks, it is relatively easy to get to. Just before you reach the main Black Rock area you will begin to encounter small outcroppings in the woods to your left. Most of these are pretty small—boulder problems, if at all. But there are some rocks that lend themselves to having ropes set up on them (and which, in this day and age, some people still would call "boulder problems"). Due to the lower level of climber traffic in these parts, you may have to clean off the spiderwebs from some places. And other than the dragstrip raceway in the distance, and the drone of traffic from I–70, this place can give you a pretty good wilderness experience—have fun with the lichen!

Black Rock is not as traveled as Annapolis Rocks, as is indicated by the amount of undergrowth located throughout the area, particularly between the Overlooks and THE TOWER OF BABYLON (wear long pants to prevent thorn damage to your delicate calves and thighs). Also, much of the rock is lichen covered (for the obvious reason that no one goes here much), and there is still loose rock in this area (again, no one climbs here much, so the looser stuff hasn't been broken off—**So be careful, dammit!**)

LOCATION/DIRECTIONS

The main and most popular way to get to the rocks is to go to and past Annapolis Rocks, although there are several other, smaller and lesser known/traveled ways in to the rocks (these other avenues of approach also have extremely limited parking, keeping their popularity down; also the up and down nature of the Appalachian Trail north of Black Rock helps contribute to fewer climbers coming in from the north). The easiest is to follow the directions for Annapolis Rocks, and just continue up the trail for 1 mile beyond Annapolis Rocks.

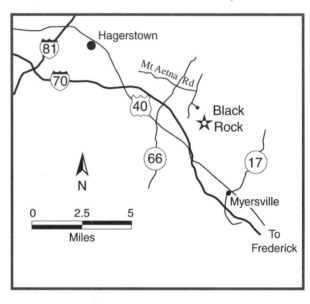

The best alternate, and quicker (and shorter at 1.4 miles), way to go is to come in from the northwest.

From I–70, get off at Exit 35 and head north on Md. 66. Then, 1.4 miles later, you will come to a traffic circle. Bear around right to Mt. Aetna Road. Take Mt. Aetna Road 1.4 miles until it ends in a T-intersection with Crystal Falls Drive. Turn right again, and head south on Crystal Falls Drive for 0.4 miles. Turn left onto White Oak Road and take that a quarter mile to its end. Park here.

Hike up the jeep trail (sparsely blue-blazed) approximately 400 feet to a four-way junction (after 200 feet there will be a jeep trail to the right; pass it by). At the junction bear right and continue until the jeep trail veers hard to the left. There will be a footpath directly before you (there are blue blazes on this path, but you may not be able to see them for the foliage). Take this footpath and follow it gently but steadily uphill to the Appalachian Trail, and the Pogo Campground (it should take approximately 30 minutes at a slow, steady pace to reach the Trail from the parking area). Turn right on the Appalachian Trail and head south for approximately 15 more minutes. You will reach a flat area on the trail and a "clearing" on your right. There will be a sign in the area indicating "Black Rock View." This is it! You are here. Time to climb.

A determined Mark "Aqua" Neubauer takes on No Surrender, No Retreat *(5.10a)*

GEOLOGY

The geology of the rock here is identical to that of Annapolis Rocks (it's the same rock band, just a mile apart). Lest I repeat myself verbatim, refer back to the Geology entry covered in the Annapolis Rocks section.

EQUIPMENT

As with Annapolis Rocks, you'll do well having long webbing (20 to 40 feet) and some gear for top-rope anchors. While the main rocks are at the edge of the woods, most good, beefy anchor trees are set far back from the edges, so medium to large pro would be something to think about carrying in if you don't have extra-long webbing anchors (such as in the 60-foot-plus range).

CAMPING

While most places in this guide do **not** have camping in their immediate vicinity, there is actually camping near here. Annapolis Rocks offers some campsites with a spring several hundred feet south of the camping area, and is only a mile down the Appalachian Trail. The Pogo Memorial Campground is much closer, though, being 0.4 miles north (and mostly downhill) on the AT. It offers a number of sites tucked away in the woods as well as an outhouse and a spring 300 feet down the main side trail to the road (Note: in very dry years the spring can dry up). But it lacks a view. There are other State Parks (Gambrill and Greenbrier) in the area that offer camping, but they cost a bit more than the free ones noted here.

RESTRICTIONS AND ACCESS

There are no real restrictions or access issues. But please don't bolt anything here; it's not necessary or needed.

LOCAL EATS

There really isn't much of anything "local" to Black Rock. Frederick and Hagerstown both offer some food places (Frederick has a fast-food/sit-down strip of restaurants along Route 40 just outside of town; head East on I–70 from Myersville until you come to the exit for Route 40 East; take it and in a mile or two you'll be in food heaven). See the Annapolis Rocks section for more details.

OTHER INFO

This is about as remote as it gets for central Maryland climbing. Be aware that if you encounter a situation requiring medical attention, help is going to be **hours** away. Be self-sufficient and prepared for self-rescue if need be. Cell phones are helpful here in case of serious emergencies, but be aware that the local rescue authorities may not necessarily be prepared for a vertical or remote access rescue.

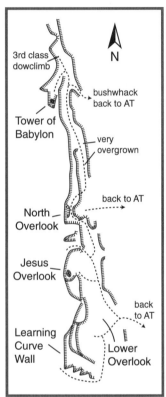

It also offers wonderful views to the west, particularly in the autumn months as the leaves are turning colors. During this time you can find quite a number of visitors to the overlooks. So far this is one of the places where there is no history of non-climbers messing with your gear/anchor setups. Most are just curious as to what you are doing. Be friendly back. It helps in the long run (and who knows, maybe you'll meet some through-hikers on the Appalachian Trail who have done some climbing, and may ask if they could catch a ride on your ropes!)

Ravens will sometimes nest in the crags here. Leave them alone and give them space. Remember, this is their home—you are the visitor.

The Routes

The routes are described from right to left at each outcropping.

LOWER OVERLOOK ROCK

Anchors for here use primarily pro/gear in cracks, though you can wrap some of the boulders with long strips of webbing. Climb descriptions start from right to left, as looking at the rock from below.

1. Well, I Was In The Neighborhood (5.9)—17 ft. Begin at the first east-facing wall/south-facing corner past some blocky overhangs. Climb the left side of the short, some-

what overhanging face without touching the wall behind you. The crux is at the top. More or less a bouldering problem, somewhat contrived.

2. The Ragged Edge (5.3)—20 ft.
Climb the blocky south-facing arête just left and around the corner from *Well, I Was In The Neighborhood*.

3. The Jagged Edge (5.5*G)—20 ft.
Climb the short, west-facing wall 4 feet left of *The Ragged Edge* to the tiered overhangs above, staying more to the left than right. Enjoyable sharp holds, but beware the loose block halfway up! A slightly harder (contrived) variation aims for the flaring notch at the upper overhang on the right (a 5.6 move). You're finished when you can grab the large knob at the top.

4. Objects In Motion (5.6*)—22 ft.
Climb the overhanging east-facing wall directly opposite *The Jagged Edge*. Large holds lend to this being a fun, if short, route. If it were four times longer, it'd be a classic.

5. Objects At Rest (5.4)—26 ft.
Climb the blunt arête just left of *Objects In Motion*. The trick is getting off the ground. Beware of the loose block halfway up that shifts unnervingly.

6. Awkward Customer (5.4)—32 ft.
Not so awkward. Grunt up the 10 feet tall chimney (crux) immediately left of *Objects At Rest* until you reach a broad ledge. Continue up the blocky corner to the top.

7. Easy Two Step (5.3)—34 ft.
This is a variation to *Awkward Customer*. Climb the broad face to the left of *Awkward Customer* until you reach a large ledge. Finish by climbing the barely discernible but blocky arête to the top, staying left of *Awkward Customer*.

8. Learning Curve (5.3–5.5* G/PG)
—44 ft. On the "main face" of the rock, facing west. Drop your rope down the middle of the clean lichen-free southwest-facing wall (there is a small 'notch' that marks the approximate center). Pleasant climbing with plenty of holds to

work with. Slightly harder if you follow the shallow groove/notch on the right side of the wall and straight up to the small roof above. Pulling the roof should be fairly straightforward (but be careful if your anchors are off to the side).

9. Snap, Crackle, And Pop Go Climbing (5.5)—44 ft. Ascend the shallow, lichen spotted arête 10 feet to the left of *Learning Curve*. Move left and up to an overhang at the top, skirting bushes and trees as you go. Be aware when setting your anchor that the lip of the roof is pretty sharp.

10. A Voice In The Wilderness (5.6)—65 ft. What your belayer will likely hear from you as you climb up through the bushes above (especially in the summer months). To the left of *Snap...* follow the short left-leaning crack opposite a Y-forked tree with a small boulder lodged partway up the notch of the two tree trunks (pretty cool, eh?) Climb the easy face above past the pine tree to the top. Drop the rope so it is on the north side (left as facing from the ground) of the pine tree. For an extra long climb, set the anchors off of the tall stack of rock at the top of the cliff.

11. Ruling From The Roof (5.6*)—73 ft. The longest "real" climb at Black Rock. Starting 5 feet left of *A Voice In The Wilderness*, layback up the flaring left-facing crack to a small triangular roof. Pull past the roof to a couple of short sections of thin edge climbing, then onward to (surprise!) a larger roof, bisected by a crack, not visible from the ground. Using some sweet holds, pull the roof at or to the right of the crack and finish the face above. Beware the tree branches when you're lowering back down again.

12. Points Of Departure (5.6+*)—64 ft. Begin just uphill to the left of *Ruling From The Roof*. Climb the obvious right-facing corner then pull through a rectangular long bulge, staying left of *Ruling From The Roof*. Climb the face to a roof split by a crack. Pull the roof to the left of the crack (slightly harder than the right side) and finish on the face above.

THE JESUS OVERLOOK ROCK

The next major rock outcropping from LOWER OVERLOOK ROCK, approximately 100 feet to the north. This is the southern of two overlook rocks you come to when traveling north on the Appalachian Trail. It's perpendicular to the trail at the point where a faded sign on a tree says "120 yards" to the Black Rock View. Follow the foot trail back and around a short band of rocks by a mini-meadow-like area, to the rocks outside the woods themselves. It is referred to as THE JESUS OVERLOOK due to the red graffiti at the edge of the overlook quoting Jesus stating some scripture.

The main face is around 60 feet tall, starting at a ledge approximately 20 to 30 feet up from the scree field (from up top it looks to be over 100 feet to the base, giving one pause for thought about top-roping the routes here). From the top scramble around down right to gain access to the belay ledge below. Alternatively go left, down around LOWER OVER-LOOK ROCK, and then 4th class it up the 20 to 30 feet from the scree field to the decent belay ledge. There are points to anchor in if you so desire.

Wrapping a couple of huge boulders with webbing and slotting some medium large sized tri-cams or hexes will help with anchors.

13. There All The Lichen Lies (5.5)—28 ft. Find the lichen-free overhanging wall at the far right end of the belay ledge. Starting at the left end of the lichen-free overhang, climb up and reach left to the shallow arête with jugs that appear just as you need them. Several moves later, surmount a ledge with more lichen than you can shake a stick at. Finish on the short upper wall to the top. Unless you have reach from hell, you may have to find an inventive manner to use the undercling two-thirds of the way up. This route has probably one of the easiest overhangs you'll ever climb.

14. Moments of Transition (5.4–5.7)—63 ft. If it weren't for all the lichen in the first half of this route, this would be a pretty nice climb. Start 7 feet left of *There All The Lichen Lies*, beneath a rectangular block on a shelf 15 feet up. Climb straight up the lichen encrusted face to a meadow (weaving left then right makes the climbing easier). Stop here, or transition to a different type of climbing by walking over to the wall with jutting blocks. Climb these overhanging blocks to the top (easier to the right, a bit more difficult to the left).

15. By Any Means Necessary (5.5* PG)—56 ft. A nice little climb, if a bit awkward at the crux. Starting 20 feet left of *Moments of Transition*, go up either the face (slightly contrived to make it a little harder) or the broken ramp/steps up to a V-notch in the

overhangs above. Squirm through here to a stance, up a ramp to a picnic-area sized ledge. Snack out, or go up the final face section to the top. Best to have your rope drop in the corner to the left of *Mind War*.

16. Mind War (5.5* PG)—56 ft. Keep your head together for this one. Starting 10 feet left of *By Any Means Necessary*, climb up the overhanging right-facing corner. Work your way through the overhangs and up to the main roof. Either traverse low, using small intermediate footholds to go up, traversing around the arête to a blind foothold, or go up directly to the huge roof flake above, angling to the left on not-so-obvious holds. Continue working your way right and up through the severe overhangs. It looks far more intimidating than it really is (but if you fall, you're in for a swing!) You can make it harder by doing the lower and middle overhangs differently. Set your rope to drop approximately 7 to 10 feet left of the "Jesus…" grafitti.

17. The Four Winds Bar (5.8*)—47 ft. Start 10 feet left of *Mind War*, up on the ledge left of the blocks forming the *Mind War* corner. Head up the ledgy face to a block bulge halfway up. Haul yourself through this bulge (crux; reach problem) onto another ledge area beneath the final roof. Pull this roof a few feet to the left of the crack splitting the roof onto the final ledges at the top.

18. Thirdspace (C1+)—29 ft. This short route starts about halfway up the wall to the left of *The Four Winds Bar*. Begin beneath the 7 foot long roof with a splitter crack heading out and right. There is also a tree growing below the roof. Climb up the back wall (overhangs 3 feet in 10 feet) next to a tree to the roof, then aid out the crack to the end of the roof. Pull past the lip of the roof onto the slabby finish and top off. You can do this clean; no need to pound any pitons.

19. Holding Out For A Hero (5.5 G)—30 ft. Said hero will have to brave numerous thorny plants and much lichen to access and climb this route! Find the south-facing wall split by a right-leaning vertical crack approximately 40 feet left of *Mind War*. Start below the large left-facing corner, climb the wall and pull through the overhangs, following the crack as you go, to the top blocks.

NORTH OVERLOOK ROCK

This rock is basically 3rd and 4th class terrain all the way (except for the overhanging section at the very top). This is the northernmost of the two "scenic overlook" outcroppings at Black Rock. You can identify it by finding one of the furthest out slab/boulders with graffiti in red paint reading: "All mighty God is Jesus Christ" (and so on and so forth; I guess vandals permeate even the Christian religion).

From here you can see to the north, low, through the tops of some trees, the upper blocks of THE TOWER OF BABYLON, about 250 feet away. There is no real good path over there; you're bushwacking it. There is a faint path that follows along near the top of the rocky outcroppings, but knowing where to drop down (and where the path itself is) is the tricky part.

There is a short wall halfway between NORTH OVERLOOK ROCK and TOWER OF BABYLON in the woods that has a number of boulder problems on it.

THE TOWER OF BABYLON

This shorter, somewhat detached outcropping with a pillar of slabs stacked atop of it like a squarish, steep smokestack, lies a couple hundred feet north of NORTH OVERLOOK ROCK. It is best and most easily found from the talus field. The outcrop is characterized by steep faces seasoned with overhangs and roofs. The large left-facing open book on the west wall has two trees growing out of the bottom, with an obvious offwidth crack above. The north face of this rock is lichen encrusted, but most of the other faces are pretty much lichen-free.

The routes are listed from right to left, starting from the wide, boulder choked chimney/gully that leads down past the east face. The rock here on the east face is of a golden brown color. The first climb is the first thing you would come to on your right by going down the gully. Long slings wrapped around boulders and strategic gear placements are the order of the day for top-rope anchors.

20. The Geometry Of Shadows (5.7)—12 ft. This is really more a boulder problem than what one might call a "real climb" (come on, it's barely 10 feet high!), but interesting in its own right. From the "ledge" of rock formed by the boulders in the gully, climb the short golden brown east-facing rock following a right-leaning crack. Beware that what at first looks like a nice finger-locking crack is actually the devil's mouth, as it is filled with razor-sharp crystals for most of its length. Working your way around it on the right allows for you to find nicer holds and a flake before topping out.

21. The Exercise Of Vital Powers (5.10b*)—26 ft. While not quite as classic as *No Surrender, No Retreat*, this route is well worth dropping a rope on. Ascend the short, steep (overhangs 6 degrees past vertical) east face from the bottom of the boulder choked gully, immediately right around the corner from *No Surrender, No Retreat*. Do watch that you don't smack the tree or pile into the boulders if you come off near the bottom! Trying not to use the boulders in the gully, work your way up to the pumpy, golden brown face above. Step left (**V1**) when you hit this golden brown face in order to exercise the crack on the left up to a small roof. Step right and finish the final few feet through the lichen encrusted holds above. Small/medium gear and slings wrapping the summit blocks work well for anchors.

V1: Vital Powers Direct (5.10c/d*) Really just a contrived variation (but then again, what isn't?) Instead of stepping left, continue straight up through the golden brown face, using small yet vital tiny little slopey finger "ledges."

22. No Surrender, No Retreat (5.10a** R/PG)—31 ft. A truly nice route, doable if you're tall or short. Start beneath the tall south-facing wall free of lichen with a roof approximately 10 feet up, split by a hand/finger crack. Work your way up the blocks toward the right to a ledge beneath a roof. Pull through the roof on the right up to a hand shelf

Pam Klinger gets up By Any Means Necessary *(5.5)*

above (there is a key heelhook here), then get set up for your attack run on the steep, sustained, lichen-free face above. A classic route with all the qualities of the standard Black Rock/Annapolis Rocks horizontal cracks. A rival to *Black Crack* and *Faint's Roof* at Annapolis Rocks. **Classic**.

23. Falling Towards Apotheosis (5.10a*)—31 ft. Located to the left around the

corner from *No Surrender...*, on the south-facing wall. Climb up through the tiered roofs and make a **long** reach to a **sharp** detached left-facing flake (a serious reach problem; much harder if you are short). Bypassing the roofs on the left is only slightly easier, but makes for a long reach to the right to gain the flake. Pass the flake by angling right to find a few holds in the mildly lichen covered wall above. Finish when you reach the ledges.

24. Epiphanies (5.5)—29 ft. Work your way up to the corner beneath the offwidth
crack. Easier if done facing right, but can be climbed facing either way. Struggle up the
offwidth crack to the top. Good use of an arm-bar helps early on in this one. Be aware of
the trees (and tree branches).

25. Signs And Portents (5.10c)—41 ft. Start at the lowest point of the rocks, and
either scramble up the clean, shallow corner on the left, or work the somewhat lichen coated
face to the right next to the nose. From the shelf above pass the roof on the right.

To the left, around the corner from *Signs And Portents*, is a wide roof; above it is a
completely lichen encrusted wall.

26. All Alone In The Lichen (5.9)—39 ft. Start at the lowest point on the rocks,
and go up the shallow corner to the shelf above. Work your way over the roof on the left
and through the sea of lichen (bring a weed whacker!) A tough little route.

27. Between The Darkness And The Lichen (5.8–5.10a*)—97 ft. This would be
a double * if it were totally clean of lichen. This route goes through the narrowest section of
the wide roof below the sea of lichen wall above. Follow the crack that cuts through the
roof, then swim through the lichen above, up the face following the jagged right-stepping
hand-jam crack or the face to the right. A variety of variations pull through the roof to the
face above (layback, heelhook, finger locks, face climbing, combination of the previous,
etc); depending on how you do it will depend on how hard the route is (e.g., the crux is
really the roof problem). The face above is approximately 5.4 to 5.5 at best (though you can
make it harder by avoiding the obvious ledges, of course) and offers several different ways
to go up (you can, for example, avoid the hand-jam crack altogether, or climb past it
without using it).

Descent Route (3rd) Twenty five feet to the left of *Between The Darkness...* is a notch in the wall. This is the easiest access area from bottom to top (or vice versa) for this area (the other option is an exposed 2nd/3rd class traverse on the west-facing wall by the boulder choked chimney on the other side of THE TOWER OF BABYLON rock. There are a couple of 3rd class steps that need to be negotiated to get through this, but otherwise no problem.

28. Beth's First (5.1)—20 ft. A nice, simple, short 20-foot route that has a tree growing off a ledge near the top, to the right of the large fissure chimney. Follow ledges with great holds to the top. Nice route for beginners who may have braved coming out this far just to climb. Still gotta deal with lichen, though.

29. A Kind Word And A Two-By-Four (5.7)—11 ft. Speak gently and carry a large stick. This is a boulder problem, but the landing is something to pay attention to, even if spotted. Immediately to the left of the fissure chimney just left of *Beth's First*, work your way up to a pointed rock to great handholds. Swing under and then pull the roundish overhang (a heelhook is key) with good (if lichen covered) holds above. Four moves and it's over.

Much of the rock bands in the woods above THE TOWER OF BABYLON are short (approximately 10 to 15 feet high) with some interesting problems. These would basically be boulder problems, and probably too easy for your true boulderer, but as practice for the general climber, there exist a number of interesting problems. But watch your landings; some of them have jagged, uneven rock below—personally I'm just as happy to rig a rope.

RAVEN ROCK
HOLLOW

Chris Bender gets in a little bouldering workout while Mark "Aqua" Neubauer spots

RAVEN ROCK
HOLLOW

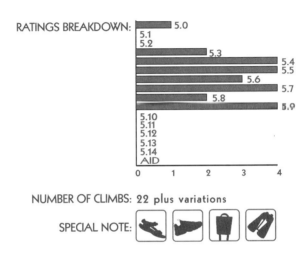

RATINGS BREAKDOWN:

5.0
5.1
5.2
5.3
5.4
5.5
5.6
5.7
5.8
5.9
5.10
5.11
5.12
5.13
5.14
AID

0   1   2   3   4

NUMBER OF CLIMBS: 22 plus variations

SPECIAL NOTE:

"Same old rock, all new climbers."—Anonymous old-timer climber

Raven Rocks is near the northern terminus of South Mountain State Park, and offers a variety of easy to moderate routes to play on. It is surprising that it is not a more popular destination due to the proximity of the rock to parking, the fact that the Appalacian Trail passes right by much of the rock, and the nearness to Hagerstown. Unlike Annapolis Rocks or Black Rock, this outcropping starts right next to the road, and heads uphill in a series of terraced cliffs. In this broken jumble of rock there are several sections that offer climbing potential. The rest are either two- to three-move boulder problems, or are too short (or low-angled) to concern oneself about. The whole outcropping does soar a couple hundred feet above Md. 491, but it is broken by ledges, large and small, giving the illusion of very tall rock which is, in fact, fairly short in sections. Nothing is really higher than 40 feet or so.

Some of the cliff is easily gotten to with almost no difficulty, but other sections are besieged by thick growths of sharp thorn bushes. Take care when attempting to gain access to these thorn surrounded rocks, lest you come away with bloody legs. These details will be noted in the route information section to follow.

LOCATION/DIRECTIONS

From Baltimore: Head out I–70 to Exit 35. Take Md. 66 north for 5 miles to an intersection with Md. 64 (there is a light). Turn right, and continue on Md. 64 for another mile to the next light (intersection with Md. 77). Keep going on Md. 64 for 0.3 miles and turn right onto Md. 491. Follow Md. 491 for 1.8 miles to the Appalachian Trail (very, very poorly marked; in fact, if you don't know exactly what you're looking for—a post with 2 white blazes on the north/left side of the road near a guard rail—you will miss it—and you might miss it still even if you know what you're looking for!) If you go 2 miles (on Md. 491 from Md. 64) you will come to Ritchie Road on the left, and will

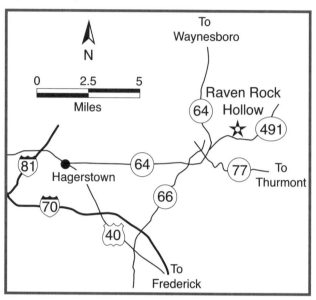

have missed the Appalacian Trail crossing by 0.3 miles. Your choices are to turn around and go back down the hill 0.3 miles (parking on the side of the road in the grass near the Appalacian Trail crossing), park in the pull-off a couple hundred feet up Ritchie Road, or pull off next to the wide grassy area just west of the intersection of Ritchie Road and Md. 491. This would put you right next to the ROADSIDE BOULDERING WALL, which gives easy access to the SIDEWINDER WALL and the RAVEN'S ROOST areas.

If you want to get to the OVERLOOK WALL area, GUNFIGHTER WALL, or DEE WALL, park at the Appalachian Trail trailhead and follow the AT north (and uphill) for a quarter mile. The Overlook Trail will take you to the top of the OVERLOOK WALL area and pass by GUNFIGHTER WALL. The AT will continue uphill and pass the backside of DEE WALL (see map on page 149).

If you are interested in the LOWER RAVEN'S NEST area, SIDEWINDER WALL, or the ROADSIDE BOULDERING WALL, park off the road in the grassy meadow just before you reach Ritchie Road.

An alternative place to park is the small pull-off on Ritchie Road, a couple hundred feet after you would turn off of Md. 491. There is a trailhead across the street from this parking area, as well as another at the corner of Ritchie Road and Md. 491. Neither of these will take you anywhere near the rocks, however, as they parallel the ridge lower down the east side of the hill.

From Washington, D.C.: From D.C. you want to take I–270 north toward Frederick, get on I–70 West, and continue on to Exit 35. Get off here, turn right and go north on Md. 66. Follow the directions noted above for this route.

From Hagerstown and points west: From Hagerstown it is easiest to head east on Md. 64 until you come to Md. 491. Follow the directions above when you get to Md. 491. The rocks shouldn't be more than 15 or so minutes from you (barring traffic and lights).

For other points west, you have the option of getting off in Hagerstown and working your way over to Md. 64, or taking I–70 east to Md. 66 (Exit 35), turning left, and following the directions from that point as if coming from Frederick/Washington, D.C.

GEOLOGY

This is another fine example of South Mountain Weverton Formation, Buzzard Knob Member rock (in fact, Buzzard Knob is that hill across the road). However, unlike Annapolis Rocks or Black Rock, whose layered strata are more or less horizontal, the rock at Raven Rocks has been folded and faulted so that the strata are anywhere from 45 degrees off the horizontal all the way to vertical. This allows for a very different type of climbing than what you have at Annapolis Rocks/Black Rock, even though the rock type is identical.

Due to the highly inclined nature of the strata layers, it weathers a bit differently than the rocks of Annapolis Rocks/Black Rock. The faces have more features, where more resistant quartz deposits remain after the softer surrounding rock slowly is eroded away. And the cracks are more broken, as the water seeps down through them, then goes through the freeze/thaw cycles every winter, expanding the cracks more and more, and ultimately causing chunks of the rock to bust off sideways.

EQUIPMENT

Due to the uplifted nature of the rock here, it is possible to find plenty of places to put gear in as anchors for a number of routes (and some places this is preferable to the trees in the area, which may either be dead or very far from the rocks). The surrounding woods also offer a number of trees to be used as anchors. So having both gear and moderately long anchors (20 to 30 feet) is ideal. Each section will have a very brief note about the best options for setting up top-rope anchors.

CAMPING

Although there is evidence of people sleeping amongst the rocks (there are a couple of fire pits next to some of the cliffs), this is not a designated camping area. Your best bet is to hump a mile or so north along the Appalacian Trail to the Devil's Racecourse Shelter (named for the riverbed of sizeable boulders just downhill from the shelter). You can pitch tents here as well. Otherwise, consult the campgrounds available around Catoctin Mountain National Park (see the Wolf Rock chapter for details) for car camping options.

RESTRICTIONS AND ACCESS

Parking is not overly abundant, but this isn't usually a problem as this section of the Appalachian Trail isn't as heavily visited as, say, the trailhead at Route 40. Still, this is something to keep in mind. Also, while not enforced, you should consider avoiding certain areas of the cliff (notably around the RAVEN'S ROOST) during nesting season. Take responsibility to police yourself in this matter.

LOCAL EATS

Raven Rocks is not close to anything in particular, food-wise. Your choices are to either head into Hagerstown, or go over South Mountain and hit Thurmont. Hagerstown has a wide assortment of fast-food and sit-down restaurants, most of which are located near and around Route 40 off of I–70. Thurmont has a couple of small "bar & grill" places in the immediate downtown region, and a half a dozen fast-food and sit-down (if you consider Pizza Hut a "sit-down" restaurant) on the south end of Thurmont (one exit south on Route 15 from Md. 77).

However, if you're coming from Pennsylvania, your best bet will be to head East on 64 for 4 miles to a flashing light/stop sign combination. Turn right onto Md. 418 and follow that for 2.25 miles to Route 16 in Waynesboro. By turning left, you will shortly come to an array of sit-down and fast-food restaurants (even a Golden Corral). There's a Pizza Hut at the far end of this run of food and car shops and other stores, where Route 16 meets Pa. 997.

OTHER INFO

Ravens inhabit portions of these cliffs, and you can find some nests that have been around for more than a few years. Take care in this area to keep away from the nests, especially during the spring, when the young are fledging.

The ridgeline seems to promise more opportunity for climbing further up the hill, but this is an illusion. All the rock further up the ridge is just a broken line of boulders. However, if you keep going far enough to the north, you'll eventually come to High Rock. There is climbing potential here, but it is usually overrun with trash from rednecks going up to party, or hang gliding (now if you want to try your hand at hang gliding, this is the place to go!)

Be aware that, while infrequent, there have been a couple reports of car windows being shot out by hooligans juiced up on testosterone and playing target practice with other people's cars (said cars have been parked by the Appalacian Trail crossing, but no reason to suspect that is a factor; it is very likely a lone car parked along the road may be a larger draw than multiple cars). One can only hope that they will find out what it is like to have something like this happen to themselves in the near future.

The Routes

The routes noted herein are generally listed from left to right as you look at the wall in question. Exceptions will be noted.

ROADSIDE BOULDERING WALL

This wide but short (17 foot tall) outcropping of rock right at the road level offers a half dozen or so bouldering problems to work out, a warm up prior to climbing higher up, or a warm down after a day up on the rocks above. Difficulties range from V0– to V3.

SIDEWINDER WALL

This is the short rock band immediately above the ROADSIDE BOULDERING WALL. This cliff offers easy top-rope setups, as there are good trees on the ledge above

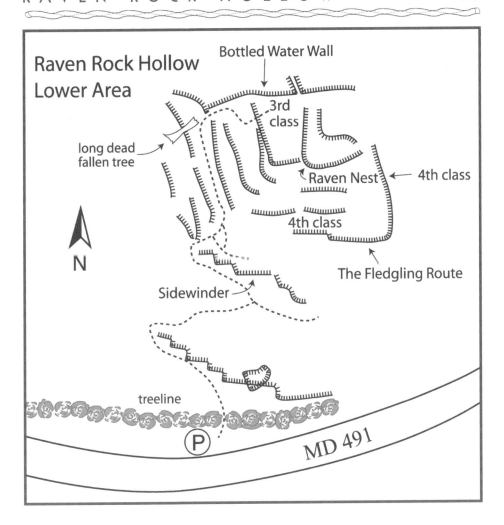

Raven Rock Hollow
Lower Area

Bottled Water Wall

3rd class

long dead fallen tree

Raven Nest

4th class

4th class

The Fledgling Route

Sidewinder

N

treeline

P

MD 491

(beware the dead and flimsy ones right near the edge!) Because of this, and the ease of access, it is often used as a rappel training area for groups like the Boy Scouts. There are several routes on this wall, along with a number of variations. They are harder than they first appear.

1. Unlearn (5.8)—25 ft. Forget all the conventional climbing techniques you've acquired; it's time for something a little different. Start on the block in the ground below the left-facing overhanging corners, 6 feet left of the tree near the center of the face (**V1**). Climb straight up the overhanging corners to the flat section above. Pull past the small overhang near the top. The last moves are the crux of the route.

V1: Unlearn Right (5.8) Start at the left-facing corner a few feet left of the tree by the rock. Climb up, trending left as you go to join up with *Unlearn*. A slightly easier start, but the finish is the same!

2. Sidewinder (5.7)—23 ft. Begin by climbing up the small left-facing corners just right of the tree by the rock. Continue up the wall, aiming for the notch just right of the

small climb of (dead) trees at the top. There is a fair amount of sideways climbing on this route.

3. AIM-9 (5.7)—22 ft. The military designation for the Sidewinder missile, an "air intercept missile." Start on the blank section of wall 4 feet right of *Sidewinder*. Climb up the blank face coated with a dusty lichen (friction? forget it!) to the small blocks above. Continue to the top block poking out.

THE RAVEN'S ROOST

This broken section rises high above the road in steps. The different sections are denoted below. The rock here is heavily encroached upon by thorn bushes, making access to the base of some routes problematic. You also should probably avoid most of this area in the spring when the ravens are nesting.

LOWER RAVEN'S ROOST

This is what is essentially the "bottom" of the broken, stepped cliffs

that make up THE RAVEN'S ROOST. It basically has one route with many variations on it. You'll need to scramble up and around the right side of the rock (3rd class) to get to the ledge to set anchors (here pro and long—20 foot or so—anchors are essential).

4. The Fledgling Route (5.3–5.5)—37 ft. This route pretty much goes anywhere up the left-slanted wall with a wide chimney. Do the chimney inverted for fun.

UPPER RAVEN'S ROOST

This broken series of rocks isn't very easy to access, partly due to the presence of greenbrier all over the place. You can get to it from either the Overlook Trail off of the Appalacian Trail, or from directly below (easier). If coming from below, start from the left side of SIDEWINDER WALL and head up the climber's trail, following the dark green blazes for about 110 feet, staying just to the left of the rock, until you come to a long-dead fallen tree. Turn right and scramble up some ramps until you are beneath a tall wall on a spacious flat area. This puts you at BOTTLED WATER WALL.

BOTTLED WATER WALL

The best way to approach this wall is by the green-blazed trail up left of SIDEWINDER WALL. If you are coming from the Appalacian Trail, this is the rightmost

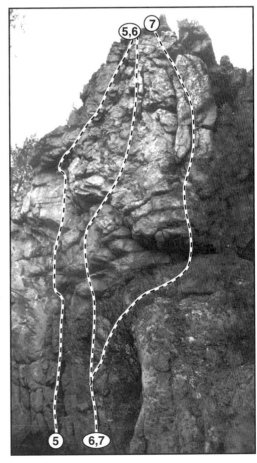

outcropping furthest from the terminus of the blue-blazed trail before you start going downhill (fast). It is not recommended that you come in that way, though, as you'd have to bushwhack through a **lot** of greenbrier, and do some funky downclimbs. Much faster coming straight up from the road. Anchors for this area use primarily gear and 20- to 30-foot lengths of webbing or static line. You can wrap a few boulders, but you'll do yourself a favor bringing gear.

5. Deer Park (5.6* PG)—38 ft.
Climb the left-facing corner past ledges to a short, blank wall below a small roof system. Continue up the blocky corner and blank wall (crux; **V1**), pulling through the roof on bucket holds. Follow the ridgeline up and right to the top.

> **V1: Deer Park Left (5.7)** Start on *Deer Park*, but traverse 5 feet left just below the blank face (optionally, start directly below the left end of the blank face on *Deer Park*). Climb through the left side of the blank face to the top.

6. Aquafina (5.4* PG)—38 ft. A real gem of a climb. Beginning a few feet right of *Deer Park* and left of the rhododendron bush, climb straight up the middle of the wall to the top. The crux is the first moves off the ground but otherwise the route is a jug-fest. If you can't find a bucket hold, you aren't looking hard enough.

7. Evian (5.4 PG)—38 ft. A somewhat contrived route. Start on *Aquafina*, but immediately begin a rising traverse to the right, aiming to be below the overhanging bulge above the rhododendron bush. Pull through the bulge on excellent holds, step right to the hand crack, and follow that until it ends (while optional, the crack makes for great practice using handjams). Finish on good holds to the top.

RAVEN'S NEST

This outcrop is up and left from the LOWER RAVEN'S ROOST. The easiest way to access it is to follow the trail up to the left of the rock to the BOTTLED WATER WALL. Once there, turn right toward a large severely leaning pine tree, 44 feet away from BOTTLED WATER WALL. Push through the rhododendron bush to the rock. Once at the tree, hop over the short wall on the left to a large, sloping ledge. Set your anchors here. Facing out away from the wall, you will note that there are projections of rock sticking out. *Nevermore* comes up from the right of these projections; *No Caws For Alarm* comes up through the notch. To get down to the base of the climbs, either rappel to the **small** ledge with a young pine tree (room enough for two; as the rock drops off precipitously through the trees below, you'll want to anchor in down there—not a place for beginners to venture) or scramble down the steep "gully" beneath the large leaning pine tree, passing the raven's nest, to the same small platform. The raven's nest is often occupied in the early summer months, so please avoid this area during that time. By late July, however, it usually has been vacated, and the climbs open up once again. Note: there are no topo photos for these two routes.

8. Nevermore (5.5)—32 ft. Thus quoth the Raven…and what you'll likely say after you've climbed this once. Climb up into the deep chimney that houses the raven's nest (assuming it hasn't already been knocked down). Squirm and struggle up the chimney to the overhangs capping it above. Pull out onto the overhangs on good holds to stance. Oh, when you're done here, be sure to wash your hands thoroughly. You'll understand why when you see the start of the route. The white stuff is not chalk.

9. No Caws For Alarm (5.7* G)—30 ft. No worries, mate! From the small stance with a young pine tree, climb up the left-overhanging corner and crack system to the blocky overhangs high overhead. Continue on through the notch to the sloping ledge. A great route, just situated in a very awkward place. Doubt it will ever see much traffic.

OVERLOOK WALL

The easiest way to get to this part of Raven Rock Hollow is to head up the Appalachian Trail from the road (otherwise you're bushwhacking it through greenbrier bushes—not recommended). Go up the Appalacian Trail for about 6 to 7 minutes (approximately 1/4 mile) until you come to a junction with the Overlook Trail (blue blazed). The Appalacian Trail will turn sharply to the left; the Overlook Trail goes directly to the right. Follow the Overlook Trail, which will angle you a bit right and take you to the overlook

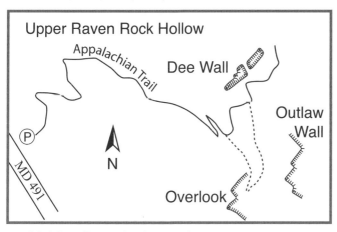

itself (enjoy the view of the Hagerstown Valley). The routes are located on the rock to the right of and below the overlook. The routes are described from left to right as you would approach from the Overlook Trail. The first four routes are located on the short 20 foot tall wall that you first walk past.

10. Hidden Charm (5.5)— 20 ft. This climb hides a couple of surprises. Beginning next to the dead tree stump embedded in the small, knee high right-facing corner at the base of the rock, climb a few thin moves up the blank looking wall using small, sharp flakes that are essentially invisible from the ground. When you gain the right-rising ramp, you also gain larger, less painful holds. A few more moves will bring you to the top, at the right portion of the horizontal quartz veins at the top of the wall.

11. Ace Of Swords (5.9 G)—20 ft. You'll need to be sharp on this route. Beginning 4 feet right of *Hidden Charm*, 10 feet left of *Cows Are People, Too*, delicately work your way up the steep wall on small, very sharp flakes past a welcome "jug" 9 feet up to some welcome relief in the form of larger, not-so-sharp holds near a small black spot on the rock. Passing right of the black spot, continue up to the top on good holds, finishing to the right of the horizontal white quartz veins.

12. Rip Talon (5.9)— 21 ft. Begin 7 feet left of the obvious vertical crack (*Cows Are People, Too*). Often where you think there are no holds you can find…something, small and sharp though it may be. Climb the thin holds to welcome buckets two-thirds of the way up the wall, staying left of the *Cows* crack. A couple of stretchy moves will allow you quick access to the top. Take care not to get your fingers slashed early on.

George "Geode" Cummings takes in a refreshing moment on Aquafina (5.4)
Photo by Rafi Reyes

13. Cows Are People, Too (5.6*)—22 ft.

Hoof up the obvious vertical and widening crack to
the top. The start might be a bit of a challenge for
shorter climbers—you may need to be a little more
innovative in your technique to gain the first good
finger slot in the crack. While sometimes dirty and
spiderweb encrusted (it is not often climbed), this
is a neat route with some interesting mooves and
challenges.

14. Cradle Corner (5.0)—24 ft. Clamber up
the blocks and ledges immediately right around
the corner from *Cows Are People, Too*. Rather
unesthetic.

15. Dr. OW Training Ground (5.5)—24 ft.

Only for those sickies who are obsessed with wide
cracks. Struggle up the rightmost of the two obvious curved off-width cracks to the top. At first
easier if you face left, but you may have to turn
around before the top. An optional way to go up is
via layback. Might be the preferred technique.

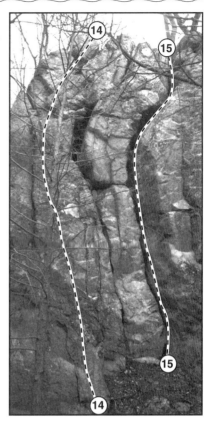

16. The Mummer's Dance (5.9*)—31 ft.

About 10 feet to the right from *Dr. OW Training
Ground* is a west-facing wall with a thin, right-rising crack, below the overlook area itself. Starting
on the right side of the tree immediately next to the
rock, pull up onto the stepped ledge and, going
through some very awkward balance moves (**V1**),
follow the ledge up and left until you can reach the
right-rising finger crack. Follow the crack to a horizontal, move right a couple steps, then stretch up
for the next major horizontal crack. With the right
hand, find the small horizontal finger ledge/crack
just left of the small tree growing out of the rock
high up (note: large hornet's nest is in the corner
immediately above this tree), then s-t-r-e-t-c-h left
to reach as high as you can in the vertical crack,
and top out.

> #### V1: The Mummer's Dance Direct (proj-
> ect) Instead of following the ledge left to the
> finger crack, climb the face directly to the hori-
> zontal cracks above. Finish on *The Mummer's
> Dance*. Has not yet seen a successful ascent that
> your author knows of.

This next route is located around the corner to the right of *The Mummer's Dance*, straight out and directly below the overlook.

17. Parallel Universe (5.9*)—22

ft. Scramble to the top of a large boulder, then climb the overhanging blocky face with two parallel cracks. Follow the left crack (excellent handjams) past a short right-facing corner to a ledge on the left. Bypass the ledge to continue up and slightly right, using the right crack to surmount the small roof, and finish on big holds to a jumbled ledge. A short enduro-fest climb.

GUNFIGHTER WALL

A couple of hundred feet north of the overlook is a tall north-south bearing wall split in the middle by a chimney, and surrounded by a large boulder field. This wall is fairly noticeable from the Appalacian Trail—it's off to the right 100 feet away as you walk by. There are two established routes here, though the wall has potential for additional climbs. However, most of these will be short, broken by ledges in between.

18. Wyatt Earp (5.6*)—35 ft. This route begins on the southernmost section of

GUNFIGHTER WALL. Shoot straight up the blocky ledges through a shallow chimney 10 feet right of the outside corner to a spacious ledge 15 feet up. Walk over to the corner, then layback and stem your way up the nearly perfect finger crack to the top. A fun route. If the corner were at least three times taller it'd be a classic.

19. Wild Bill Hickok

(5.3)—24 ft. This route boasts some interesting moves, but isn't as tough as the reputation of its namesake. Begin around the corner and 28 feet feet north of *Wyatt Earp*, just past the split in the GUNFIGHTER WALL. Climb up the ever so slightly overhanging blocky southwest arête to a ledge. Continue up the face on decent holds

to the final jug below the dead tree that hangs out over the top of the rock. The crux is a reach problem for shorter folk. Belayer, stay sharp for loose rock and holds as the climber goes up. You don't want to end up with a Dead Man's Hand.

DEE WALL

The band of rock is on the west side of the Appalachian Trail, west of the rest of the rock outcroppings in this area. It doesn't offer anything overly tall, nor overly hard. Mostly a bouldering wall tucked away off the trail (though if you're talking, you can be heard from passersby on the AT). To find it, continue up the AT, passing the Overlook Trail accesses to the right. Continue for another 200 feet up the AT and come to a band of rock on the left. As the AT turns sharply to the right, there will be a large cleft in the rock band. Push through this break, turn left again on the other side, and 20 feet later you'll come to a small right-facing corner with a crack running up it. You are here. Watch for thorns and poison ivy in the area. Requirements for anchors include gear of moderate size and some moderately long slings (approximately 20 feet) to tie off to some small trees. If you have no gear, then use longer slings (approximately 30 feet) and tie off to the larger trees!

There are three noteworthy routes on this band, described from left to right.

20. Tweedle Dee (5.4)—18 ft. Starting 18 feet right of the break in the rock band, climb the crack and right-facing corner to the bulge above. Continue following the crack through the left end of the bulge. Short and sweet.

21. Tweedle Dum (5.3)—18 ft. Begin 6 feet right of *Tweedle Dee*, immediately right of the tree. Looks harder than what it is (but if you're wearing floppy tennis shoes, it's as hard as it looks). Climb the face to the bulge, trending left towards the block in the bulge with two vertical cracks. Pull the bulge at this block.

22. Deedle Dee (5.4)—24 ft. Begin next to and left of the vertical crack at the base of the rock, 6 feet left of the tree next to *Tweedle Dum*. Scamper up the face to the right end of the bulge. Finger ledges mostly. Pull past the bulge on the right. A nice little climb… with the operative word being "little." Named after a climber's mom.

WOLF ROCK

After incessant heckling, Daniela Stricklin cries out
Screw You Guys, I'm Going Home! *(5.3)*

WOLF
ROCK

RATINGS BREAKDOWN:

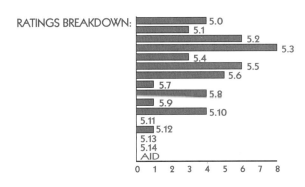

NUMBER OF CLIMBS: 46 plus variations

SPECIAL NOTE:

"It seems stupid that climbers who know what they're doing have such restrictions, yet non-climbers can scramble all over the rock being dangerous to themselves and others."—Deimos

Catoctin Mountain National Park is situated about 20 miles north of Frederick off of Route 15. It offers some pleasant hikes throughout the hills, as well as some relatively easy climbing on 15 to 30 foot tall, good quality rock for the novice and intermediate level climber. While there are quite a few outcroppings of rock scattered throughout the Park that offer routes ranging from "5.way-easy" to "5.incredibly-hard," the Park Service restricts climbing to only the Wolf Rock area. Because of this, a number of climbers have either "pirate climbed" (slipped off into the woods somewhere quietly) or, more often than not, went off to climb elsewhere in Maryland rather than deal with the restrictive nature of the climbing here (see **Restrictions and Access** below). This chapter will cover only the rock that the Park Service has set aside for climbers (and rappellers) to play on.

The crag here is unique due to the "fissure caves," or crevices, that cut the center portion of the rock (see **Geology** below). These crevices allow for ideal crevasse rescue practice for those knowledgeable in such rescue techniques. And the crevices offer some of the harder routes to climb on (if you don't use chimneying techniques, that is!)

Wolf Rock is so named due to the fact that the pillar formation at the very north end of the rock outcropping has a vague resemblance to a wolf sitting upright, facing east (you may or may not need some imagination for this). From space the whole outcropping looks less like a wolf and more like an elongated protozoa. Kinda cool that you can see it from space, eh? (See photo on page 160.)

LOCATION/DIRECTIONS

From Baltimore: You have two options. You can head out on I–795 to Md. 140. Follow Md. 140 for approximately 32 miles, going through Westminster and Taneytown, until you reach Emmitsburg. At Emmitsburg, get onto Route 15 South. Take Route 15 for 8 miles to Thurmont and exit onto Md. 77. There will be signs for Catoctin National Park and Cunningham Falls State Park. Head west on Md. 77 for 2.5 miles to the Catoctin Mountain National Park Visitor Center.

The second option is to head out to Frederick via I–70, then head north on Route 15 for 18 miles until you reach Thurmont. Get off of Route 15 when you reach Md. 77. There

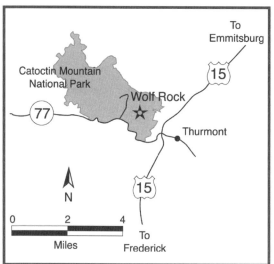

will be signs for Cunningham Falls State Park and Catoctin Mountain National Park. Follow Md. 77 for 2.5 miles to the Catoctin Mountain National Park Visitor Center. These directions are valid for those of you coming from Washington, D.C., Frederick, and Hagerstown.

From the Visitor Center, you can hike up the trail 1.5 miles (30 to 40 minutes for most people) to Wolf Rock. Alternatively, you can go up the Park Service Road past the Visitor Center for half a mile and park at a small parking area on the right side of the road, then follow the trail there for .9 mile to Wolf

Rock (half of it is uphill). There is a "climbing by permit only" sign here. Although the parking is limited at this latter location, the hike in is much shorter (you can save 10 to 15 minutes) and not as steep.

Note: whenever the President or Vice President is hanging out at Camp David, the shorter hike in is **not** an option! Suck it up and hump it in from the Visitor Center. Many other trails will be closed as well. If this is too much of an inconvenience, Raven Rock Hollow (see previous chapter) is only 10 miles away….

GEOLOGY

Wolf Rock is an isolated, 800 foot long exposure of Weverton Formation Quartzite (as are most of the exposed rock outcroppings in the area). It represents the approximate location of an overturned syncline (the other part of this syncline is South Mountain). The center of this particular outcropping is sliced by "fissure caves" (not caves in the "true"

sense where one would get aphotic, however), the longest of which is 80 feet long, 5 feet wide, and as deep as 35 feet. What appears to be slickensides and fault breccia on the walls of these "fissure caves" suggests that the said fissures are actual faults in the rock structure. Pretty cool, huh?

EQUIPMENT

You'll need standard top-rope gear for these climbs. There are plenty of trees, boulders, and cracks for you to set ropes using medium to long slings (10 to 30 feet). You will need gear for some of the top-rope setups.

CAMPING

There are several designated camping areas in Catoctin Mountain National Park and Cunningham Falls Sate Park across Md. 77. These are generally open from April to either October or November. Check at the Visitor Center for details.

RESTRICTIONS AND ACCESS

Of all the places in Central Maryland, Catoctin Mountain National Park has perhaps the most draconian and restrictive set of regulations for climbing. As noted earlier, climbing is **only** permitted at Wolf Rock. Permits are required and may be gotten at the Visitor Center (if desired, you may make reservations up to 5 days in advance: 301-663-9388). You may **only** climb during the hours the Visitor Office is open (10:00 a.m. to 4:30 p.m. weekdays, 8:30 a.m. to 5:00 p.m. weekends). You must check in and out at the Visitor Center when you climb here. No more than 25 people (total!) will be issued permits on any given day, be it individuals or one large group (you could **lose** 25 people around these rocks without them bumping into each other). At least there is no cost for these permits. Permits will **not** be issued during "high visitor weekends" (October) or when conditions appear to be unsafe for climbing (as determined by the largely non-climbing park staff). Solo climbing (and "high-ball bouldering") is not permitted, but scrambling all over the rocks by non-climbers seems to be quite acceptable.

In addition to your other, regular top-roping gear, the Park requires you have helmets for the belayer as well as the climber. But it's up to the ranger on duty whether or not everyone else in the party needs helmets as well. They will want to see helmets when you sign in.

The rules and regulations were drawn up years ago by a well-known climbing ranger, but were intended for some dinky park out West, **not** for Catoctin Mountain National Park! Said ranger had a fit when he found out the Park Service took what he drew up and adapted them to Catoctin. However, the Park Service, like so many government agencies, was unmoved by his protestations, and the regulations remain in place to this day. Hopefully, one day the Park Service will reexamine its policy on the legitimate use of this park by climbers. In the meantime, be aware that some friction exists between climbers and some (but not all) of the rangers.

LOCAL EATS

The nearest place to get food is in and around Thurmont, just off Route 15. Other options include heading north on Route 15 to Emmitsburg, south on Route 15 to Frederick, or west on Md. 77, working your way to Hagerstown.

OTHER INFO

Back in the mid '30s, what is now Catoctin Mountain National Park was considered submarginal land—land that had its resources overutilized by the settlers and those who followed. It was purchased by the government to show how the land could be reclaimed and restored, and thus was born the Catoctin Recreational Demonstration Area. The restoration project also provided people with work during the Great Depression. A number of camps for crippled children were built in this area, as were retreats for federal employees.

Then President Franklin D. Roosevelt, seeking a new retreat from the hot, muggy Washington, D.C. summers (partly due to his health, and partly to avoid U-boats which might make their way up the Potomac and skewer him on his yacht) discovered what was then called Camp Hi-Catoctin. Being 10 degrees cooler than Washington and relatively close (less than 100 miles away), the camp seemed an ideal spot for a retreat. The President made his first visit in 1942, naming the camp "Shangri-La" (from James Hilton's 1933 story "Lost Horizon"). After World War II had ended, most of the land was given to the National Park Service and the Maryland State Forest and Park System. Camp Shangri-La was retained as a retreat for the President, and was renamed "Camp David" by President Eisenhower in 1953 for his grandson.

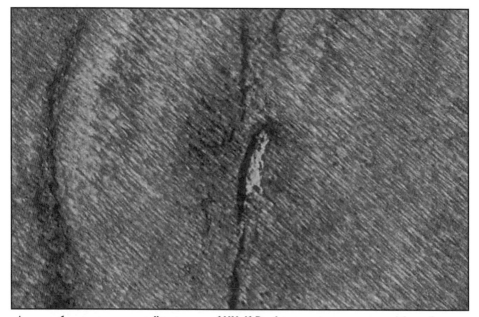

As seen from space: a satellite image of Wolf Rock on a winter morning. Note the shadow along the west edge of the rock and the diagonal shadows of the leafless trees.
(GlobeXplorer, 2002)

Just up the road on Md. 77 from the Visitor Center is Cunningham Falls, at 78 feet the tallest cascading falls in Maryland. Cunningham Falls State Park is the part of the original Catoctin Recreational Demonstration Area given to the Maryland State Forest and Park System. It offers numerous trails for the hiker to explore. In addition to the hiking (and the limited climbing in Catoctin Mountain National Park), both Parks offer a wide variety of other activities for the outdoor enthusiast, including horseback riding, swimming, fishing, hunting (Cunningham Falls State Park only), snowshoeing, and cross-country skiing. However, neither park permits mountain biking.

While climbing along the main wall, notice that near the cliff and in the woods around is a type of flower called Indian Pipe. It looks like a tall, milky-grey, thin-stemmed mushroom with no cap.

One word of warning: there are timber rattlesnakes in the area, and they love the little crevices and cracks on the top of this outcrop of rock. Be careful where you stick your hands when setting gear for anchors, or when climbing in or around the Fissure Caves area.

The Routes

The routes are generally described from left to right (unless otherwise specified in a given section), as if viewed from the trail. It is refreshing that there is a marked lack of broken glass and cigarette butts along the base of the rock here, unlike so many other places in Maryland. There is a walking trail to the top of the rock about two-thirds the length of the rock band to the right. The climbing areas are broken up into sections, starting with THE WOLF'S HEAD PILLAR and ending with EBOLA MONKEY WALL. The FISSURE CAVES are tucked in between the main wall area and the EBOLA MONKEY WALL.

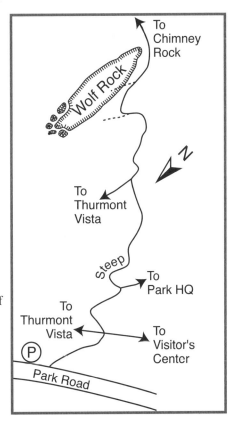

THE WOLF'S HEAD PILLAR

If you look at the pillar from the northeast side, with a little imagination, you'll see the arête appears as a wolf's head, and the main part of the pillar itself being the body and front legs...you'll need a little imagination.

The Pillar is at the far left end of the main wall, and offers some of the harder routes in the area. It is possible to lead some of the routes here to gain the top, but it is almost easier (although rather exposed) to 4th class climb it on the right side. The routes are described starting with the left side of THE WOLF'S HEAD PILLAR, and working around counterclockwise to the back.

1. Eye Of The Mind (5.9* PG)—27 ft. Use your imagination. Starting on the pointed rock sticking out of the ground just right of a couple of large stacked boulders, boulder up the first move (crux) to a relatively horizontal crack. Follow the crack and flow of white quartz up the shallow corner to a small alcove, step left, and pull directly through the notch in the roof (**V1**) without stepping to the right. Finish when you reach the top. If you step on the blocks to the left at the start to gain the horizontal crack, the rating drops to about 5.6. The "PG" rating comes only from protecting the first move. After that, it's G.

V1: Eye Of The Mind Sidestep (5.5) Instead of pulling the roof (5.6), traverse out right onto the slabby face and go up from there. This is basically a two-move variation.

2. Spinal Tap (5.4 G)—31 ft. From the front of the Pillar, follow the vertical crack and quartz vein up the low-angled face past a small tree to easy ground near the top. This basically would be the spine of the wolf. The crux is getting started on this route.

3. Wolf's Head Pillar Access (5.0)—29 ft. It is possible to gain the top by making an exposed scramble up the right side of THE WOLF'S HEAD PILLAR, then traversing left when halfway up to the easy terrain of *Spinal Tap*.

4. Wolf's Head Left (5.7*)—24 ft. Start in the center of the wall on a large, pointed boulder. Climb the shallow left arête up to a ramp, then work left and up to the final corner, and top off. Several variations exist for this route. A little awkward in places.

5. Wolf's Head Right (5.10b*)—20 ft. Starting on the backside of the Pillar, among the lowest point in the boulders, climb the right arête and face immediately left of the arête

to a large platform immediately below and to the right of the Wolf's Head Arête (the knife-edge feature). For added fun, tweak your way up the left side of the wolf's face (the knife-edge feature) to the very top. Starts out sustained, pumpy, and steep, then gets worse.

THE MAIN WALL

This is the main section of rock that can be easily seen from the trail. Most of it is very easy bouldering, ranging from 4th Class to 5.1 scrambling, and most of it is 20 feet or less. However, there are spots where the rock is taller, and there are worthy routes to drop ropes on. This area offers the highest density of easy climbs per square foot in Maryland. In essence, it's a perfect place to bring beginners. The real climbing starts at the first tall section of rock 170 feet to the right of THE WOLF'S HEAD PILLAR. This is one of the more popular climbing spots, as well as a favorite among rappellers.

6. Ghostwalker (5.3 G)—34 ft. Slightly contrived. Silently drift up the obvious major vein of white quartz to the end, staying within 6 inches of the quartz vein, then finish on the steeper but easier section near the top. The crux is within the first 10 feet off the ground.

7. First Hard On (5.3)—32 ft. The hardest thing about this climb is just getting **on** it! It also is an excellent route for virgin climbers to practice using those small holds. Starting 5 feet right of *Ghostwalker*, climb the green face to the blocky wall above. Easier than it looks.

8. Just Another Hold On The Wall (5.1)—32 ft. Start below a shallow, right-facing corner, 3 feet right of *First Hard On*. Scamper up to and past the shallow right-facing corner to the blocky wall above. Finish on great holds. Perfect for the fledgling climber.

9. A Round Peg In A Square Hole (5.2)—

32 ft. Can you find the square hole? Beginning immediately next to the tree 4 feet right of *Just Another Hold…*, follow the sporadic quartz vein up to the parallel cracks near the top. The holds up high are not quite as good as they are a few feet to the left. But that shouldn't pose much of a problem for you…right?

10. Cate's Crawl (5.0)—25 ft. Find the large

crack 15 feet right of *A Round Peg In A Square Hole*. Clamber up the blocks to and through the notch above. This is an easy way to reach the top of the rock here without going down to the walk up path couple hundred feet to the right, or bouldering up one of the other cracks nearby.

The next set of routes are at the next tall section of the wall 80 feet right of *A Round Peg In A Square Hole*. There is a downed tree lying along the base of the cliff here.

11. Pack Mentality (5.3)—35 ft. Climb the face

and crack past a couple of small right-facing corners to easier ground above. Don't crowd anyone else while climbing this.

12. Wolfman Jack (5.6)—36 ft. Start below the incipient crack 4 feet right of *Pack Mentality*. Howl up the incipient crack, staying within 1 foot of the crack (yes, contrived; if you don't like that, use all the holds you can find). Finish on the steeper but easier wall near the top.

13. Hungry Like The Wolf (5.5)—36 ft. Eat it up!

Beginning 3–1/2 feet right of *Wolfman Jack*, climb the wall between *Wolfman Jack* and *Benjamin Bunny*, without using either crack. The crux is halfway up. Once you're past the hard part, finish on the blocky wall above.

14. Benjamin Bunny (5.1 G)—36 ft. This route is 7 feet

right of *Wolfman Jack*. Hop up the long, left-leaning crack to a ledge 20 feet up. Finish on *Hungry Like The Wolf*. This is a perfect route for the novice leader to learn placing pro for lead climbing.

15. The Y Crack (5.0 G)—

29 ft. Located 20 feet right of *Benjamin Bunny* is a prominent Y-shaped crack. Climb the crack, following either the left or right fork (or both). The climbing basically ends after 18 feet.

16. Spirit Wolf (5.5)—29 ft.

Begin several feet right of *The Y Crack*. Climb the face following the intermittent white quartz vein to the top, without using the cracks to the left or right.

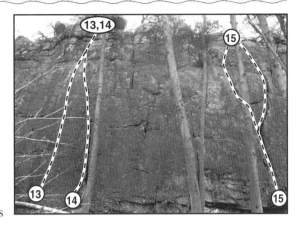

17. Step In Wolf (5.5 G)—28 ft.

Like a true nature's child, born to be wild. Adventure up the finger crack 3 feet right of *Spirit Wolf* until it ends at a short horizontal crack. Rock on the stepped crack system up and right a few moves, then shoot for the top.

18. Wolf Tracks (5.3)—25 ft.

Start in the center of the overhang a few feet off the ground, 5 feet right of *Step In Wolf*. Climb straight up the face on inobvious finger ledges to easier ground and top off. Tricky getting your foot placements at the beginning, but everything is there.

19. Arachnophobe's Nightmare (5.1)—25 ft.

Begin 3 feet right of *Wolf Tracks*. Climb the crack, or the face immediately left of the crack if the crack is full of spiders, to the top. If you're not a fan of spiders, particularly daddy longlegs, this climb ain't for you.

DARTH VADER DOME

This short dome-shaped section of rock vaguely resembling Darth Vader's helmet is located at the extreme right end of the main wall. Since the main trail passes right by it, access is very easy. The routes, some of the more difficult at Wolf Rock, are described from left to right.

20. May The Force Be With You (5.8*)—20 ft. This route begins a few feet to the left of the tree growing out from underneath the left section of the Dome. Starting under the bottom of a large right-leaning notch, climb up the smooth face to the roof. Begin to pull through it on a good hold, but work right to the small left-facing corner with more good holds. Feet get tricky; use your imagination—or the Force! Eventually you need to work yourself into a position so you can reach straight up to the top of the block in the middle of the notch and grab a two-handed bucket. Yard on up to a stance. The large holds vanish at this point, but the angle of the rock also eases back. Finish up the notch.

21. Chewbacca (5.12d)—22 ft. This one's a bit hairy. Starting between two trees about 15 feet right of *May The Force...*, climb up the slick and smooth face to and through the lowest roof. Struggle up right until you can gain the bucket hold near the outside corner in the lichen encrusted face. Pull up and finish.

22. Project 1 (unrated)—24 ft. Starting in the middle of the wall, follow a seam and climb the blank face to a roof. Pull through it and angle slightly right until you come to a lichen encrusted notch. Finish by going up the notch.

23. Project 2 (unrated)—24 ft. From the boulders at the right side of the Dome, climb the blank face to the highest roof. Work your way through the roof to the next one. Claw your way through the forest of lichen and slopers to the top.

24. Han Solo (5.2)—12 ft. Done solo, of course. Climb the short crack that forms the right side of the Dome. It's probably less effort just to walk around 20 or so feet further to the right to get to the top.

THE FISSURE CAVES

Within the fissure cave system of Wolf Rock are numerous routes and boulder problems. A rope is recommended even for the boulder problems, for a fall in these fissure caves could prove detrimental to your health. Some of the routes listed below are contrived, and were rated for climbing without using the back wall of the fissure. Most of the routes in this section will need gear or clever use of slings around blocks, boulders, and distant trees for anchors.

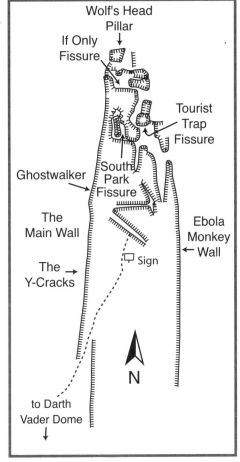

One word of caution: while in this area, be careful that you don't drop anything while on the boulders or in the fissure caves. It is very likely you won't get it back again.

IF ONLY FISSURE

This first fissure cave is an opening (not even a fissure, really) located 30 feet south of THE WOLF'S HEAD PILLAR, where the jumbled blocks meet the solid rock that forms the fissure caves. Look for a copper brown right-facing corner capped by some blocks. A small tree is growing out from near the top of the corner. The routes here are described from right to left.

25. *Kal-if-fee* (5.8*)—20 ft. You'd probably have to be up on your **Star Trek** trivia to know this is the Vulcan word for "challenge." Starting 4 feet right of the prominent right-facing corner (*If Only It Were Taller*), climb the shallow corner and face to ledges near the top. You cannot use the wide crack of *If Only It Were Taller* (i.e., this is slightly contrived), but all the rest of the holds on the face are "on." The challenge is finding the hand match partway up.

26. If Only It Were Taller (5.6)—20 ft. Climb up or layback the prominent right-facing corner, following the wide hand jam/arm bar crack to the overhanging blocks above. Jug past the blocks to catch the sun.

27. If Only I Were Taller (5.10a)—20 ft. Seriously contrived. Without using the wide crack of *If Only It Were Taller*, climb the copper brown, right-facing wall and arête on thin holds (there are a few holds on the wall inside the wide crack that you can use) to the

block above. Yard around the block to the top. Challenging for shorter people.

THE SOUTH PARK FISSURE

This fissure is located 25 feet south of the above fissure routes, near the west wall that is broken by numerous square blocks. Either rappel into the fissure (which isn't anywhere near as deep as it might appear), or downclimb through the notches to a large, sloped ledge on the west, then chimney the last 6 feet into the fissure. Really these are easy boulder problems, but spotting is difficult and a fall could be bad if you smack your back on the opposite wall. These routes are described from left to right.

28. Anal Probe (5.4)—18 ft. Starting at the lowest point possible, follow the deep handjam crack, bypassing the first roof by stepping onto the right wall, then up jugs to pull through the second, upper roof.

29. Eric Cartman (5.2)—17 ft. Climb the easy face immediately right of *Anal Probe*.

30. They Killed Kenny! (5.3)—17 ft. You bastards! Located 5 feet right of *Anal Probe*, work up the wall and shallow left-facing corner with a hand crack. Either climb the corner to the top, or halfway up, traverse right under a small roof (watch your head!) and finish on the last moves of *Screw You Guys...*.

31. Screw You Guys, I'm Going Home (5.3)—18 ft. Power up the large notch 5 feet right of *They Killed Kenny!*, following the large crack to the top. Look around; there are big handholds all over the place once you pass the initial overhang. Good, but short.

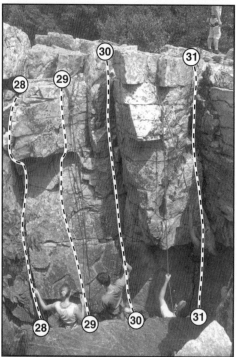

32. No, Kitty, This Is My Chicken Pot Pie! (5.2)—19 ft. Starting at the far right end of this fissure, 13 feet right of *Screw You Guys...*, scramble up the wall to a ledge

Mark "Aqua" Neubauer hugs the curb on Roadside Distraction *(5.8)*

(alternatively, to crank up the difficulty level a couple notches, do a sit-start and layback against the left-facing corner). From there climb up through the notch just right of the large roof to the top.

TOURIST TRAP FISSURE

This cavity is fairly large, though navigating through it can be a little tricky due to drops in the "floor" in spots. It is one of the more easily accessed fissures in the area (either by downclimbing from the top or scrambling up a 3rd class ramp from the east side of the rock), and heartier adventuring hikers/tourists can often be seen scrambling around in this area on weekends. Sometimes they can't figure out how to escape again. There are a number of uncharted short boulder problems along the walls of this fissure. There is a sizeable detached block on the west side of this more or less north-south fissure, located 15 feet east of THE SOUTH PARK fissure.

33. The Tourist Trap (5.2)—20 ft. Climb the left side of the face, using the left arête when necessary, to gain bomber holds halfway up. Trend right on easy holds to the top.

34. Roadside Attraction (5.6*)
—20 ft. Be sure to pull over and check this route out. Beginning near the center of the face, next to a small bush, climb the thin crack up past a small right-facing corner to a small ledge. Continue following the crack up to another ledge where it ends. Finish on easy moves to the top.

35. Roadside Distraction (5.8)—20
ft. Weird, balancy moves are the order of the day here. Begin at the right arête. Climb the arête and face as you can until you gain easier holds three-quarters of the way up. Finish in a body length on big holds. A fun little climb.

EBOLA MONKEY WALL

This area is a tribute to the mutant monkeyboys who play with the "fun stuff" down at Fort Detrick. Situated on the opposite side of the rock from THE MAIN WALL, this section sports the tallest routes in the area (some are up to nigh 50 feet high). If you want a little seclusion from the

masses on the trail, this is the place to go. There are several ways to access this area. One way, from the top, is to locate the "Geology of Wolf Rock" sign. From there bear 45 degrees to the right and you will quickly come to a wide, flat area with some trees growing out of it just before you get to the edge of the cliff. This is the top of the EBOLA MONKEY WALL. Find a way to scramble down to the base. Or you can walk on the ground around the main rock until you come to the tallest stuff you're able to find. If you come around from the south end of the rock (from the DARTH VADER DOME area), walk north along the cliff approximately 475 feet until you reach a boulder field. The walls to your left will have grown. If you come around from the north (from the WOLF'S HEAD PILLAR area), scramble south through the boulder field for a couple hundred feet until you reach the taller and less broken band of rock on the right; at this point the boulder field tapers off dramatically. You'll have passed by a number of good, short boulder problems prior to this wall from either direction.

The routes in this section are described from right to left, as if you were coming from the north.

36. Monkey See, Monkey Do (5.5)—20 ft. Climb the short wall just right of *Vee-Da-Woo-Hoo*. At first it looks a lot easier than it really is, but it's still not that hard. It is legal to use the left edge of the wall when you run out of holds on the face.

37. Vee-Da-Woo-I loo (5.6)—25 ft. Climb the obvious hand crack that widens to offwidth size. Beware the sharp flakes and edges. As the crack widens, step right onto the face for better stability (or for those prospective Dr. OWs out there, continue up the crack offwidth style!)

38. Bad-Ass Undead, Inc. (5.10a/b)—25 ft. A reference to extra strong/durable skeletons, zombies, and other undead from **Dungeons & Dragons.**™ Deft balance and a strong arm will swiftly dispatch this ghoulish little route. Climb the wall immediately left of *Vee-Da-Woo-Hoo*. Good holds ar⸍ few and far between. Using the left or right edges of the wall i legal; without them tack on ə er grade or two. Use both aʳ a grade or so easier.

39. Monkey Wall Α (5.0)—15 ft. This iˢ

direct of the numerous ways up or down the EBOLA MONKEY WALL area, soloed without much thought. From the bottom, scramble up to the top of a ℏ small rhododendron bush on the left. Go up and right to a ledge; step up to ˊ above as you are most comfortable doing. Reverse this to go down.

40. Marilyn Monkroe (5.2)—47 ft. Start at the right end of the sˊ left of the *Monkey Wall Access* and some boulders, by the trees (some ˙ slab to the right of the tree growing immediately next to the rock untˀ Monkey Ledge with a large blocky boulder, beneath an obvious rigˡ hand crack. Stepping onto the boulder for a moment (beware updr

Fabrizia Ｃ

Guglielmetti wishing If Only It Were Taller (5.6)

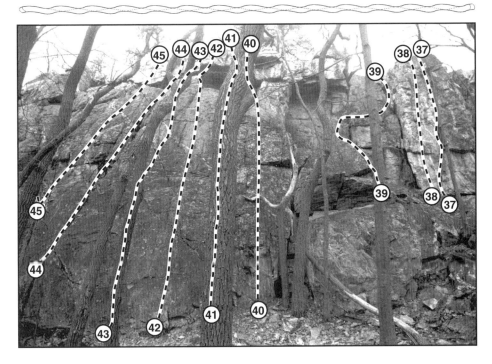

skirt), make a few easy moves up the corner to finish the route. If you choose to **not** use the boulder, the starting moves for the corner are a little trickier than 5.2. Enjoy!

41. Monk Daddy (5.10a*)—46 ft. Who's your daddy! Begin immediately to the left of the tree growing right against the rock, 5 feet left of *Marilyn Monkroe*. Step up the slab until you reach the huge Monkey Ledge, beneath a wide, 5 foot deep roof. Without stepping onto the block to your right, haul through the roof by following the left-leaning white vein of quartz with a crack running through it. When you can get your feet under you again, stand and gain the top.

42. Grease Monkey (5.6)—46 ft. Start 5 feet left of *Monk Daddy*. Work your way straight up the slab (slippery) to the Monkey Ledge 36 feet up. Stepping left onto the boulder with your left foot, pull through the left side of the roof to finish (significantly harder if you eliminate using the boulder).

43. Flavour Of The Weak (5.4)—49 ft. This bland line never gets very difficult. Beginning 5 feet left of *Grease Monkey*, climb the slab up to the boulder on the Monkey Ledge, and continue upwards through the 5 foot wide "notch" to the top.

44. JUMP (5.3)—49 ft. Justified Use of Military Power. Justified use of a machete or a flame thrower would be more appropriate! Starting 5 feet left of *Flavour Of The Weak*, climb the variable sized crack up the slab through a few trees until you reach the large ledge. Finish by continuing up through the 5 foot wide "notch." A better, optional finish would be to step left and climb the final moves on the white headwall of *Monkey Mouse*.

45. Monkey Mouse (5.5)—49 ft. Climb the crack 3 feet left of *JUMP* until it ends. Continue on past a small ledge area to the large Monkey Ledge. Finish by climbing the short, white headwall to the top.

46. Typhoid Monkey (5.3)—44 ft. You won't get sick on this one. Start 15 feet left of *Monkey Mouse*, where the rock has a cave-like opening at its base. Climb above the cave and follow the moss covered ramp (**V1**) up left for a few feet until you find holds that allow you to gain the sloping ledge above. From the ledge, work up the next headwall to another sloping ledge. Easier rock will lead you to the top at this point.

V1: Typhoid Monkey Direct Start (5.8) Instead of following the ramp up left, climb straight up the face over the cave. You can use the bottom and right-most part of the ramp for your left foot if need be. Once you gain the sloping ledge, finish as normal.

To the left of *Typhoid Monkey* the rock begins to ease off dramatically in difficulty and height, allowing access to the top from the bottom (and vice versa). There is some bouldering along this area, but eventually it's just scrambling until the end of the rock.

Brian Walker sinks it deep on Anal Probe *(5.4)*

RIGHT FORK
ROCKS

Jody Powell enjoys a little Jam Crack (5.6)

RIGHT FORK ROCKS

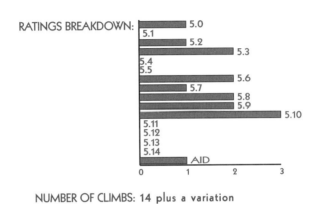

RATINGS BREAKDOWN:

5.0
5.1
5.2
5.3
5.4
5.5
5.6
5.7
5.8
5.9
5.10
5.11
5.12
5.13
5.14
AID

0 1 2 3

NUMBER OF CLIMBS: 14 plus a variation

SPECIAL NOTE:

"I don't fall a lot…I am just gravitationally challenged."—Ex-local climber **Thom Iwancio**

The Frederick Watershed offers a number of small areas tucked away here and there. This secluded set of rocks is quietly situated in a serene wooded setting…which, unfortunately, has been marred by the presence of thoughtless and uncaring people (there are other words for them, but unprintable here). The whole area resembles a back alley of an inner city. Graffiti adorns many trees and much of the rock walls, even more so than at Ilchester. Broken glass coats the ground around the first outcrop of rock. Trash is strewn carelessly about the woods (mainly confined to the first outcropping of rock, where the ground is flat and conducive to spending the nights or hosting parties). Some of this can even be found up in the trees at times. It is a sad testament to humans in general that they feel the need to turn sections of the world into their personal garbage pit. If the Watershed Authorities decide to crack down on the abuse that has been heaped on this place, climbers are sure to suffer. And lose yet another area to crank on rock.

Nice rock, great climbs. Distressing how the area is treated in general.

LOCATION/DIRECTIONS

These directions assume you are **coming from the Frederick area** (or that you made your way from Baltimore/Washington to Frederick). From I–70 take Route 15 north for 9 miles. Exit from Route 15 (to the left) when you come to a sign that reads "Hansonville Rd to Mountaindale Rd." Turn left onto Hansonville Road, travel a couple hundred feet, and turn right onto Mountaindale Road.

Follow this back a few miles until you come to a small residential community nestled in the woods at the base of the mountains you were approaching. Mountaindale Road will have a 'T' intersection in this community. Turn left and continue.

A minute or so later you will enter The Frederick Watershed proper (complete with sign and gravel road, which may be closed during the winter months due to people who are not so mountain savvy going up there with their vehicles and getting stuck in the snow). Proceed 0.4 miles up this road until it forks. The right fork is imaginatively called Right Hand Fork Road and will take you to Right Fork Rocks. The left fork is likewise imaginatively called Left Hand Fork Road, and will take you to Left Fork Rocks.

To reach Right Fork Rocks, bear right at the split in the road and go 1.1 miles. The road will curve hard to the left, and there will be a small pull off on the right—enough room for two to three cars (with some creative parking you can squeeze 4 cars in here). Park here, cross the stream, and bear right or go straight ahead (depending where you cross the stream). You should be able to see the outcrop of rock as soon as you cross the stream, if not before. It is, after all, less than 100 feet away.

GEOLOGY

These quartzite boulders are part of the Weverton Formation quartzite. They have weathered differently than the outcrops that make up Annapolis Rocks, Black Rock, and Raven Rock Hollow; hence the strata layering that is characteristic of the South Mountain ridge rocks is not evident. This rock is essentially the same as Wolf Rock up in Catoctin Mountain National Park. There are even a couple of "fissure caves" hidden here.

EQUIPMENT

Slings from 10 to 40 feet will suffice for most of the top-rope setups here. There really aren't many places to put gear, and pretty much all the routes are top-rope problems, anyway.

CAMPING

You can find camping at Gambril State Park. Just continue up Right Fork Road to the ridge, turn left and in about 3 or so miles you'll come to the camping area.

RESTRICTIONS AND ACCESS

There are no official restrictions to climbing in the Watershed. However, see the Left Fork Rocks chapter for some potential concerns.

LOCAL EATS

Heading back into Mountaindale, you will come to the T-intersection. Turn right and cross the bridge. After going 0.1 mile, you will come to the Mountaindale General Store. You can get hot and cold sandwiches here, as well as find your typical "general store" assemblage of food and miscellaneous items. A mile further east on Mountaindale Road is the Mountaindale Convenience Store, complete with a small deli and the usual odds and ends one can find in a general store type environment. These are the only local eats. If you want something more…sophisticated (or greasy fast-food), Thurmont is 10 miles to the north on Route 15, and Frederick is 9 miles to the south.

OTHER INFO

The rocks are often damp, because the surrounding trees keep the moisture in the area contained. The best time to climb here is after it's been dry for a week or so. Otherwise, you can add a grade or three to the ratings when the rock is wet.

Beware of mosquitoes that seem to live here longer than in most places in Maryland. Bring plenty of bug repellent!

There are some rocks off on the right in the woods behind the gun club that you pass as you drive through Mountaindale. These rocks host some of the nicer routes in the area, but unfortunately, access is no longer permitted (you have to park at the gun club then walk through their range into the woods beyond to get to the cliffs). There were a number of established routes up there. Maybe someday these rocks will be open again? Maybe one of you fine readers can look into getting this area accessible for climbers once again….

The Routes

Many of the routes here were established 15 or so years ago by George King, Greg Nerses, and other members of the "Open Sky Adventurers" group. The routes are described from left to right, as you would approach the rocks from the parking area.

DEATH ROCK

This massive chunk of Weverton Formation quartz sits a mere 80 feet from the small parking area. It is so-named from an early outing when a climber had pulled off a multi-hundred pound block, that missed smashing into the belayer (who was anchored to a tree, unable to run) by inches. Graffiti can be found on much of this rock, as well as on some of

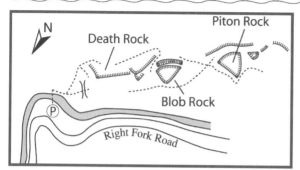

the surrounding trees. Ashes from fires can be found around the base as well as the top of this rock. Often you will be crunching through glass that covers the ground.

1. Games People Play (5.7)—30 ft. Really a one-move wonder route, this never-

theless has good climbing from bottom to top. Begin to the right of a tree next to the rock, 6 feet left of *Witch's Tit*. Dance up the steep quartz-covered face on jugs to the crux in the middle. Once past this, continue up on fun moves to the top. If you get tired early, you can step off right onto a ledge 20 feet up for a break. Some of the moves are a bit reachy. The original route made a rising traverse up left to the top, but it is mostly done straight up nowadays.

2. It's All In The Fingers (5.10a)—25 ft. A fun route to tweak on. Climb the face a
few feet left of *Witch's Tit*, following the thin crack up to the top. There are plenty of sidepulls for you to play with on this route. The upper section is the crux of the matter.

3. Witch's Tit (5.10a**)—26 ft. This route is pretty straightforward. Climb the promi-
nent arête past a small ramp three-quarters of the way up to the large ledge at the top, using holds on either side of the arête itself. A variety of holds, from buckets to thin to sloper, are the order of the day. Note that the higher of the two holds near the top is the one you want. A little easy for a 10. Fun moves; don't miss this climb.

4. Jam Crack (5.6* PG)—28 ft. Begin 11 feet right of *Witch's Tit*. Step up on the
blocks to a shelf below the obvious hand crack. Jam or layback up the crack with sweet holds to the dirty jugs above. Finish in the square notch. This would be an area classic if the jam crack was longer and the dirty jugs weren't so dirty.

5. Corner Crack (5.6*)—30 ft. Start
5 feet right of *Jam Crack*. Clamber up the initial blocks to a ledge, then layback the crack in the left-facing corner to blockier stuff high up. Pull through this to the top. It's surprisingly easier than it looks.

6. Unknown (5.9+)—30 ft. Starting
just a couple feet right of *Corner Crack*, work your way up the face and some blocky left-facing corners. The holds are all there, somewhere. At the final bulge, stepping off to the right makes for an easy finish, but staying left offers a different challenge.

7. Dirty Chimney (5.0)—25 ft. There is a grungy chimney located 17 feet to the right of *Corner Crack*. It is very likely one of the first routes ascended in this area (probably by partiers before climbers found the rock). It's dirty and rather unpleasant. Not recommended for an enjoyable climbing run, this route is noted only because it is there.

BLOB ROCK

This outcrop is located 75 feet away from DEATH ROCK, and because of this does not see as much partier traffic (there is still some graffiti in the area, but nowhere near as much trash).

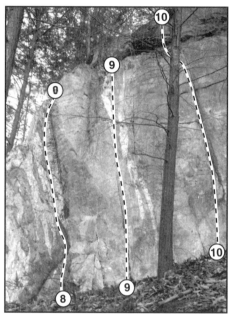

8. The Ugly Duckling (5.3)—17 ft. Nicer than it looks! Start at the grungy crack a few feet right of the lowest point on this outcrop of rock. Climb the crack and left wall (**V1**) the short distance to the top.

V1: The Swan (5.9) Begin on *The Ugly Duckling*, but halfway up "mature" to the right into a shallow corner, and continue on to the top. Some nice holds are on here.

9. Unknown Aid Route (A2)—20 ft. Starting 5 feet right of *The Ugly Duckling*, aid up the quartz vein on various seams paralleling it. Think RURPs. When the seams end, either stand up high in your stirrups for a good hold, or tentatively hook the final few moves. Check out the naturally formed crystal-laden *mono-doigt* a bit more than 5 feet off the ground.

10. The Boulder Problem (5.10b**)—18 ft. One of the cleanest routes here (outside of spider season, that is) and the area testpiece. Beginning 3 feet right of *Unknown Aid Route*, crank up the smooth off-finger crack until it tapers down to a seam. Utilizing a painful toe jam, make that reach for the jug at the top of the seam. Finish by going up and left. The main wall is essentially frictionless; find small edges and sloper nubs to stand on. For a slightly easier start, climb the wall immediately right of the finger crack to the horizontal crack 7 feet up, then step left and finish on the main crack. This only makes the start easier; the finish is still bouldery.

PITON ROCK

This detached outcrop is 60 feet to the right of BLOB ROCK. It seems to be detached from the hillside by the "fissure chimney" formed between it and the short rock wall uphill. A few noteworthy routes adorn this rock. Anchors here are long (20-foot plus) slings from trees, or in a very few spots, small to medium-sized gear. Be creative. The east face of this rock sports a few short boulder problems. Take care, as there is a lot of glass hidden under the leaves all around the base of this rock (not to mention other assorted bits of trash; hooligans like to sit up on top and throw things off—this is Big Fun for them).

11. Footloose And Fancy Free (5.8)—25 ft.

As the trail turns steeply downhill on the west (right) side of this rock, locate the right-leaning crack on the left side of this wall that heads up to a short left-facing corner. Climb up the crack, using fancy footwork until you gain the left-facing corner halfway up. Work up the corner to a good hold. Then, following a short horizontal crack, traverse several feet to the right to the broad main corner sporting a large chunky deposit of white quartz with great holds. Climb up this shallow corner to the top. Not the best route in this area, it's above average overall.

12. Slapshot (5.8+)—32 ft.

Begin 6 feet right of an overhanging right-facing corner, or 15 feet right of *Footloose....* Claw your way up thin holds and thinner edges to a small, blocky shelf. Continue up the steep face and left-facing corner to a steeply ramped section. From there, drifting slightly left, aim for a small notch at the top.

The next two routes are located around the corner and uphill on the south-facing wall.

13. Nature Boy (5.2)—17 ft.

Begin below a parallel crack/flake system halfway up the wall. Climb through the white quartz and black rock zone to the parallel crack/flake system. Continue up between the two until you reach the top.

14. Nature Girl (5.3)—16 ft.

Start a few feet right of *Nature Boy*, just left of the arête. Climb up through the white quartz and black rock zone on easy holds until the wall steepens and the good holds run out. One or two interesting moves will bring you to better holds once again. Finish on easy moves to the top.

There is a fourth outcrop of rock just beyond PITON ROCK, but it is small, and hosts only one or two boulder problems. There are also some rocks on the other side of the road, a few hundred feet before the parking area, which offer some tall bouldering problems. They are not far back from the road, but are not visible until after the leaves have dropped off in the fall. Then they are quite noticeable as you drive past.

LEFT FORK
ROCKS

Donna Childress playing in the midwinter sun on Stairways (5.5)

LEFT FORK
ROCKS

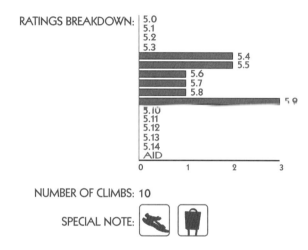

RATINGS BREAKDOWN:

NUMBER OF CLIMBS: 10

SPECIAL NOTE:

"Remember: climb like a gecko. Knees out."—Andy Nichols to a student climber

This extensive little area is littered with fractured and broken boulders on both sides of the creek. The more heavily visited climbing area is on the road side of the creek, but if you want to brave crossing the water and the hike uphill, you can find some nice routes in the line of rock that rises up the hill behind the trees, hidden from the road.

Primarily easy to moderate level climbing, Left Fork Rocks is not often visited by those seeking harder routes to test themselves against (that is usually reserved for the Right Fork Rocks). Usually the local climbers here are just out to quietly play.

LOCATION/DIRECTIONS

These directions assume you are **coming from the Frederick area** (or that you made your way from Baltimore/Washington to Frederick). From I–70 take Route 15 north for 9 miles. Exit from Route 15 (to the left) when you come to a sign that reads "Hansonville Rd to Mountaindale Rd." Turn left onto Hansonville Road, travel a couple hundred feet, and turn right onto Mountaindale Road. Follow this back a few miles until you come to a small residential community nestled in the woods at the base of the mountains you were approaching. Mountaindale Road will have a 'T' intersection in this community. Turn left and continue. A minute or so later you will enter The Frederick Watershed proper (complete with sign and gravel road, which may be closed during the winter months due to people who are not so mountain savvy going up there with their vehicles and getting stuck in the snow). Proceed 0.4 miles up this road until it forks. The right fork is imaginatively called Right Hand Fork Road and will take you to Right Fork Rocks. The left fork is likewise imaginatively called Left Hand Fork Road, and will take you to Left Fork Rocks.

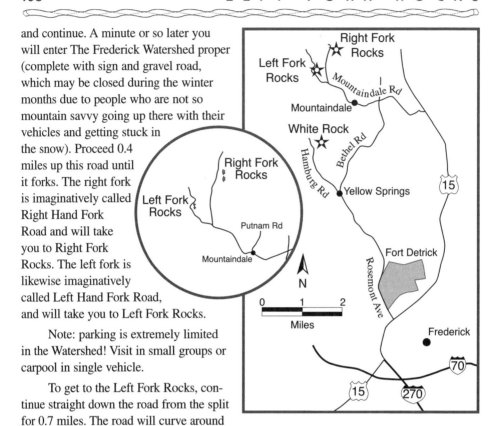

Note: parking is extremely limited in the Watershed! Visit in small groups or carpool in single vehicle.

To get to the Left Fork Rocks, continue straight down the road from the split for 0.7 miles. The road will curve around towards the right, with a serious drop-off to the left. Uphill on the right will be outcroppings of rock, visible from the road. This is it! You are here. There is parking on the outside of the curve (left side of the road) next to the drop-off, and very limited parking on the right immediately before the road curves right.

GEOLOGY

This rough, sharp rock is part of the Weverton Formation family (not the familiar Buzzard Knob member that makes up Annapolis Rocks and most of the crest of South Mountain, though; most probably it is Owens Creek member rock). It is a bit prone to breaking (this mainly applies to "good holds," not slopers) due to weathering, which also produces flared cracks and those rounded holds. Not always the best for lead practice, but if you need to work on your friction sloper techniques, this is an ideal place to play.

EQUIPMENT

Anchors in the 20- to 40-foot range will reach most all the sturdy trees near the tops of the cliffs. If you want more (in some cases you might), throwing in a cam or two, or a hex or nut, will do the trick as an additional anchor point, particularly for GYMNASTICS WALL. Bring stuff in the medium-to-large range for this. Note: be careful about the rock as some of it is not as sturdy as you might like it to be.

CAMPING

See Right Fork Rocks for more information

RESTRICTIONS AND ACCESS

While climbing is permitted here, occasionally a Watershed ranger will come along and chase climbers out. Local climbers have tried working with the City of Frederick on this matter but the situation remains unchanged. Sometimes it seems you can, sometimes someone gets a burr up their butt about climbers and evicts them from the rocks.

By the way: do **not** swim in the small reservoir near the entrance to the Watershed! There are many small pools in the creeks and streams up in the Watershed you can avail yourself to in order to cool off during the hot summer days.

LOCAL EATS

See the Right Fork Rocks chapter for more details.

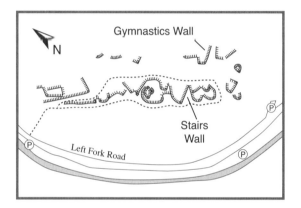

OTHER INFO

Be aware that you may get quite dusty here from other vehicles going up and down the road, kicking up dust clouds. Your car will definitely need a wash after a visit here.

A class working out problems on Stairs Wall

The Routes

There is a **lot** of rock here, but most of it is in the 3rd to 4th class range. George King and members of the Open Sky Adventurers group established a number of climbs here, and were working on a small rag guide to the Watershed nearly 15 years ago for the local climbers, but it never got out into the community. The routes noted herein are located on the right side of the rocks as you face them from the road. Boulder problems abound on most of the rocks here, but they are not covered in any detail at this time.

The routes are noted from left to right. See the overview map on page 187 for orientation.

STAIRS WALL

This is the first outcrop of rock you'll see from the road as you arrive (or, if you as the driver cannot see it—trying to keep your eyes and car on the road—your passengers will, assuming they are looking!)

1. Greg's Birthday Gift (5.6+)—37 ft. Climb the juggy overhanging arête to ledges and finish on easier moves. Greg Nerses cranks this every year on his birthday.

2. Get The Point (5.4 G)—37 ft. Climb up easy moves to shelves halfway up on the left side of this wall. The crux is near the bottom. Makes for an excellent route to practice lead climbing.

3. Stairways (5.5 G)—32 ft. This one is a bit harder than it looks! Wander up the right side of the wall, staying left of the V-notch corner. Enjoy the rounded and sometimes sloping holds. This is also a popular route for beginners to learn rappelling.

4. Ladder (5.4)—approx. 30 ft. Climb up the easy face opposite *Stairways* to the top. A great route for beginners.

GYMNASTIC WALL

This outcrop is located uphill to the right of STAIRS WALL. From the top of STAIRS WALL, facing down at the climbs, turn left 90 degrees and you'll be looking straight at a narrow overhanging wall.

5. All Around (5.8)—19 ft. Climb the left arête of the overhanging wall to the top.

6. Middle Man (5.9+*)—20 ft. Climb straight up the center of the seriously over-hanging face to the notch at the top. There is a key heelhook move you may want to try in the final moves of the climb.

7. Swinger (5.9+)—20 ft. Haul your way straight up the right arête of the overhanging wall. You may find a heelhook near the top helpful. Or not. If you climb halfway up *Swinger*, then traverse halfway to the left and finish on *Middle Man*, the climbing isn't really any harder than 5.8.

These next routes are located to the right around the corner from *Swinger*. While these are the basically established routes here, you can climb pretty much anywhere (but that should go without saying anywhere, no?)

8. OSA (5.5)—26 ft. Stands for "Open Sky Adventurers," what some of the original climbers in the area back in the '80s called themselves (and who have long since gone different ways in life). Climb the face anywhere between *Swinger* and the first big left-leaning crack system 15 feet to the right. If you look you'll find an occasional good under-cling, and opportunities to practice hand jamming in some of the horizontals higher up.

9. Paul's Path (5.5–5.7+)—25 ft. Near the center of the wall is a wide, left-leaning crack system, a few feet to the right of the left-leaning crack system right of *OSA*. Follow this crack up to the bottom of the overhang. You can keep going past it, keeping the climbing no more than about 5.4 or so (tricky), but if you stop and pull through the overhang just left of its lowest point onto the featured (but mostly useless!) face above, you're in the 5.7+ range. A fun route. Don't bonk your head when you get under the overhang. There used to be a bolt on the wall halfway up in the dim past. It was used as a handhold (a finger hold, actually—urk!) in the early years of climbing this route.

10. Gymnastic (5.9+)—22 ft. This climb begins 9 feet right of *Paul's Path*. It's a fairly stout route. Starting directly below the triangular shaped roof, work your way up the blank face (crux) until you reach the horizontal cracks beneath the roof. Pull around the left end of the point of the roof to quickly finish. Interesting balance problems. The wall is punctuated with a couple of decent holds amidst all the slopers until you reach the horizontal cracks (but unless you can jam, they aren't bomber, either—surprise!)

There is additional rock across the creek and uphill from the left end of these rocks. Most of it is either boulder problems or 3rd to 4th class stuff, but there are a few nice lines tucked away over there. Your mission, if you choose to accept it: go find and play on them.

WHITE ROCK

WHITE
ROCK

RATINGS BREAKDOWN: Unknown

NUMBER OF CLIMBS: Unknown

SPECIAL NOTE:

"This isn't the Gunks, but for something close it looks good."
—**Anonymous climber**

There are at least three areas in central Maryland called "White Rock(s)," and two of them have climbing. This is the second one. It also doubles as a canvas for defacers. You will find more graffiti here than you can shake a stick at (go ahead, try it…nope, you missed some; look around the corner…). Even though some of it is good, it's a sad fact of life that people feel they need to do this here.

LOCATION/DIRECTIONS

From I–70: Take Exit 53 for Route 15 north. Exit a short time later onto Rosemont Avenue (Exit 14, approximately 1 mile north of the Route 40 exit). Bear right at the end of the off ramp, and take Rosemont west. The trailhead is approximately 6.25 miles away. After a couple of miles, near Fort Detrick, Rosemont Avenue changes its name to Yellow Spring. Its name changes again after you leave the Yellow Spring community (and enter the Watershed) to Hamburg Road. For landmarks, in Yellow Spring you will come to a four-way stop with Bethel Road. The trailhead is now a bit more than 1.6 miles ahead. As you proceed into the Watershed, the road will begin twisting and turning quite vigorously,

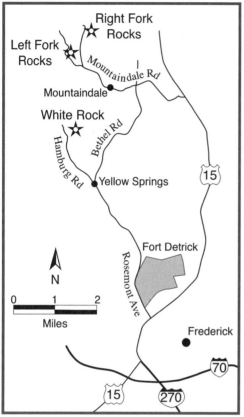

and soon the double yellow centerlines will disappear. Just 0.4 miles later, you will come to a driveway on the right; the address is 9639. The trailhead is right here to the left of the driveway, on the right hand side of the road. There is a pulloff for one car across from the driveway, and another pull off immediately to the left of the driveway. **The driveway is private property—do not block it!** There is blue paint on the telephone pole next to the trailhead.

The trail climbs steadily uphill to the rock ridge. You should be able to reach it in 5 to 7 minutes at a steady moderate pace. You will cross a series of rotted, long-dead fallen trees about a minute before you come to the rocks themselves. When you cross these trees, the rocks will be directly in front of you, through the woods. Continue straight until you find them.

Once there, turn left and follow the path gently uphill, paralleling the ridge of rock. This is the backside of the crag, but it does host a few boulder problems along the way. The height of the outcrop will steadily increase. The main climbing routes are on the opposite side of the rock when it reaches its highest point. Immediately after this there is a 10 foot wide gash in the rock that allows you to see to the other side.

GEOLOGY

This ridge of rock is **identical** to that of Wolf Rock. See the Wolf Rock chapter for some of the geological details (there are no "fissure caves" here, however).

EQUIPMENT

You'll need a mix of gear and slings measuring upwards of 40 feet to rig some of these routes.

CAMPING

There is no camping allowed here. The closest place is Gambrill State Park.

RESTRICTIONS AND ACCESS

There are no known access issues for this area.

LOCAL EATS

The closest eats are back down Hamburg/Yellow Spring Road/Rosemont Avenue, near Fort Detrick. You will find a small selection of fast-food and sit down restaurants, even a Pizza Hut. If what you're looking for is not here, jump on Route 15 and head south for 1 mile to the exit for Route 40. Take Route 40 west, and in short order you will find a larger selection of food establishments on both sides of the road.

OTHER INFO

Of the climbing spots in the Watershed, White Rock offers something none of the other places have: a view! From the top of the rock the Frederick Valley spreads out before you, and Sugarloaf Mountain is plainly visible some 15 or so miles to the south. In the fall the colors of the valley are simply superb. Sunrises are also quite nice from up here.

Just don't fall off, okay? Rescues are a bitch to do from here, and it's very likely no one will know you were up there for a long time, anyway.

The Routes

This outcrop of rock stretches for nearly a thousand feet from end to end, giving promise to a great deal of climbing potential. However, most of the rock is low-angle (3rd/4th class at best), and much of it is not very tall. There are only a few potential lines here, and even then much of the base of the rock is choked with foliage (reinforced by the infrequency of visitors). The nigh impossibly hard stuff is located on the opposite side of the rock from where the bulk of the graffiti is located, and pulls through the blocky roofs. The easy stuff is located to the right (as you face the climbing side of the rock), and is mostly one-move wonder stuff up 4th class rock covered in lichen. Currently no information is available for established routes on this cliffband.

Getting down to the base of the rock here can be problematic in and of itself. You can either rappel down, find a way to scramble around the ends and bushwhack back to the center, or down climb one of the 3rd/4th class ramps or gullies. Either way, once down, you are in a veritable jungle. Most of the routes start on a small ledge about 25 feet up from the very base of the rock.

There are some bouldering problems scattered all along this band of cliff. Take care, though—some of the landings are a wee bit nasty!

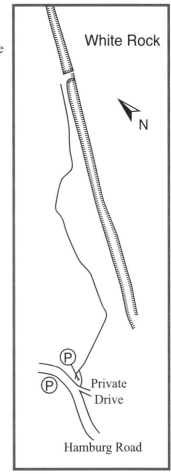

White Rock

N

Ⓟ

Ⓟ   Private
     Drive

Hamburg Road

THE FIN

George "Geode" Cummings works on the Outer Limit (5.5)

THE FIN

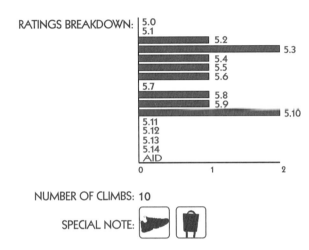

RATINGS BREAKDOWN:

NUMBER OF CLIMBS: 10

SPECIAL NOTE:

"This is a handhold?"—Anonymous beginner climber

Situated a mile or two downstream from Pretty Boy Dam and a few hundred feet uphill from the Gunpowder Falls River in the Gunpowder Falls State Park, this quiet little blade of rock is just that: quiet and little. While the total height is nigh 70 feet from very top to very bottom, the nature and positioning of the rock does not allow for any routes that are much longer than 40 or so feet. However, do not let that stop you from visiting. Despite the shortness of some routes, there are quite a few real gems to play on here.

The outcrop here has several different names given to it by different locals: The Fin and The Blade being the more common ones (with "The Fin" being more common than "The Blade").

Just a short ways away from this outcrop, maybe 50 yards or so, is a bouldering area that offers some nice problems to practice on. These are not covered in detail at this time.

LOCATION/DIRECTIONS

From Baltimore: Take I–83 to Exit 31 (Middletown Road). Turn left at the end of the off-ramp and proceed down Middletown Road a quarter mile to the first road you come to just past the highway. Turn left onto Falls Road and follow that for about 1 mile to a stop sign. Continue down Falls Road for about a quarter mile to a one lane bridge. Cross over it

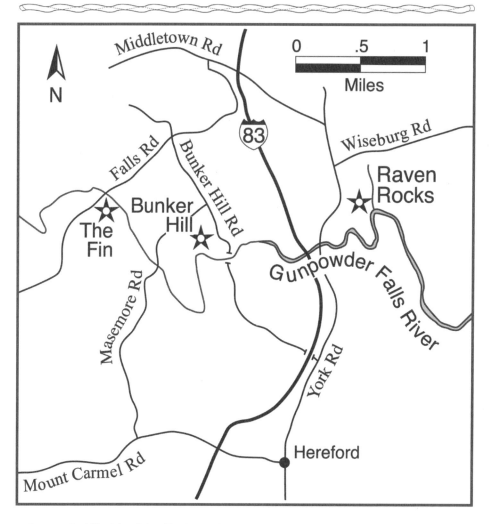

and go up the hill. After 0.1 mile there will be a small parking area (for about 10 or so cars) on the right. Park here.

From the parking lot walk back down the road towards the one lane bridge. Just before the bridge the Gunpowder Falls South Trail crosses the road. Head right (downstream) on this trail from the road. Follow the trail for about 260 feet and there will be a faint "climber's path" heading due right, into the woods. The rock will be visible high on the hillside in the woods from here. Head up the "climber's path" until it vanishes, then work your way over breakdown and through foliage. After a couple hundred feet you will be at the base of the knife-blade rock.

Alternatively from the parking area, you can strike out southeast through the woods across the road until you are atop the ridge. There is a faint path from this direction (easily found near the road, but quickly lost in the undergrowth partway to the ridgeline) that you can try to follow. Once you are bushwhacking you may need to use dead reckoning in order to get to the spot on the ridge where the rocks are.

GEOLOGY

The rock here is known as Pleasant Grove Schist. It is a fine grained plagioclase-chlorite-muscovite-quartz schist. The numerous thin veins of milky quartz and beds of quartzite give it that seamed appearance (the thin veins of quartz are particularly evident where *Fenway* goes up), though it doesn't really have any "seams" (beyond the flakes and cracks). You don't typically think of schist as being frictionable, but the mineral combination allows for you to get a better grip here than, say, on the mica-schist rock of Carderock and Great Falls. However, you still might find the tiny edges and quartz crystals better to stand on.

EQUIPMENT

You'll need anchors that reach upwards of 30 feet, and then you will need to be creative with some of your anchor setups. Some are relatively straightforward; others will require more imaginative use of the nearby trees.

CAMPING

The Gunpowder Falls State Park is a **day use only** park—there is no camping here!

RESTRICTIONS AND ACCESS

There are no real restrictions, other than the number of people you can bring here. The rock is small, and the stances for belayers and other climbers are not the best.

LOCAL EATS

See also Bunker Hill Rock for more information.

OTHER INFO

With the exception of the occasional car driving along Falls Road, this is very likely to be one of **the** quietest areas you will experience climbing in central Maryland. And it's a very pretty place to be at during the fall when the leaves are changing color.

The Routes

As this is a blade of rock sticking out from the side of a hill, the routes are described from right to left, starting at the level landing on the lower northwest section of the rock, where you logically end up if approaching from the riverside trail below.

1. Kryptonite (5.9*)—35 ft. Don't be weak! Starting next to the large left-facing corner, ascend the partially green moss covered wall on sustained crimpers to the huge detached flake. Layback past the flake on the left finishing at the large tree.

2. Hawkeye (5.8* PG)—35 ft. Stay sharp. Starting 5 feet left of *Kryptonite*, climb the thin left-facing flake system until the holds run out. Aim for the depression in the wall directly below the huge detached flake and finish

Action Man™ *free soloing* *Hawkeye (5.8)*

on *Kryptonite*. There was a fixed wire stopper partway up the flake system. This is the best route on the rock.

3. Ethics Gradient (5.10c*)—38 ft. Climb the face between the two flake systems that make up *Hawkeye* and *Outer Limit*. Contrived; do not use any of the flake holds. Thin.

4. Outer Limit (5.5* PG)—

38 ft. Depending on where and how you set your anchors, the swing could be **bad** if you fall on this one. Climb the large left-facing flared flake system near the arête until it merges with the arête two-thirds of the way up. Follow the arête to the upper ledge. If you chose to lead it, careful your gear doesn't strip out of the crack in the event of a fall.

5. Charitable View (5.3)—

45 ft. Located around the corner to the left of *Outer Limit*, climb the cracks and face up the moss covered east buttress arête. Nice exposure, plenty of handholds hidden by the carpet of moss.

The next four routes are located on the south face of the rock.

6. Crystalline Lizard (5.10c)—27 ft.

No fooling around on this one! Start at the lowest south-facing wall on the southeast corner of the rock. Delicately climb the steep face on small, sharp quartz crystals. Finish on the mossy ramp above.

7. Dirty Chimney (5.2)—17 ft.
Climb the blocky chimney to the left of *Crystalline Lizard* to the top. Very dirty and full of lichen and moss. Not really recommended.

8. Avoiding Temptation (5.3*)—19 ft.
At the right end of the south-facing upper wall, follow the right-facing flake to jugs, following those to the top.

9. Tree Of Temptation (5.6*)—19 ft. A height dependent start (and crux). Starting immediately right of the large tree, climb the tallest part of the upper south-facing wall to the top. No fair chimneying off of the large tree as you go up.

The next route is located on the opposite side of the wall from *Avoiding Temptation* and *Tree Of Temptation*, and uphill right from *Hawkeye*.

10. Fenway (5.2—5.4*)—28 ft. On the upper wall on the north side, climb anywhere on the slightly tilted, green moss covered slab wth tiny holds. A nice route for beginners to 'learn the ropes'—or how to deal with slanting holds. Named after Fenway Park in Boston (which sports a green wall that is apparently easy to hit homeruns over).

BUNKER
HILL

Ron Drimmel makes that reach on Pocket Poser *(5.7)*

BUNKER
HILL

RATINGS BREAKDOWN:

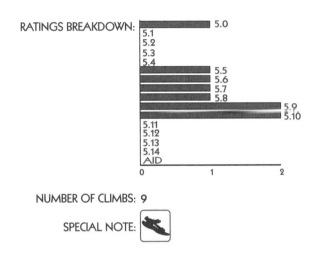

NUMBER OF CLIMBS: **9**

SPECIAL NOTE: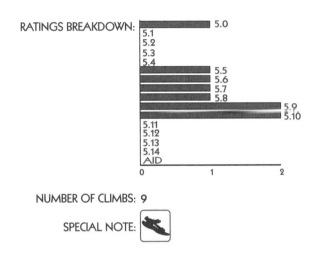

"I don't think there's anything harder than 5.3 there."—**Anonymous beginner climber**

This small outcropping of rock is gently nestled along the banks of the Gunpowder Falls River in the Gunpowder Falls State Park, a few miles downstream from Prettyboy Dam in northern Baltimore County. It is a relatively quiet, peaceful setting, a plus for weekday afternoons during the spring and fall. Think 'babbling brook behind belayer.'

This crag doesn't see a lot of traffic, despite the short and easy stroll from the cars. Part of the reason is due to the fact that the rock is often dirty. Another reason is that few people know of it, as the proximity of Rocks State Park overshadows most stuff in this region. Finally, the vertical strata of the rock itself is unlike a lot of other places in Maryland where one can climb. In addition to the composition of the rock, the way it is exposed and has weathered does not allow for many good holds, so most of the climbing usually involves pinch holds on sharp edged flakes (where if you fall you might slice your palm open—or at the very least that flap of skin between your thumb and forefinger), sloping erosion pockets, or desperately tiny nubs on the face (which have the annoying tendency of busting off). Top this off with the fact that the outcropping is small, and thus doesn't offer a large number of routes. On the flip side, it is very easy to get to from the car (5 minutes flat walk), is in a scenic area, and the top-rope rigs are not at all difficult to set.

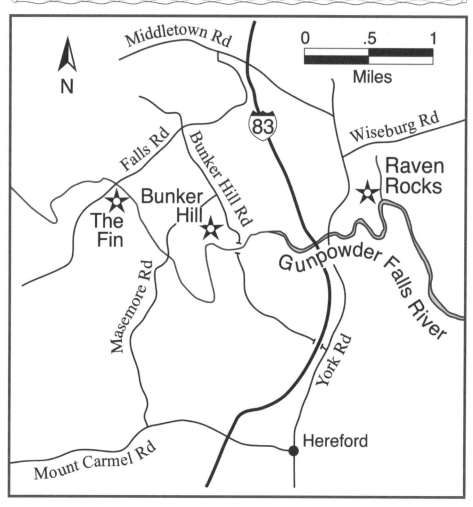

This area is usually only visited by climbers from the Hereford or Cockeyesville/ Towson area. Most other climbers who have to travel further tend to focus their attention at other, larger areas, such as Rocks State Park, or Chickies Rock near Lancaster, Pennsylvania

LOCATION/DIRECTIONS

From Baltimore: Take I–83 north to Exit 31 (Middletown Road). Turn left at the end of the off-ramp and proceed down Middletown Road a quarter mile to the first street after crossing over I-83. Turn left onto Falls Road and follow that for about 1 mile to a stop sign. Turn left onto Bunker Hill Road and proceed down it for 1 mile to where the bridge is washed out (from a flood years and years ago). Park in the gravel parking area on the left.

Head upstream along the small footpath. After a 5-minute leisurely walk you will suddenly come to a block of rock on the right. This is it; you are here!

GEOLOGY

This outcrop is made up of the sedimentary rock known as alluvium. It is a combination of clays, silt, sand, gravel, and other materials, molded as deposits in rivers and flood plains. It originally formed during the wetter climates of the glacial times. As the glaciers receded, the climate dried and the rivers and streams cut narrower channels in the region. The old upper surface of the sediments that used to be underwater became the river banks, and as the streams carved narrower channels, the sediments along the banks became terraced above the rivers. This particular outcropping has been tilted upward over time due to the slow, ever-grinding motion of the ground beneath your feet.

As has been mentioned earlier, this rock is not very strong, and you will find it disconcerting when flakes flex and holds break off on you while you are climbing. Climb gently when playing here.

EQUIPMENT

You won't need much more than some 15 to 40 foot long slings for anchors (depending on which routes your want to set up). This is primarily a top-rope area; lead climbing is not recommended on this friable rock.

CAMPING

The Gunpowder Falls State Park is **day use only**—there is no camping here!

RESTRICTIONS AND ACCESS

There are no major restrictions. The parking lot isn't overly huge, and the rock not overly wide, so not a great place to bring hordes of people (i.e., probably not a place for bringing large climbing classes), but other than that, no major issues.

LOCAL EATS

There really isn't much in the immediate area here. The nearest source of food is a few miles South on I–83 to Hereford (Exit 27) where there is a convenience store and a local pizza shop (which also serves breakfast!) Barring that, or for more variety, continue south a few miles on I–83 until Exit 20 and head east on Shawan Road. In short order you'll come to the Hunt Valley Mall on the left that has a few sit-down restaurants around it, and a food court inside. Continue another half mile and you come to York Road. Turning right to head south on York Road you'll find a broken string of restaurants (fast-food & sit-down), gas stations, grocery stores, etc.

For the Pennsylvania climber, your best option would be to head north on I–83 approximately 10 miles to Exit 1 in Pennsylvania. There are a small number of food establishments just off of this exit.

OTHER INFO

This is the northernmost section of the Gunpowder Falls State Park, which extends from the Prettyboy Dam area all the way down to the Gunpowder River, covering over 16,000 narrow acres of land in Baltimore and Harford Counties. Here, the Hereford/Prettyboy Dam section, along with having a few areas for climbing, also offers catch-and-release fly fishing, bowhunting (permit required) and archery practice, hiking

(with miles of trails in the woods and along the Gunpowder Falls River), canoeing almost
year-round (the water is generally deeper than on the upstream end of the Patapsco River just
west of Baltimore), and horseback riding. Be careful in the woods during hunting season.

After a hot afternoon of climbing, be sure to take advantage of the proximity of the
Gunpowder River. Wade in, and cool off (just be careful that there aren't any stray hooks
laying around from fly fishers).

The Routes

The routes are listed from right to left as you would approach them given the directions above.

1. Beginner's Chimney (5.0*)—27 ft. Don't miss it! At the far right end of the out-
cropping, at the nearest point the rock gets to the river, find a short, prominently V-shaped
chimney. Climb it using buckets and ledges on both walls. Or you can practice your stemming techniques (in preparation for a climb up Devil's Tower, perhaps?) by **not** using the
hand and foot ledges the entire way up—friction stem up the wall to the top!

The following routes are located 30 feet to the left on the main wall.

2. Pocket Poser (5.7)—38 ft. Start on the right end of the main wall, 6 feet from the
right edge. Follow the wide crack stacked with pockets the entire way up. Skirt around the
overhanging section by stepping onto the gray rock on the right for a few moves, but then
work back over into the crack just below where it widens into arm-bar size. Follow the
crack to the end. This route has the only known "handle" holds in central Maryland (several
of them, in fact!) The pockets are not as useful as they first appear.

3. Fly Fishing (5.9)—38 ft. You'll be fishing for some holds on this route before you
land the big ones. Follow the crack 5 feet left of *Pocket Poser* to the overhanging flakes.
Pull around and through the jutting overhang by creative use of laybacks and pinch holds
onto the blank face above (thin feet). Use even smaller holds to follow the face and shallow
groove on the left until you can reach the bomber handholds higher up. Beware that the
delicate flakes down low flex and will break off if enough force is applied. Full-on layback
moves will do this.

4. Tramontane (5.8)—39 ft. Named after a '70s **Foreigner** song. Start immediately
left (4 feet) of *Fly Fishing*, just right of *V Reel Theorm*. Climb the deep, flaring crack and
flakes, pulling past and through the left side of the roof/overhang at its lowest point. Climb
up the blank looking face above (no, really, there are holds to use), passing just right of the
deep crack (dirty) at the top of *V Reel Theorem*. You get a little of everything on this route
(jams, pinches, edges, nubs, slopers).

5. V Reel Theorem (5.5*)—39 ft. Climb the chimney just left of *Tramontane* until it
ends halfway up. Continue up the face towards a right-facing corner (using it if you have
to), gaining the large, dirty erosion crack near the top, and finish. Good opportunity to practice some hand/fist jamming. Step right at the very end for a cleaner exit. Just a little awkward, but pretty cool when you work the moves out.

6. Tweedle Beetle (5.9)—35 ft. Start at the base of the large left-facing open book, left of and around the corner from *V Reel Theorem*. Climb the blank corner straight up to the smaller right-facing corner above. Continue to the top.

7. Klingons On The Starboard Bow (5.10b/c)—35 ft. Start 3 feet left of the *Tweedle Beetle* corner, where a horizontal crack begins 6 feet off the ground with good holds. Climb up the face (crux), aiming for the rectangular alcove. Gain the alcove, then pull through the jagged overhang on the right.

8. Wipe Them Off, Jim (5.10a)—33 ft. Begin 9 feet left of *Klingons On The Starboard Bow*, where the horizontal crack ends. Climb the blank looking face on tiny holds to a shallow comma shaped hollow. Continue up to the right-rising/facing overhang, and follow it up and right until you can squeeze through a narrow notch (beware the thorny plant life) to the left of *Klingons*...Beware of loose rock to the left.

9. Poetry In Motion (5.6)—20 ft. Start below the lowest point of the right-arching overhang on the left side of the wall, 3 feet left of *Wipe Them Off, Jim*. Dance up the lichen encrusted face to a shallow chimney, passing the lowest part of the aforementioned over-hang on the left. There are some nice moves buried beneath the lichen and dirt. Be aware that the rock is also very rotten in this section of the cliff. Loose holds and easily broken rock abound. Be careful where you belay.

212

RAVEN
ROCKS

Gary Lay's reach is a Natural One *(5.8)*

RAVEN ROCKS

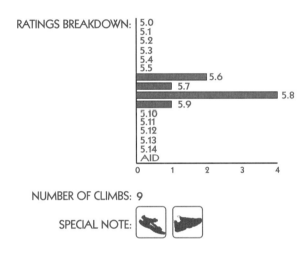

RATINGS BREAKDOWN:

NUMBER OF CLIMBS: 9

SPECIAL NOTE:

"This is insane…if this were better rock this would be a really good climb…put me down. This is ridiculous."—Anonymous climber on "Unfinished Symphony"

Raven Rock is yet another area to climb in Gunpowder Falls State Park. But…while it has huge potential for hosting many routes (the main outcrop measures 140 feet from end to end!), the quality of the rock ensures that not many people come here. Thus development of this crag is still in its early stages. The center wall, the main draw to the eye when one is here, has poor rock quality. The left and right ends of this band of rock, however, have better rock quality (though this is not to say you will not bust loose any holds—just fewer than from the middle!) However, the left end of this band of rock is often overlooked because, well, it's…shorter.

While the setting for these rocks is remote, the sounds that funnel down the river valley from I–83 remind you that civilization is not terribly far away. This is especially true when trucks are engine braking down that long hill on the highway.

LOCATION/DIRECTIONS

From Baltimore: Head north on I–83 to Exit 27 for Hereford (Mt Carmel Road). Bear right at the off ramp and go 0.5 miles to a light at York Road. Turn left onto York and proceed north a total of 1.7 miles to a parking area (you will pass Hereford High School on the right after 0.6 miles). After the first mile, you will find yourself going down a long, somewhat steep and somewhat curvy hill. Just as you get to the bottom, there will be small parking areas on the left and right. Most people park on the left by the kiosk (it is the larger of the two).

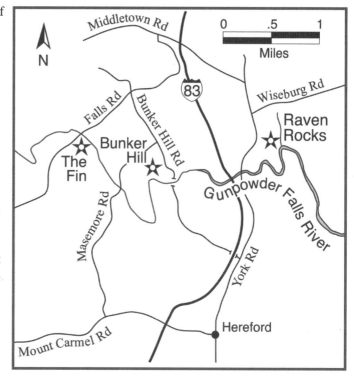

From points north: Head south on I–83 to Exit 31 (Middletown Road). Turn left (east) on Middletown Road and follow it until it ends 1 mile later at York Road. Turn right, and go south on York Road for 1 mile. You will go down a steep, twisty hill and cross over a bridge at the bottom of the road. Just as the road starts to go up again, there is a parking area on both the right and left sides of the road.

From the parking area, walk north on York Road and cross over the bridge. About 120 feet later, there will be a green sign that reads "Wiseburg" on the right hand side of the road. There is a break in the guard rail just past the sign and a trail that leads steeply down and into the woods. Follow the blue-blazed trail downstream. It is mostly flat, but there are some up/down sections. After about 20 to 25 minutes, you will spy a broad outcropping of rock a few hundred feet uphill to your left in the woods just before you cross over a small tributary. Continue down the path for another 200 feet until you come to another stream coming in from the left. There is a path that follows this tributary upstream past a series of small waterfalls. Take this path up a couple hundred feet until you come to a small 12 to 16 foot tall boulder. Turn left here and follow the faint path to the main band of rock.

On the final approach, be aware of thorn bushes and poison ivy, especially in the late spring to mid-autumn time frame. Wearing long pants will help. The base of the cliff is fairly clear of foliage—though you will have to contend with spiders during the warmer parts of the year.

GEOLOGY

The rock is exactly the same as that at Bunker Hill Rock. See the preceding chapter for geological details. However, instead of climbing the strata edge on, you are climbing the face of the strata. It also is notoriously loose and prone to breaking—not the best rock in the area to be climbing. In fact, you need to be pretty desperate to be climbing here often.

EQUIPMENT

This is primarily a top-roping area. All you will really need are slings in the 10- to 60-foot range (depending on what you want to set up). There is only one area that can also take gear, but since it is such a small spot, and you can use 40 foot slings off of trees, you can skip humping your rack in with you (besides, the quality of the rock is poor enough that lead climbing is **not** recommended!)

CAMPING

Nope. None here.

RESTRICTIONS AND ACCESS

There are no real access problems with this crag. Other than the thorn bushes that seem to spring up everywhere, making it difficult sometimes to get to the tops of the rock.

LOCAL EATS

The closest thing for food is the Pioneer Pub three-quarters of a mile south on York Road. Further down the road in Hereford is a small shopping plaza, and therein is a small pizza joint (Michael's Pizza). After that, there are food establishments down in Cockeysville and up in Pennsylvania. See the Bunker Hill chapter for more information.

OTHER INFO

The Gunpowder Falls State Park in the Hereford Area offers a number of hiking trails, both immediately along and away from the river. If you want a break from climbing and want to have a nice, serene stroll through the woods, this has some ideal areas to get away from things. In the immediate vicinity is Raven Falls, a small cascade fall a few hundred feet away from the rocks. While it's not very impressive as waterfalls go, if you go far enough upstream you can actually get away from most of the droning coming down the river valley from I–83. It can almost be a quiet and peaceful place to sit and relax!

When climbing here, keep a sharp eye out for poison ivy that can trail down the cliff, and be aware that the woods are **infested** with ticks. If you bring dogs, they will bring passengers home. The best time to be here would be mid to late autumn or early to mid spring, before the ticks (and other insects) get ramped up for the warmer weather.

The Routes

This broad band of rock is 140 feet from end to end, and ranges from 20 to 40 feet in height (the shorter section is to the left, the taller to the right). The routes are described from right to left, as you would encounter them approaching the rock.

1. Eye Of The Beholder (5.6)—46 ft. Start in the center of the far right-end face below two "eye" holes. Climb up the center of the wall, passing the "eyes" on the right. The rock here is reasonably secure, unlike most of the rest of the outcrop. Maybe it's not the prettiest route, but remember: beauty is in the eye of the beholder.

2. The Dragon's Tooth (5.8*)—

46 ft. If any route can be considered
"popular" here, this is it! It is also the one
least prone to having holds shear or break
off. Beginning 4 feet left of *Eye Of The
Beholder*, layback up solid rock using the
left-facing flakes below the left "eye" and
hauling up on the pointed "stalactite"
flake (the dragon's tooth! don't let it bite)
just up and left of the same "eye." From
here, follow the left-facing corner ramp
up to a ledge, then easy climbing gets
you to the top.

3. Snaggletooth (5.8*)—45 ft.

Climb the outside left corner (the arête)
to a "tooth" flake 12 feet up. Snag it and
pull past using additional flakes above,
maintaining the arête until you reach a
ledge. Scamper up the final few moves to
the top. It's a bit more sustained than
The Dragon's Tooth.

4. Dirty Chimney (5.6)—39 ft.

Climb the ramp up to and into the broad

chimney around the corner to the left of *The Dragon's Tooth*. Climb up the chimney, paying
careful attention to loose, rotted rock, especially near the top. Struggle up to the left to
finish.

5. Unfinished Symphony

(project)—39 ft. Unfinished is right.
Beginning between the chimney and the
tree, climb the left-arching downward-
pointing flake system up and left until it
ends. Reach up for some good finger
buckets. Move up and left across the
blank looking face until you are below
the overhang with brown rock. Somehow
struggle up through the overhang to the
rotten brown rock above, then finish in a
small, dirty left-facing corner. Belayers
should stand clear as the brown area of
rock is completely rotten and large flakes
can bust loose with little pressure. You do
not want to stack your rope directly
below this route while belaying, either.

6. Natural One (5.8)—43 ft. Nothing artificial here. This route begins around the corner 33 feet left of the tree by *Unknown Symphony*. Climb the inside of the left-facing corner with an arm-sized crack in it until you reach the ramp 8 feet up. Walk up the ramp until it ends at a series of left-facing flakes. Some of them are…sensitive to being used as holds. Layback up these flakes, trending right until you reach an overhang near the top (with great but nearly useless layback underclings). Pull around to the left of the overhang on large side-pull holds to gain the top. Watch for poison ivy trailing down from the bushes.

The next set of routes ascend the wall 42 feet left of *Natural One*, not quite at the far left end of the band of rock. This area is often overlooked because it is shorter (half the height of the main wall) and more covered with spiderwebs. However, this is unfortunate as there are a number of decent routes on decent rock on this end of the cliff. The routes start to the left of a 6 foot wide left-facing corner, 42 feet left of *Natural One*.

7. I Lichen It (5.8)—21 ft. You may or may not lichen it; your tastes will vary. Begin at the first left-facing flake system 6 feet left of the 6 foot wide corner. Lieback and climb the flake up to a stance, then continue up the corner to the top. The first half of the route is great. The last bit leaves a little to be desired.

8. The Blind Leading The Blind (5.9)— 21 ft. Great opening moves! Start 2 feet left of the large *I Lichen It* flake, at other smaller left-facing flakes and corners. Feel your way up these smaller left-facing features, making a long reach to a huge upturned flake system. Haul yourself up onto that and head up the steep wall with smaller holds above. The crux is in the last few moves, when you hit the dusty lichen and moss covered holds. Take care when reaching up near the top, or you will very likely knock enough lichen and dirt down into your eyes to effectively blind you. There is one move past the lichen/dirt section that is a good exit hold. You won't need eyes to know that you have it when you grab it.

9. Bucket Brigade (5.7*)—21 ft. Steep, pumpy, and fun! Possibly the second best route at Raven Rocks. Locate the large left-facing flake system 14 feet left of the corner, 6 feet left of *The Blind Leading*….Grab large holds and start climbing! Follow the flake up to the steeper wall above, then pull straight through the slight overhang. to a bucket finish hold.

ROCKS STATE PARK

Leslie Goldberg enjoys the great moves on Strawberry Jam *(5.8)*

ROCKS
STATE PARK

RATINGS BREAKDOWN:

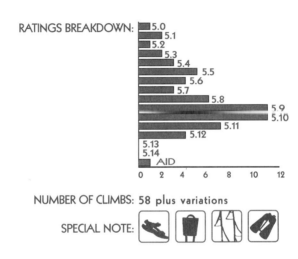

NUMBER OF CLIMBS: 58 plus variations

SPECIAL NOTE:

"It's the exact opposite of Carderock! There are holds and things."
—**Matthew a hang gliding climber on his first visit to Rocks State Park.**

Rocks State Park (also called Rocks of Deer Creek, although this name has fallen out of usage) is located about 50 minutes north-northeast of Baltimore. The land making up the Park used to be part of the Susquehannock Indian Nation, who once used the KING & QUEEN SEAT area for ceremonial gatherings. Now the land is a place for many types of recreation—including rock climbing.

Almost every square inch of the rock has been touched at one time or another. There are even some two-pitch routes (the rock is over 100 feet high in places). A number of the routes can be led safely, so most of the routes have been given a "protection grade" in addition to their normal difficulty rating. For top-roping in most areas here a 50 meter rope will be more than sufficient, but if you are climbing in the BREAKAWAY WALL area, be **sure** that both ends of your rope touch the ground!! The wall here is just at 25 meters at its tallest. It would suck if your rope was not centered properly and one end was dangling 20 feet in the air (it would suck even worse if you didn't tie knots at the ends of your rope and you rappelled down, too!)

The Rangers are climber-friendly. They feel that climbers are as legitimate a user-group as anyone else, and if you work with them, they will work with you. Bearing this in mind, there are four hard and fast rules that the Rangers will enforce on you (and other Park users):

1) **The Park Closes at Sunset!** Please, please, **please** be down, off the rocks, and **out** of the Park by sunset! Sunset is published daily in the papers, and there is a sign at the upper parking area (the King & Queen's Seat parking lot) indicating what time the Park closes. The Rangers like the climbing community, but they also want to keep things safe for everyone. They also want to go home, too. If you are in the Park after dark and a Ranger finds you, you **will** be issued a "$70 autographed invitation" (euphemism for ticket). Don't worry; they will be waiting.

2) **No new pitons or bolts are to be placed in the rocks!** If you feel for some reason that there absolutely **has** to be a bolt/piton driven in somewhere—**check with the Rangers first!** If you can make a valid case…maybe they'll let you. But don't bullshit them; some of the Rangers are climbers, too, and know the rocks pretty well.

3) **No pets!** This isn't much of an issue for most climbers, but some feel they have to bring their pets (dogs, cats, ferrets, goldfish, whatever) to the rocks with them. The Park has a blanket policy on pets—they are not allowed. Please leave them at home. And even if the weekend "gatekeeper" people tell you that you're allowed to have pets on the trails but just not in the picnic areas, don't believe them.

4) **Alcohol is strictly prohibited!** This is Park policy. Deal with it.

In case of any emergencies in the Park please call 800-825-7275.

LOCATION/DIRECTIONS

There are a few ways to approach Rocks State Park from Baltimore. Herein are two of them.

From the Baltimore beltway: From I–695, head over to I–95 North, continuing until you reach the Bel Air exit for Route 24 (Exit 77B). Continue north on Route 24 (take note of all the strip malls and food areas you pass in the next 6 or so miles). After you go approximately 6 miles, you will pass the Business Route 1. Route 24 will split to the right a quarter-mile later (continuing on Route 24 North; the left fork sends you down Route 1 South). This puts you onto Route 1 North for a bit. Take the second exit, which continues Route 24 North (the first exit is for Route 924, and brings you to downtown Bel Air). Follow Route 24 for another 6 miles (despite the signs saying 7 or 10 or whatever) and you'll enter Rocks State Park. After 1.5 miles, there will be a large parking area on the left. You can park here (follow the left-trending purple-blazed trail up the steep hill) or continue up Route 24 another 0.3 miles, turning left onto St. Clair Bridge Road, and then 0.7 miles later, turning left again onto the King & Queen Seat access road. Go up the steep hill for 0.5 miles and take the first parking area on the left.

From Towson: You can take Dulaney Valley Road/Route 146 north out of Towson (it crosses I–695, so you can exit from the beltway here if desired). Stay on Route 146 when Dulaney Valley Road splits off after you cross over the Loch Raven Reservoir. About 16 miles after getting off of or passing I–695 (you will swear the edge of the world will be just over the next rise!), you will come to an intersection with a stop sign and flashing red light. This cross street is Route 23. Turn right and go down Route 23 for 2.5 miles into "downtown" Jarrettsville. Turn left onto Route 165 at the light, and head up the road 4.8 miles until you come to St. Clair Bridge Road (it will be on the right at the bottom of a steep hill; turning left here puts you into someone's driveway). Turn right onto St. Clair Bridge Road and continue on for another 2.5 miles to the access road on the right for the King & Queen Seat Parking. Head up the steep hill and park in the first parking area on the left. (Additional parking is available on Route 24.)

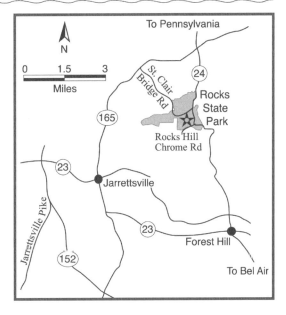

From the King & Queen's Seat parking area, it is a quick walk down to the top of the rocks. The King & Queen's Seat are two side by side curved "seats" atop a large boulder near the trail at the start of the rock outcropping.

The Ranger's office is located on Rocks Chrome Hill Road, 0.2 miles off of Route 24, south of the large parking area on Route 24. There is an optional parking area a few hundred feet prior to the Ranger's office, and a trail that leads to the upper areas of the park, including the King & Queen's Seat area.

GEOLOGY

There are a number of exceptional routes here. Even the so-so routes are not so bad (except for a few, but every place has those). This is due to the nature of the rock, which is a Wissahickon formation schist (note: this formation is being reevaluated by geologists as being very different from other "Wissahickon formation" rock, so this name may not be applicable in the future). It is characterized by quartzite and serpentine crystals, allowing for some nice, sharp holds (there are some excellent examples of the small, sharp serpentine crystals on the second pitch of *Chardonnay*). The bedding plane is primarily vertical, but if you look around (particularly over near the MOBY DICK boulder and elsewhere along the purple trail that leads to/from the parking area on Route 24), you can see areas where the bedding has folded. Also, if you look closely around THE PINNACLE, you'll see larger deposits of quartzite.

EQUIPMENT

You will need a combination of slings and gear to set up anchors for most of the routes in the Park. A rack consisting of medium to large gear and a few lengths of 20 to 25 foot slings should suffice for most top-rope anchors. But use your best judgment as to what to bring and where to climb given what gear you have available. Different areas here have different requirements for anchors and anchor-setting techniques.

If you want to do any lead climbing, a standard rack will more than suffice for most routes.

CAMPING

There is no camping in the Park. Period. The closest camping can be found at the Susquehanna State Park on the south side of the Susquehanna River from Port Deposit.

RESTRICTIONS AND ACCESS

There are no access issues with the Park. The Rangers are climber-friendly and will work with you on any issues you may have. The only restriction is on the placing of fixed gear in the rock. Oh, and the Park closes at sunset. You've been sufficiently warned.

Most of the rocks across the road are **private property**, and the landowner does not wish to entertain climbers on these rocks. Stay off of them. Rumor has it he has been known to shoot at people who have been found over there. Besides, there are very few decent sections of rock to climb over there; much of it is low-angle or is loose or is over-grown with plant life. The rock that is on Park property over there is closed to climbing. Treat it as if it were private property, too. Besides, there's plenty of rock to be climbed on this side of the river.

LOCAL EATS

There are a number of eateries scattered along the 6 mile stretch of Route 24 that is between Route 1 and I–95. You can find a bevy of sit-down restaurants and fast-food places, the bulk of which are located within a half mile radius of the strip malls a mile or so east of Route 1 on Route 24. There is a Pizza Hut near the intersection of Routes 24 and 23, on the left tucked back in a small complex as you approach the intersection coming from Rocks State Park, as well as a few other fast-food places on Route 24 just northwest of Route 1. If you came through Jarrettsville, there are a couple of delis, some convenience and gas/food stations, and a Subway scattered around the small town. If you have a hankering for some **real** Italian foods, Di Pasquale's is an Italian grocery store located 4.75 miles south on Md. 165, 0.1 miles past the intersection with Md. 152. They offer not only real Italian foods/ingredients at a reasonable price, but also good pizzas, salads, and sandwiches (primarily an order-out/take-out service, though).

OTHER INFO

The Park allows users free access during the weekdays, but charges $2 per person for those who wish to park at the KING & QUEEN'S SEAT area on the in-season weekends (generally April through October/November). Note that there is a small shack at the KING & QUEEN'S SEAT parking area indicating the time that the Park will close **on that day**. Pay heed to this.

The Park Service is currently working to rebuild the rescue trail and build/maintain climber access trails. They would dearly appreciate volunteers. Please contact the Volunteer Coordinator at 410-557-7994 or 410-836-6735.

The Rangers take a dim view of people throwing **anything** off the cliffs. This is a criminal offense, and the Rangers will charge offenders (if caught) with reckless endanger-ment and assault. So, if you catch any bastards throwing things off, feel free to notify the authorities. This is for your protection, too.

The Park is a Trash Free Park! If you pack it in, pack it out. Bring an extra bag to put your trash in if you need to. And be helpful; pick up any extra trash you find lying around.

Other climbers and the Rangers will definitely appreciate it.

There are copperheads (the snake variety, not climbing gear) in the Park. They like the rock, especially to warm themselves on during chillier days. The BREAKAWAY WALL area is one of the more popular areas to see snakes. In the 14-plus years of climbing there, your author has not yet encountered one (now next week I'm sure I will!), just some evidence of their passing. Just be warned. Forewarned is forearmed, and you don't want your forearms on the receiving end of a couple of poisonous fangs—do you?

In the spring and early summer, be aware that wasps and yellow jackets love to make their homes in the clefts and corners of the south-facing rock here. This tends to impact routes such as *Vertical* a lot. Take appropriate precautions when they are out and active.

There is a micro moss that grows on the rocks (what kind, I don't know; that's not my forte). This moss, after it rains or mists, suddenly comes "alive" and causes the rocks to be slicker than oil. I know of a couple of people who have face-planted while walking along the base of the cliffs here, but the moss is not restricted to just the bottom. Be aware and extra careful when the conditions are wet.

Please climb safe! This should go without saying no matter **where** you climb, but bears repeating. People die at Rocks State Park almost every year. Until recently (1998 and 1999) most of these have not been climber deaths (just stupid people doing stupid things). But the sudden demise of two climbers (who were soloing) in recent years here has woken some people up to how dangerous this recreation really is. **Know your limits** and **take responsibility for your actions!** Self-rescue if possible. The Rangers will assist in true emergencies, but they are not babysitters. If you solo, know that if you fall you are going to get seriously injured or killed. This could potentially jeopardize the future of climbing in the Park. No one likes to do body recoveries (been there, done that). I'm not telling you not to solo climb. I **am** saying be extremely aware of the consequences your actions may have on the area.

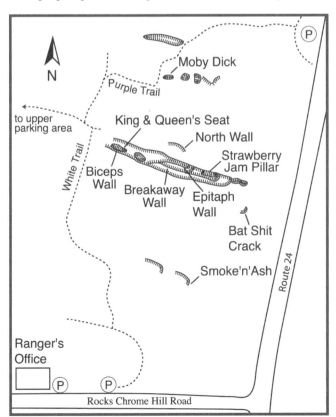

On hot summer days, you can take a dip in Deer Creek, which runs parallel to the road a couple of hundred feet below the rock. This creek is also popular for fishing and tubing. Note, the Park has the standard disclaimer that you swim/tube at your own risk.

And if it's too chilly to climb/swim, or too wet to climb, there are always 3.5 miles of hiking trails in the park that one can explore. Who knows, maybe you'll find a "forgotten" outcropping of rock somewhere….

The Routes

The King & Queen's Seat area is the main outcrop of rock in the park, protruding from the side of the hill toward Route 24. The Seats themselves are a couple of depressions in the first high stack of rocks you come to on your right as you approach from the top (95 percent of the people who visit here come from this direction). Below and to the left is a short wall capped with a small roof leading to a short slab. This is one of the main boulder problems here. To the left of this is a large notch formed by the rocks of the King & Queen's Seat boulders and the next tall stack of rocks known as BIG MOMMA BOUL-DER. Ofttimes rappellers will have rigged BIG MOMMA BOLDER for those long rappels (just make sure your rope reaches the ground, because from the top it's nigh 140 feet to the ground!) The lower right corner of BIG MOMMA BOULDER is another fun but small boulder problem, this one with a sit start.

BICEPS WALL

This is the wall located directly behind and below the King & Queen's Seat.

Anchors are generally off the boulders behind the King & Queen's Seat block. Access to the base of the climbs descends down the steep erosion trail to the right of the rocks, cutting back to the cliff face at your best opportunity. Routes here are listed from left to right (as you would logically approach the wall).

1. Exhibition (5.11b/c X)—23 ft. Begin 10 feet to the right of a stack of blocks forming a right-facing corner at the far left end of the rock. From the green slab, climb up to and through a crescent shaped flake to reach the roof. At the small, left-facing corner pull through the roof and continue up on small, tiny holds. This route used to be 5.9 or so before the flake above the roof was broken off (well, according to some of the original pioneers, anyway!)

2. Fever Dream (5.12b)—31 ft. Someone had a feverish dream to come up with this route. Begin next to the large tree near the center of this wall. Climb up the overhang to the thin face below the roof. There are a couple of tiny underclings in the roof. Pull the roof just right of *Exhibition* and continue up on holds bordering on imaginary. Relax when you get to the large ledge above.

3. Biceptennial (5.10a* X)—43 ft. Start a few feet right of the tree, at some right-facing corner blocks. Climb up through the overhang at a right-facing notch to the sloping ledge. Keep going up the steep face, trending slightly right, to the roof. Crank through the roof at the left-facing corner system to some larger holds, then to the top. Fun route. A dyno may be warranted for some.

4. Golden Arches (5.11b/c*)—43 ft. Start 6 feet right of **Biceptennial** at a small stance with a good finger flake, or on the ground 4 feet lower, directly below the golden brown arch high above. Climb up to the arch and pull through with small holds (**V1**). Finish on the face above.

V1: Golden Arches Right (5.10b/c*) When you reach the arch, it is possible to pull around it on the right on better (read: larger!) holds.

5. Beginner Flake (a.k.a., The Flake, Critter Crack, or Peanut Brittle; 5.5* PG)—51 ft. Begin pretty much anywhere 4 to 10 feet right of *Golden Arches*. Climb the bulging face and obvious left-facing flake (**V1**) to the top. The variety of starting points gives a little jazz to this route.

V1: Beginner Flake Direct (5.9*) There are actually several variations you can pull out of the main route. This one is the hardest and goes straight up the face to the right of the flake.

6. Beginner Corner (a.k.a. The Crux) (5.5 G)—53 ft. Starting 12 feet right of *Beginner Flake*, climb up the sloping ledges following a thin crack past the small, blocky right-facing corner to easier ground above. Not always the cleanest or most graceful route to play on, it is a popular route for beginners to cut their teeth on, especially when the rest of the rock is overrun with tourists and other climbers.

There are a couple routes located downhill and to the right of BICEPS WALL, between BICEPS WALL and the BREAKAWAY LEDGE.

7. Unnamed (A2)—40 ft. This is an old aid route just left of *Chardonnay*. Don't climb it. Not recommended. It is only included here for historical completeness. The rock is rotten, the gear bad to worse, and the seams too thin. There is no place for solid clean gear, and you are **not** allowed to hammer anything in on the rock. Trust not the pins! They are 30-plus years old. It was first attempted in the late '50s/early '60s, but it wasn't until Eric Cook came along (during his crazier years) that the line was completed, topping out where the bushes of grass exist today. It had only ever seen a handful of ascents after that and is never climbed anymore.

8. Chardonnay (5.7 PG–R/X)—110 ft. So named when the first ascent party topped out at 6:00 a.m. to find some guy on the summit draining a bottle of Chardonnay wine. This route is often the rappel spot for those who come here just to rappel (nice long drop for it—just make sure your rope(s) touch ground!) To climb this route, start on the ground, below and a little uphill from the BREAKAWAY WALL, near a large tree, at a right-facing corner/crack/chimney-like "notch."

Pitch 1: 58 ft. Follow the crack through the chimney 'notch' (crux) to a ledge. Step right a move or two, then follow up and left on easier ground to a ledge with a sizeable tree (beware the greenbrier!) You know you're close when you reach the grassy ledges.

Pitch 2: 52 ft. Climb straight up the face (**V1, V2, V3**) above to the top of the BIG MOMMA BOULDER. Protection is sparse to nonexistent at best. There is a chicken-head you can sling about 12 feet or so up, but a fall before, and most of the way after, will have you hitting the deck. Suck it up and don't fall, rappel off, or choose one of the variations. Pitch 1 is often wet because it is a natural drain for water in the rock. This route doesn't see a lot of traffic, so the greenbrier bushes have been growing thick on some of the ledges. Take care.

V1: Chardonnay Variation Finish (5.9) Head right and a little up to a small roof (the "cave"). Pull to the right around this and follow the offwidth crack above to the top. Awkward as hell (duh, it's an offwidth!) There is almost nothing for your right foot except…air. At least initially.

V2: Chardonnay Escape (5.5) Traverse straight right to a cave. Continue past this opening around the corner and then up to the top.

V3: The Prow (unrated) Not a recommended finish, noted here only for historical purposes. Difficult to top-rope, dangerous to lead. There is no pro, really. Step left from the belay and work your way up the overhanging arête, going through three roofs. Underclings and left side pulls are the order of the day here. Maybe 3 people have ever climbed this variation (and no, that was not an offer for a challenge!)

BREAKAWAY WALL

This is the "main wall" of Rocks State Park, accessible only by an exposed 4th class/5.1 downclimb scramble down past the Strawberry Jam Pillar. Please be very care-ful when going down/up this area (especially when it's wet). A fall could be terminal (see earlier note about body recoveries). Rope up if you have to, okay?

The BREAKAWAY WALL hosts the longest top-rope routes in this guide, pushing 80-plus feet in length. Be sure both ends of your rope reach the ground before trying these climbs! **A 50m rope is the minimum length you want to use in this area!**

Routes are described from left to right, starting to the far left after you've descended the downclimb. You'll need gear for most anchors here, and the anchors are usually set from either the EPITAPH WALL (for those climbs left of *Vertical*) or the platform 15 feet lower down (for *Vertical* and *Piney*).

9. Unnamed (5.6)—approx. 130 ft. This oft-overlooked route has some nice moves to it, and if done, is usually done as a two-pitch lead climb. The first pitch is "the" pitch. The second pitch just gets you off the rock (as rappelling from the small trees might make you a little nervous). Climb up the wide gully to the left of the huge Breakaway corner until you come to the roof. Pull around to the left at the lowest point of the roof and climb out on the face (crux) up past a horizontal crack and to a tree ledge (pitch 1). Finish by continuing up and left over easy 4th and 5th class ground to the top, finishing where many hikers and tourists come to look out from the rock.

10. Cave Crack (a.k.a. Bat) (5.9 PG)—45 ft. Same start as *Unnamed* above, but instead of heading left under and around the roofs, follow the crack that splits the roof above you. After you drop a couple of large nuts for pro in the crack, wing off the end and finish by either climbing the last pitch of *Unnamed* above, scrambling left and climbing the last pitch of *Chardonney*, or climbing up the last part of *Breakaway*. First done by Eric Cook and Sam Spice long ago.

11. Green Subtrafuge (a.k.a. Centrifuge) (5.7+* PG)—85 ft. Climb up the gully until you come to the *Cave Crack* roofs. Cut right under the roofs and go up the flakes. Mostly liebacking, but with good holds. This would be nicer if the lichen and other foliage were consistently cleaned out of the bottom part of the route.

12. Green Subtrafuge Direct (a.k.a. Centrifuge Direct) (5.8 X)—85 ft. Start up the gully and climb the outside corner to the left of *Breakaway Left* to a ledge 30 feet up. Either traverse right and finish on *Breakaway Left*, or nudge over left onto *Green Subtrafuge*.

13. Breakaway Left (5.9* R)—83 ft. As *Breakaway Right*, climb corner to block roof, but move left onto the left face, pulling up onto a long and narrow ledge, left of the block roof. A sequency three-move layback pulls you past and atop the block roof. Finish on good holds to the top. Note: using the same anchors as for *Breakaway Right* could set up quite a swing if you fall while pulling the crux.

14. Breakaway Direct (5.11*)—83 ft. Start as *Breakaway Right*, but instead of traversing out right, pull the block roof directly. Finish on *Breakaway Right*.

15. Breakaway Right (5.9** R)—83 ft. Climb large right-facing corner/crack system to the block roof approximately 35 feet overhead. Traverse out right on the narrow foot ledge with thin handholds (one was "modified" in the early to mid '90s to be slightly better than what it was; bastards) until the ledge runs out. Angle up and step past the roof on your left, following the thin finger crack to the corner again. Finish by working your way through the upper half of the wall on moderate to good holds (although your hands may not have the grip-strength left to hold onto them). A nice forearm pumper.

16. Breakaway Green Scar (5.10a** R)—83 ft. Climb *Breakaway Right*, but once past the roof and the heavily chalked layback flake, step right (not on the piton!) and follow the steep and unrelenting face to the top. About halfway up, you'll encounter the green colored part of the rock for which this route is named. Basically a variation to *Breakaway Right*. No single move is harder than 5.9, but the sustained nature and very sequency face on the upper half of this route make it feel more difficult. **Ultra classic**.

17. Superbulge (5.12c/d* X)—83 ft. Climb the slightly bulging and somewhat blank (for Rocks State Park standards) wall to the right of right-facing Breakaway corner. Do an iron-cross or pull a tight, low-angle layback (saves you a move) through the crux. Hugh Herr considers the route 5.11d at best. Your mileage may vary. Finish on or to the right of *Breakaway Green Scar*.

18. Breakfast Of Champions (5.11d* X)—67 ft. A contrived route left of *Mike's Finger Buckets*. Go up the wall halfway between *Mike's…* and *Breakaway Right* to a large downward-facing notch in the flake. Using this as a left-side upwards pull, stretch far right to about two o'clock to a hold. Then go up the wall immediately left of *Mike's…*, following a sharp, left-facing flake system, without using any holds on *Mike's*. Finish on *Mike's* or end it here (since the hard part is over after 30 feet of climbing).

19. Mike's Finger Buckets (5.10a* X)—(35 ft.) (67 ft. to top of cliff) A short "boulder problem" working up the semi-blank face left of *Vertical* following a right-arcing seam below and to the left of the small roof above. Continue through face holds and flakes until you reach a large ledge (well, you can sit on it, anyway) about 35 feet up. End it here or just keep climbing up to the top (the original ascent moved right to join with *Vertical*). The climbing tapers off dramatically after you reach the left edge of the roof, although your fingers may be a bit fried. There is a contrived 5.8 variation that goes up immediately next to *Vertical* (without using any holds right of the crack on *Vertical* or the crack itself) to the roof above, then angles hard left, rejoining *Mike's...* First ascent was Mike Endicott in the early to mid '70s.

20. Vertical (5.6** G)—67 ft. Super-positive holds all up and down this classic route make it an extremely popular climb. Follow the prominent crack/flake system that starts in the center of the wall, about 15 feet beneath a small overhang. Pull through it and follow the parallel left-leaning cracks up to the next bulge. Work your way over or around the bulge near the top to the large platform (**V1**). Great pro, an excellent route for practicing leads. There are many variations possible. Some follow the parallel cracks exactly, some work the face on either side. Whatever you want to do, go play and have fun (that is the name of the game, right?) One fun variation is to traverse left until above *Mike's Finger Buckets* before you pass by the first overhang and then climb the featured green face to the top. The climbing doesn't get any harder than 5.6 or 5.7, whatever you opt to play on.

> **V1: Vertical Extension (5.4* PG)** An excellent optional finish is to continue climbing up the right-facing wall/arête to the Slimey Ledge. This gives you another 15 feet or so additional climbing.

21. Bone Jacker (5.7*)—67 ft. As this is really just a right variation to *Vertical*, some people do not recognize it as a separate route. Climb the featured face between *Piney* and the cracks of *Vertical*, staying to the right of the overhang and crack system on *Vertical*. The hardest part is pulling through the final wall just left of the *Piney* roof. Easily avoided by going left up the ramp to finish on *Vertical*.

22. Piney (5.10a/b)—67 ft. Start to the right of *Vertical*, up to the right-facing corner to the flat body-length roof split by a horizontal flake/crack. Pull the roof on the left side near the end of the crack, using less than optimum holds. Finish on the slabby face above.

EPITAPH WALL

The following few short routes are located above the Slimey Ledge, and access the summit section directly. You will need medium to large pro in order to set up top-rope anchors for these routes. There is a quick and exposed two-move 4th class traverse (don't fall!) on the north side of the rock that will allow you easy access to this broad ledge. Routes are from right to left as you face the rock.

23. Slimey (unrated*) The bouldering area to the right of *Virgin Crack*, named for the scooped out section that fills with water periodically after rains (but mainly because the original climbers used to all pee in this depression before doing their bouldering sessions— great incentive **not** to fall!) Basically do laps on the awesome holds in and around this overhang until you can't hold on anymore.

24. Breakaway Escape Hatch (5.5)—32 ft. Instead of making the exposed 3rd class moves on the backside of the wall to leave this ledge, you can climb up the jugs of *Slimey* to a spacious ledge. From there make a few quick, exposed moves to gain the summit.

25. Virgin Crack (a.k.a. Divirgin Crack) (5.9 PG)—31. Climb the obvious smooth, upward flaring right-leaning crack. Awkward. This route was first put up during the Vulgarian period of climbing, and the name was derived from how the climbers hands would bleed like...well, you figure it out. The crack actually forms the detached block for *Slimey*, as is evidenced by the fact you can see clear through to the other side.

26. Goblin Eye (5.8* X)—26 ft.

This fun little route is mostly a one-move 5.8. Climb the short, overhanging face 5 feet to left of *Virgin Crack*, following the zigzag crack first left then right on good holds. There is a nice hand jam about halfway up in the crack as it cuts right. There is also a piton halfway up the route (you won't see it from the ground, though).

27. Epitaph (5.8* R/X)—26 ft.

Climb the short, featured, overhanging face a few feet left of *Goblin Eye*. There are a couple of variations to this route to the left that are strenuous and pumpy. Beware of rampant thorn bushes that block access to the bottom of this route (they can be skirted around on *Goblin Eye*). Bring a weed-whacker.

THE PINNACLE

The only way to set top-ropes up here is to do a lead or solo. Easiest is to clamber up from the notch formed by THE PINNACLE and the main rocks. Second easiest is to follow the crack left of *Better Balance* on the north face of THE PINNACLE (medium to large pro; watch for the loose block near the crux). The anchors at the top are a couple of bolts.

Routes are described starting from the south side of THE PINNACLE, starting with the *Strawberry Jam* crack, and working around clockwise.

28. Strawberry Jam (5.8** PG)—32 ft.

Crank up the prominent left-leaning hand crack on the south side of THE PINNACLE (**V1**). If your jamming technique (feet and hands) needs help, this is an ideal route to work on. So named because you get "strawberries" on the backs of your hands from the jams. A very nice climb, and the crack lends itself to being led, but be warned: a number of prospective leaders have decked when they fell and all their pro zippered.

V1: Strawberry Jam Direct (5.10a*) About two-thirds of the way up the *Strawberry Jam* crack, step right and go straight up the face on small holds and a flake. This is leadable, but be warned that the flake flexes when pulled on, and your gear will easily fall out.

29. Creaking Eyelids (5.11c/d)—33 ft.

Climb the center of the steep and featured face left of *Strawberry Jam*, staying left of *SJ*, until you intersect with the *SJ* crack as it turns hard left and is on easier ground. Finish by angling right toward the summit.

30. Armless Ambidextrian (5.10b)—33 ft.

Start at the thin left-facing flake/crack between *Creaking Eyelids* and *Rick's Way*. Climb up to the small roof, and pull past it onto a short, steep wall, and continue on to the top when the angle eases off dramatically.

Christian Kammer breaks into Breakaway Green Scar (5.10a)

31. Rick's Way (5.4 PG)—35 ft.

About the easiest, and really, shortest
climbing-wise, route to the top of THE PIN-
NACLE. Often used by those who want to set
up top-ropes here, and quite often soloed.
Start on the southwest corner of THE PIN-
NACLE, just right of the notch. Climb up the
gray painted face just left of a finger crack to
a horizontal, then work your way up left to
another vertical finger flake. Follow the small
flake up to the overhang, step left, and up
onto the ramp above. Climb 4th class to the
bolts.

The next few climbs work the north
face of THE PINNACLE, left around the corner from *Rick's Way*.

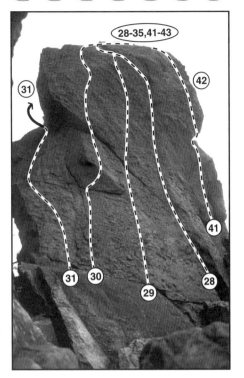

32. Scared Straight (5.9)—49 ft.

Begin at the very green rock between two
pairs of parallel thin vertical cracks. Climb up
and slightly right to the grey rock on the right
of another parallel pair of thin cracks 3 feet
left of the right edge. Following this set of
parallel cracks, work your way straight up to
the center of the small roof above. The obvious holds above the roof are not as nice as
they might seem from the ground. Once past
the roof, finish on the easy slab and scramble
to the chains at the top.

33. Better Balance (a.k.a. Peanut
Butter) (5.6 R)—49 ft. Beginning at the
first hand crack left of the right edge of the
wall, follow it up along right-facing corners
to a small roof. You can either traverse left
here onto *Chickenhead Crack* or step right
and continue up a few more feet to the next
roof, traversing left onto *Chickenhead Crack*
at this point.

34. Chickenhead Crack (a.k.a. First
Line and Cracker Jack Crack) (5.5
PG)—51 ft. Follow the obvious
crack/chimney system a few feet left of
Better Balance. Beware the loose block just
before the rock tapers off to 4th class terrain.
The nicer start begins with the small finger-

sized crack right of the wide, main crack. Scamper up to the small roof-capped right-facing corner, step left, then follow two parallel thin cracks through the chimney-like cut to the loose block. The PG rating is only for the loose block at the top of the wide crack. There is a small "chickenhead" hold halfway up the route. You can do a variation on this route by climbing the small right-facing corner left of *Better Balance* until you get to the roof, then traverse left back into the main crack/chimney system.

There are some easy cracks on the northeast side of THE PINNACLE, left of *Better Balance*, but almost no one climbs these anymore.

35. Wandering Wall (5.4 G)—58 ft.
This is a "lost" climb at Rocks State Park, as almost no one does it anymore. Starting 7 feet to the left of the Chickenhead Crack, work up fairly easy and blocky moves to a bulge (crux) below a parallel crack system high up. Crank past the parallel cracks (or step left and walk up on knobs) to the 4th class terrain above. Be careful of loose rock here.

The next three routes begin on the slab well below THE PINNACLE, facing the road.

36. Toast (5.8 PG)—115 ft.
Following the left-facing corner blocks, climb the slab to the right side of the headwall where a roof is split by a hand crack. Crank through the roof using the awkward hand/fist crack until it ends, then angle hard left to a ledge (optional belay point if you are leading). From there, follow easier ground up and left to the blocks right of the start of *Strawberry Jam*.

37. Stripes (5.10a/b* PG/R)—
approx. 115 ft. Starting anywhere on the slab, gain the headwall with a splitter crack rising up the center following a light

"stripe" (water streak). The crack has a couple of old (20-plus years) pins in it halfway up. Climb up and pull through the small roof to the blocks above. Finish by climbing up to the base of THE PINNACLE. You can top-rope this using gear, but be careful with your placements and take care you don't torque them out if you fall (at least one climber has cratered, ending up in the boulders below the slab, when he fell and pulled his top-rope pro out).

38. Pegasus (5.12d)—approx. 115 ft. This is **the** hardest (free) route in the Park, and sees very few ascents. Climb the seam a few feet left of the Stripes crack to a ledge. Mantle (not bad if you don't mind scraping your face against the rock above) through this ledge and pull the small roof above. Finish on *Shark's Tooth*.

The next route climbs the wall up and left of the slab, around the corner, below THE PINNACLE.

39. The Bouldering Wall (unrated)—approx. 30 ft. Start pretty much anywhere on the lower wall below *Shark's Tooth*, 15 to 20 feet to the left of *Stripes*. Work the face or arête as you see fit. Some folks have other names for this, but it was climbed back in the '60s and '70s before the '80s trend of naming things came into play, and was always referred to as "The Bouldering Wall."

40. Shark's Tooth (5.9)—29 ft. This route begins on the broad but fairly inclined ledge above the Bouldering Area, and 25 feet below and to the right of the base of *Strawberry Jam*. Climb the face, following a vertical, right-facing flake to the blocks above that mark the start of *Thumb Tack*. The upper rightmost block is the *Shark's Tooth* itself.

41. Thumbs (5.10c)—15 ft. This is really a portion of two routes. To the right of the

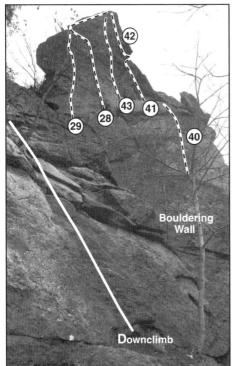

prominent *Strawberry Jam* crack is a system of smaller cracks, beginning on some large blocks. Climb these cracks and the right-facing corner that has a broken pin to an overhang. It is possible to set a nut or two in the crack here for an anchor.

42. Tack (5.11c/d)—15 ft. This route is "tacked" onto the top of *Thumbs* (and when combined called *Thumb Tack*). Climb *Thumbs* to the small overhang at the right edge of the wall, then step left and continue up the thin face to the top.

43. Hugh's Face (5.12c)—30 ft. Starting atop the block to the right of *Strawberry Jam*, climb the narrow over-hanging face between *SJ* and *Thumbs* using seriously small edges. When the size of the holds improve (not by a lot), slip a little right and finish on *Tack*.

BBB WALL

This is along the mostly rounded wall that most people either walk past without a second look or set up some very easy stuff for beginners to play on. There are some short but keep-your-attention routes here, also. The main access to the top of *Vertical* is the chimney behind this wall.

Routes are described from left to right, starting from the notch in the rock that separates THE PINNACLE from the main rock to the west.

44. In A Pinch (5.9)—16 ft. As you move up the hill from the notch, away from THE PINNACLE, there is a short but steep wall on your left. Climb the left-half part of this wall, several feet right of the left-most edge. Pinch your way through the crux using the very small right-facing "corner" to gain the low-angle ledge with a large tree above. Mostly a "high-ball" boulder problem.

45. Bob's Butt Buster (5.9)—16 ft. Some people are starting to call this "Bertha's Butt Buster," but a guy named Bob did it long before any mythical Berthas came along. A few feet right of *In A Pinch*, climb the center of the face, following a couple of short, shallow parallel cracks to a blocklike protrusion above. Mantle onto the low-angle ledge to finish.

46. 360 (5.10b)—14 ft.
A few feet right of *Bob's Butt Buster*, climb to the flake, then body hug it, using your left hand/foot on the left-facing flake, right hand/foot on the right-facing flake. It's a bit tricky.

BEGINNER AREA

This is approximately 70 feet uphill from THE PINNACLE, where the rock is a low-angled round wall cut by a right-arching crack. This is a popular spot for beginner classes to set up. There are four routes here, described from left to right. Each follows a crack.

47. Beginner Crack #1 (5.0)—34 ft. This is the most obvious and straightforward route here and probably the most fun of the four. Start at the base of a chimney/corner formed by a large boulder and the main wall. Climb up on big holds to the right-facing corner and crack system. Follow the crack and corner to the top.

48. Beginner Crack #2 (5.1)—35 ft. Start below the first small crack 5 feet right of *Beginner Crack #1*. Climb up the blocky wall to the small left-leaning crack. Step up and follow the crack until it ends. Merge with *Beginner Crack #1* and climb to the top.

49. Beginner Crack #3 (5.2)—28 ft.

Probably the most technically difficult of the
four routes here. Beginning 11 feet right of
Beginner Crack #2, friction up the face to a
thin crack system. Follow it until it ends and
continue to the top.

50. Beginner Crack #4 (5.1)—22 ft.

Start in the notch formed by the main wall
and a portion of buried rock strata, 5 feet
right of *Beginner Crack #3*. Climb the obvious crack to easier ground. End either at the
large ledge, or step up one move to the summit. A little tricky at the start (when all you
have for feet is frictioning). Follow the crescent shaped crack until it ends, then finish on
easier ground above.

NORTH WALL

Hidden from just about everybody, this
outcropping is directly across from BBB
WALL. The lone route here is on the other
side of the outcrop, and on crowded days, it can be worth a visit. When facing directly at
Better Balance on THE PINNACLE, turn around 180 degrees. On the other side of the
rock fin directly before you is this route (you'll have to go uphill a bit to get around to the
other side).

51. Unnamed (5.10c R)—22 ft. Yet another unnamed route in the Park. Follow the

seam (there is a pin bashed in deeply halfway up) to the sloping ledge above. You can lead
it, but it's tricky until after you pass the pin (which is 20-plus years old, by the way; use it at
your peril).

MOBY DICK

This is the short, long, and narrow boulder located to the north of the main rock outcropping, opposite the notch forming THE PINNACLE. You pass by it on the purple-blazed
trail coming up from the parking area on Route 24. It is an obvious standalone overhanging
boulder, and it sports an old one-inch eyebolt with a ring at the top that you can sling for
anchors. The whole thing roughly resembles the tail of a whale arced out of the water—
only without the tail fins.

52. Moby Dick (B2)—One of the two routes in this book still rated using John Gill's

"B" system (see "The Ratings Game" chapter). Climb directly under the overhanging face
(it'd almost be considered a roof), hugging the rock using both arêtes (similar technique that
you need to employ on *360*). Have a whale of a good time.

Pete Mosiuk works up the Vertical Extension *(5.4)*

BOULDER GARDEN

This is a bouldering area directly downhill from the MOBY DICK boulder. There are a number of large boulders here to play on, some of which you can circumnavigate as many times as you'd like— some without even touching the ground (look out for the exposed moves over the OLD QUARRY, though). The first block of the GARDEN is barely 20 feet east of the MOBY DICK boulder, and has some sweet steep face climbing problems.

OLD QUARRY

There is a small, old quarry immediately below the BOULDER GARDEN. It offers some interesting aid climbing practice (mind the restriction on pitons—no hammering!) and an overhang to play on. This area is often wet from the water draining down through the hill. When dry, it is a nice place to go to avoid the crowds on the main rock.

BAT SHIT CRACK

Well below THE PINNACLE's southeast corner, down in the boulder field where the rescue trail comes up from the road, is a small cave.

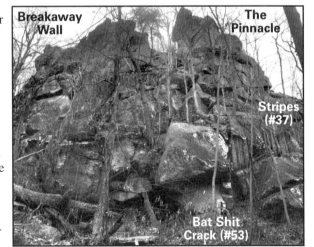

53. Bat Shit Crack (B2)—

Climb out the cave following the crack in the roof. Rarely done these days, partly because no one knows about it (lost because the "word of mouth" theory of passing on information didn't). You can guess where the name comes from—the other reason why it isn't climbed much.

SMOKE 'N' ASH

This outcropping is about 300 feet south of *Vertical*, buried in the woods. When the leaves are off the trees, you can catch a glimpse of rock out there. From the main rock, follow the trail to Rocks Chrome Road (left trail as you leave the King & Queen's Seat area). The trail will make a hard turn to the left, then approximately 100 feet later sharply turn right again. At this right turn, continue straight into the woods, angling left toward some boulders pushing up from the leaves and ground (if you continued on the trail and crossed a footbridge, you went too far—turn around and go back approximately 150 feet). Follow these increasingly numerous boulders until you come to the climbing area. This is the SMOKE 'n'ASH area.

If you are coming from Rocks Chrome Road, follow the White Trail, bearing right at each intersection. About 150 feet after you cross a footbridge, look for the trail to turn sharply left. From here, veer off hard to the right and follow the growing number of boulders to the climbing area. After 50 feet, you will cross the old original trail that used to run through here. About 50 feet after that, you'll start coming to some boulders. Follow these down and right, staying to the left of them. The routes are described from right to left as you would approach them from the White Trail.

As you bushwhack past the boulders, a short wall will appear on your right. This wall offers a number of short boulder problems, but they are mostly ignored. At the end of this wall is a wide crack forming a detached block in the rock. Immediately around the corner are the first two routes. These climbs are often passed by, as the bulk of the people who come here are "hardmen" and are generally interested in climbing *Smoke 'n' Ash*. But for someone wishing to learn jamming techniques, the aspiring lead climber wanting work on placing gear, or for the not-hardman climber, this rock offers a couple of easy routes.

54. Quisp (5.3 G)—25 ft. Named after a popular kids cereal from the '70s (which can still be found out there somewhere today). This route starts just left of the prominent

parallel cracks. Follow the horizontal crack around the corner to the right, then continue along the beautiful finger/hand crack vertically to the easy and featured slabby blocks above.

55. Quake (5.3)—23 ft. Another cereal from the '70s. Climb up the two parallel curved cracks up to the top. Short but fun.

As you continue east past *Quisp* and *Quake*, you will come to the SMOKE 'n'ASH buttress itself approximately 40 feet later. There are two bolts at the top of the rock for the first three routes. The bolts are better utilized to top-rope *Ash Arête* and *Ashes To Ashes*; they are not well suited to top-rope *Blowin' Smoke*. For *Smoke 'n'Ash*, you'll probably need to be creative with gear, lead it, or use anchors at least 40 feet long.

56. Ashes To Ashes (5.9)—24 ft. This route is often ignored, as is evidenced by the amount of lichen and dark green moss adorning the rock. Climb the face just right of *Ash Arête*, left of the left-facing corner to the top.

57. Ash Arête (5.8)—96 ft This route climbs the cleaner face to the left of *Ashes To Ashes*. Note the two old rusty pitons on this route from days long gone by. Trust/use them at your peril.

58. Blowin' Smoke (5.6)—(30 ft). Just around the corner to the left of *Ash Arête*, but right of the left-facing ramp (that leads to a foliage choked cavity), climb up the face following the slightly curved crack to the top.

59. Smoke 'n' Ash (5.11a* G)—27 ft. An excellent route, located 10 feet right of *Blowin' Smoke*. Jam your way up the curved hand crack through the overhanging wall to the top. This climb is the reason people come over to this area.

PARKING LOT BOULDER

This is a nice little 13 foot tall rock outcropping right near the upper parking area, and a good place to warm down after a hard day of climbing on the main rocks. From the far parking area (the one labeled "Rock Ridge Amphitheater Parking," by the bathroom building), locate the handicapped access parking area. From the right pair of picnic tables at the end of the parking area here, head south into the woods, passing a telephone pole about 60 feet away. As you pass the telephone pole, about 60 feet in front of you down the hill is this small outcropping of rock. The south face (far side of the rock from where you approach) offers some excellent friction/balance practice. The east face offers steep, harder than it looks flaring cracks and face climbing.

ROUTE ONE
ROCK

George Chapman battles his way through Bug Wars *(5.8)*

ROUTE ONE
ROCK

RATINGS BREAKDOWN:

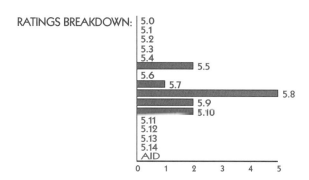

NUMBER OF CLIMBS: 11 plus a variation

SPECIAL NOTE:

"This shows you how desperate East Coast climbers are."—E. Hörst

There is a small set of rocks just northeast of Baltimore, off Route 1 in the Big Gunpowder Falls State Park, "discovered" in the mid '90s by Toby Marchand. The outcroppings are not very large, however, and are tucked in the woods less than a hundred feet off of the trail on the north side of the river. These southwest-facing rocks are heavily overgrown by late spring and summer, and host colonies of huge red and small black spiders (the rock doesn't see a lot of climber traffic).

The tallest rock here is barely 20 feet high; most of the rest are anywhere between 10 and 20 feet tall. For some people these would be considered boulder problems. Others less inclined to risk ankle breakage may want to drop ropes. The rest of the climbing public may not even bother coming here, as there are other areas to go climb within an hour's drive that offer more/better climbing potential. However, those who do visit, provided the thorns aren't covering the rock and spiders don't abound, will find some quality routes to play on. This will likely be a spot for those near or around northeast Baltimore to visit immediately after work for a quick bouldering session when the sun sets too early in the late fall or early spring to allow travel to areas further away.

LOCATION/DIRECTIONS

From Baltimore: Take the beltway (I–695) to Exit 32B north toward Bel Air (you can also take the White Marsh Blvd exit—Exit 31C—to get to Route 1). Once on Route 1, head north just under 5.7 miles (less if you took the White Marsh Blvd exit) to the Big Gunpowder Falls State Park. The parking area will be immediately on your right after you drop down a hill and go over the bridge that spans the Big Gunpowder Falls River. There are two adjacent sections of the parking lot; the one further from the road puts you closer to the rocks.

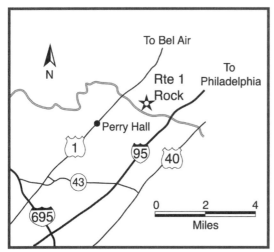

NOTE: While there are speed traps all over Maryland, there are a couple along Route 1 here that seem to be manned more often than not. One is in the residential section after the first three miles of shops, gas stations, restaurants, etc. The second is as you are going downhill toward the turnoff to the park—but they are usually facing the opposite direction, tagging southbound traffic as they speed into Perry Hall. Pay heed to the speed limits in any event and pay attention to what's around.

From the parking lot, take the blue-blazed trail (Lost Pond Trail) east out of the far end of the parking area (there is a map on the kiosk at the first parking area to give you an overview of the immediate vicinity of the Park). After 160 feet, the trail hits a junction; turn left and follow the main trail (still blue-blazed) that parallels the river downstream. Go down just under 0.7 mile (12 to 15 minutes at a brisk walk with a pack on; you will pass the yellow-blazed Sawmill Loop trail on the left after 0.4 miles) and there will be a trail off on the left that leads you to the rocks, barely 100 feet away uphill in the woods. If you come to the Broad Run (which is 0.7 miles away from the parking area), you missed the rocks by 100 feet; turn around and find the trail to the rocks (it will be on your right now). Most likely this side trail was formed and "maintained" by folks who like to sit up on top of the rocks and drink (evidenced by the glass and beer cans strewn about the base of the rocks here). The rocks should be obvious from the main trail at any rate.

GEOLOGY

The rock here is composed of Bradshaw Layered Amphibolite, an interlayered amphibolite and hornblende-quartz-plagioclase gneiss mix. This offers pretty good frictioning and large, pumpy holds. However, weathering of this rock causes many of these holds to eventually bust off. Take care when climbing here that a hold you once used might suddenly drop you on your butt.

EQUIPMENT

If you want to set up top-ropes, bring a few lengths of webbing, no more than 20 feet or so long. No need for any gear; the few cracks are either too short or are too shallow and flare too much to make for a good lead. And there are no provisions for gear placements up top for anchors. There are, however, plenty of trees (and thorn bushes).

Otherwise if you just want to boulder the routes, bring a crash pad. You won't need anything else.

CAMPING

There is no camping in the Park. This is a day trip destination. Besides, there isn't enough rock here to warrant an overnight adventure, anyway!

RESTRICTIONS AND ACCESS

The Park closes at sunset, as do so many others. Other than that, there are no access issues here. Only overgrown foliage and a metropolis of spiders. Just be safe, okay?

LOCAL EATS

From the parking lot, heading south (left, back toward the Beltway) on Route 1, you will come to the first eating establishments after about 1.7 miles. The choices here are few, so if you want other options, continue down the road another mile or so and you'll hit "the strip"—which consists of fast-food and sit-down restaurants, grocery stores, convenience stores, gas stations, car dealerships, furniture warehouses, etc., for the next 3 miles. Hopefully you can find something to your liking around there.

OTHER INFO

The best time to climb here is mid to late fall and early spring (and winter if it isn't too cold for you). The spiders will have all gone "to bed" and the foliage will have died off, opening up the rock for climbing opportunities. You'll likely want to bring a brush or something to clean off the holds from the accumulated grit and dirt.

The hiking trails extend for miles in either direction along the Big Gunpowder Falls river, with a few side trails that can take you to an interesting historical site or on loop trips. Mountain biking isn't overly popular (most of the trails are flat, flat, flat), but a number of people do ride the trails, and you may also spot the occasional horse and rider. Fishing is allowed in the river, but please observe posted dates/hours in which fishing is restricted. If you bring pets, they must be on a leash.

The Routes

There are several individual rock outcroppings here, noted as THE BOULDER, THE RIGHT BOULDER, TOBY ROCK, and STARSHIP TROOPER ROCK. The individual outcroppings are basically described from center to right then left.

THE BOULDER

This is the first boulder that you come to from the Lost Pond Trail. The access path splits left and right around this rock. There are no established problems on this rock, but the potential for a few exist—once the overgrowth has been cleared from the face of the rock, that is.

THE RIGHT BOULDER

This blocky clump of rock is located approximately 20 feet back and to the right of THE BOULDER. This, too, has a couple of very short boulder problems on the side facing the Lost Pond Trail, but nothing established.

TOBY ROCK

More than 20 feet tall and over 30 feet wide, this is one of the largest rocks here. Its main feature is the large and deep roof that starts most of the routes right off the ground. It is about 25 feet left of and uphill from THE BOULDER.

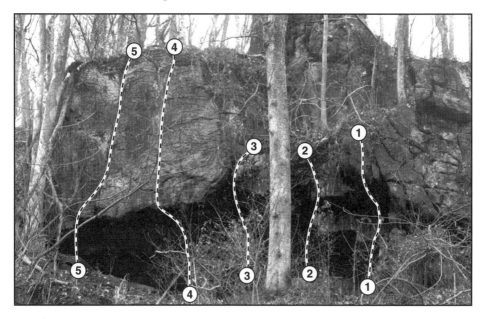

1. Spiderman (5.9)—10 ft. Funky moves on small holds. Start on the right side of the roof in the rock, 3 feet left of the left-facing corner that forms the rightmost end of this rock. Step up to the ledge and pull the roof at its most pointed part. A grunt-fest.

2. Shelob's Lair (5.10a)—16 ft. This route is 5 feet left of *Spiderman*. Start halfway back (sit down start) at the inside inner left-facing corner, layback out the roof and turn the edge on jugs. Continue up on big holds a few feet to the dirt and bush encroached top. A glorified boulder problem. The climbing is pretty much over once you reach the jugs.

3. Toby (5.9)—11 ft. Begin 6 feet left of *Shelob's Lair*, at the center of the wall. Reach up and climb through the roof at its highest point, following big holds to a stance. At this point the climb is over; scramble up and walk off to the right past the trees.

4. Trix Are For Kids (5.10b/c*)—22 ft. Located 5 feet left of *Toby*, near the graffiti "Trix," start using good, sharp holds on the face near the lip of the roof (or, alternatively, make life a lot harder for yourself and start somewhere underneath in the back of the roof). Pull up onto the rough face above. Finish by climbing sustained crimpers on the fossilized dinosaur skinlike face to the top (gotta love this rock!) An excellent boulder problem.

5. The Incredible Hulk (5.5*)—21 ft. Get burly! Haul yourself onto the ledge 4 or 5 feet off the ground, then follow the inviting but somewhat dirty (because no one climbs it) crack to the end. There are some very nice handjams in this short crack. If said crack were five times longer this route would be a classic.

STARSHIP TROOPER ROCK

Located 30 feet to the left of TOBY ROCK, this large outcropping rivals TOBY ROCK in size. It also starts as a low overhanging wall/roof, but overall the wall rises much higher up than TOBY ROCK does. Have fun, as the overhangs here are fairly continuous and more than one route overhangs 7 feet in 20. There is a small trail that heads downhill from the base of the rock to intersect with the Lost Pond Trail, but from late spring to mid autumn it is choked with foliage. If you do take it, be aware of the marsh moat at the base of the hill (might this be the "lost pond"?)

6. Klendathu (5.5)—12 ft. While the easiest route on this rock, it isn't necessarily the best to play on. Climb up the short offwidth chimney to the foliage choked notch above.

7. Johnny Rico (5.8*)—20 ft. Start at the left-leaning curving finger crack and climb up the thin face immediately left of *Klendathu* and pull through the large overhang above on good holds. The crux is getting off the ground.

8. Starship Troopers (5.8+*)—20 ft. Using the same start as *Johnny Rico*, immediately begin a left-rising traverse to the blocky corner. From the corner aim up and pull through the overhang above on jugs.

9. Bug Wars (5.8*)—20 ft. Go 8 feet left of *Starship Troopers*, and start where there are four somewhat vertical cracks low on the wall. Climb up to the overhang above, then

angle right (**V1**) to go through the higher section of the overhang (the finish is essentially the same as *Starship Troopers*).

V1 Bug Hunt (5.8–*) Instead of heading right, go straight out the lower overhang directly above the start. A shade easier than *Bug Wars*.

10. Milky Way (5.8*)—18 ft. Start just left of Bug Wars and climb the overhanging wall by following the flaring offwidth filled with a large vein of quartz to the top. Be aware of loose rocks near the top (belayers may want to stand off to the side).

11. The Wasp (5.7)—15 ft. This route is located at the far left end of the rock. At the corner, layback up the overhanging left-facing wall to the bushes at the top.

There are several additional rock outcroppings further left of STARSHIP TROOPER ROCK, but they are not explored at this time due to the incredible amount of foliage covering them. They may yield additional climbing opportunities. However, you'll need more than a mere weed-whacker to gain access.

LEAKIN PARK

Jody Powell spots Patrick Polvinale as he floats off Alice In Wonderland *(5.7)*

LEAKIN
PARK

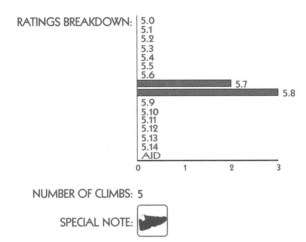

RATINGS BREAKDOWN:

NUMBER OF CLIMBS: 5

SPECIAL NOTE:

"The only time we see 'outsiders' around here is when we find 'em in the park and hafta put 'em in body bags."—**Anonymous Baltimore cop in 1994**

This is a very small crag, basically one rock sticking up 24 feet out of the ground, noteworthy because it is the only climbing area that exists within the boundaries of the Baltimore city limits. The neighborhoods are not always the nicest, though. The first **recorded** ascents in this area were done by John Kelbel and Mike Grims back in late 1988 and 1989. It is entirely likely this rock was scrambled up/over/on by others before them, but those early feats have been lost in unrecorded history.

Prior to 1999, the area was not the safest to visit. However since spring of 1999, with the opening of the new Gwynn Falls/Leakin Park trail system, the area has vastly improved.

The rock, however, is still off the beaten path and dirty from lack of climbing visitors.

LOCATION/DIRECTIONS

From Ilchester: Go east on Frederick Road toward the Beltway (I–695). Turn left onto Ingleside Avenue (before you actually reach the Beltway). After crossing Security Blvd, turn right on the first road you come to (this is North Forest Park Avenue). This will end at Franklintown Road in one block. Turn left onto Franklintown Road. After 0.2 miles you will enter Gynn Falls/Leakin Park itself (there is a stop sign).

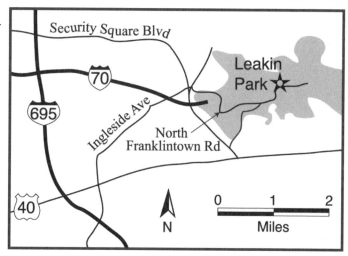

After 0.8 more miles of winding road in these woods, you will encounter a second stop sign (oncoming traffic does not have to stop!) Go straight for another 0.3 miles on the winding, twisting road in the woods, and suddenly you will come to a newly developed area: the Winan Meadows trailhead for the Gwynn Falls/Leakin Park Greenways trail system. This opened up in the spring of 1999. Pull into the parking lot (room for 35 cars, including two handicap spaces). There is a building right nearby—these are the new bathrooms.

An alternate way to come is from the west side of I–695, any direction, to I–70, but go **east** on I–70 toward the Park 'n' Ride. Take the final exit for Security Blvd and bear right onto Ingleside Avenue. Follow the rest of the directions above.

Follow the **paved** trail west past the kiosk and over the bridge spanning Dead Run. Bear right at the fork in the trail and aim for the building partially hidden by trees and overgrowth approximately 100 feet away. At the stone building the paved path turns right; you want to bear left off of the path and past the stone building, bushwhacking to the hill behind the building.

There is a faint trail system that rises along the left side of the hill. Take it if you can find it. Otherwise you're bushwhacking through thorn bushes and other unpleasantness. After you've gone approximately three quarters of the way up the hill, make a sharp right

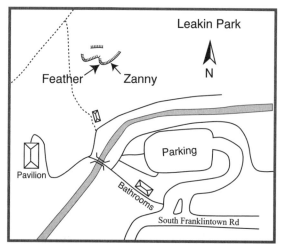

and bushwhack over to the rocks, approximately 100 feet away. Alternatively, if you can find the faint trail, it will continue up the hill and intersect with another trail system. Bear right and hit some stairs. Go up 8 steps shy of the first landing and cut hard right, following a faint trail down to the top of a rocky outcropping. The lowest and furthest point of rock sticking out is the top of the climbing area. There is a 3rd class scramble down the right side corner as you face out from the rock.

GEOLOGY

The rock here is a mix of Cold Spring Gneiss and Mount Washington Amphibolite. It has a sharp, rough texture that allows for decent frictioning. The gneiss in the area used to be quarried in the 1850s for building materials.

EQUIPMENT

Other than the standard rope, harness, and shoes, all you'll likely need are some moderately long lengths of webbing, maybe 10 to 30 foot long for rigging off of a couple of trees set back from the rock. You'll need to be creative with your rigging if you want to set a rope on *Flying Nut*.

CAMPING

There is none in the park—at least not for you. There is very primitive camping for youth groups, but that's it. For the nearest camping you'll want to go to Patapsco State Park (see the Ilchester section).

RESTRICTIONS AND ACCESS

No special issues to note.

LOCAL EATS

Your best bet for food would be to head west on Security Blvd a few miles until you reach the Security Square Mall area. There are a few fast-food places here. Alternatively take I–70 West (or Security Blvd) to the Beltway (I–695) and head south to Route 40. Getting off either exit, you will find food places (sit-down and fast-food) within a couple miles of the Beltway.

OTHER INFO

Originally part of the land of the Seneca Indians, the Gwynn Falls/Leakin Park system is bounded by a diverse array of neighborhoods—some good, some not so friendly. The park system is one of the largest urban parks east of the Mississippi, with a total acreage between 1,400 and 2,000 acres. Different sources quote different acreage, so it's not clear that anyone really knows. Either way, all sources agree that this is currently the largest urban park system east of the Mississippi. This area is unique in that there are wildlife communities within the park that are rarely found in an urban environment (much less one the size of Baltimore). These wildlife communities, however, tend to stay away from the more heavily used sections of the park as those areas see a variety of activities, from festivals to Live Steamer trains to general recreation. Other parts of the park are very isolated and rarely see human visitation. The climbing area is in one of the less visited sections of the park.

Historically, the park land was part of the "Crimea" Estate, owned by Thomas Winans, a very well-to-do individual who, with his brothers, had made his fortune by building a railroad system between St. Petersburg (Leningrad) and Moscow. Thomas's father, Ross, was a southern sympathizer during the Civil War, and built a rock wall with six fake cannons covering the southern end of the property in order to "protect" the estate from nearby Union troops (who pretty much left the property alone, anyway). It is interesting to note that part of what is now Leakin Park (the Jahi/DuBose Trail) was used as part of the Underground

Railroad in an effort to free the slaves from bondage in the South. It was very likely used as such before the Winans purchased their portion of the land.

In 1942, Baltimore City purchased the lower portion of the Crimea Estate, thanks to a significant donation by J. Wilson Leakin, and in 1948 the remaining portions of the property were purchased, buildings and all. The buildings were turned into offices for the Baltimore City Department of Parks and Recreation. The Crimea Mansion and other buildings are still in good repair, and you can visit these stone constructs off of the Windsor Mill Road, east of North Forest Park Avenue.

A few hundred feet further down Windsor Mill Road, just before the bridge that seems to be under perpetual construction (i.e., may never be completed), there is the Carrie Murray Nature Center, which operates a rehabilitation facility for disabled or injured birds and animals (in 2001 they had several hawks and an eagle in residence, in addition to other animals) that you may want to check out.

In the spring of 1994, some climbers who went to check out Leakin Park in search of a new place to climb were confronted and told by a substantially sized cop that the only time the police had ever seen outsiders in this section of the park was when they were dead and in need of an autopsy. This attitude and perception has long been the bane and reputation of the park.

However, since the upgrade of the trail system in the park complex, the area is far, far nicer. The revamping of the park came about in 1999. With the first step completed, linking Leakin Park and Gwynn Falls, the proposed 14-mile Greenway Trail will ultimately reach the Middle Patuxant River and the Inner Harbor without crossing a single street. You'll be able to walk, rollerblade, and/or bike from Leakin Park to the Inner Harbor. Neat, huh?

There are a ton of other activities that occur in the park throughout the year, far too numerous to list here. Check your local paper or online source for posted schedules of events.

Be aware that in the summer months ticks live all over in the woods. Be sure to check yourself thoroughly after your visit here for these little buggers.

The Routes

The routes are described from left to right.

1. Feather (5.7)—20 ft. Be as light as one. Begin on the left outside corner. Strenuously layback a few moves until it is possible to pull onto the left face. The climbing ends about 20 feet up.

2. Alice In Wonderland (5.7)—24 ft. Work the left side of the main face, just left of a small left-facing corner, like a Mad Hatter until you are about three quarters of the way up. Step left onto the left face and finish.

3. Rock Dance (5.8)—24 ft. Be sure to have your dancing shoes on. Begin in the center of the main face, 3 to 4 feet right of the left corner. Follow the outside edge of the small left-facing corner, aiming right to the larger left-facing corner above. Finish on buckets.

4. Zanny (5.8)—24 ft. Below the large left-facing corner, follow the right-leaning groove to a ledge. Finish on the face to the left.

5. Flying Nut (5.8)—15 ft. Begin on the right side of the rock above the second "R" in the word "WARLORDS." Using the first bucket, dyno for a second. Yard onto the ledge above. This is basically just a boulder problem. You can scramble easily to the top of the rock from here.

ILCHESTER

Long-time local Mike Carroll enjoying a little late-season afternoon climbing on Blue Rose (5.8+), Charles Danforth belaying

ILCHESTER

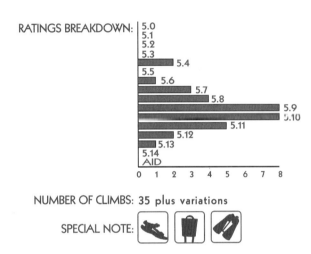

RATINGS BREAKDOWN:

5.0
5.1
5.2
5.3
5.4
5.5
5.6
5.7
5.8
5.9
5.10
5.11
5.12
5.13
5.14
AID

0 1 2 3 4 5 6 7 8

NUMBER OF CLIMBS: 35 plus variations

SPECIAL NOTE:

"It comes from the discolored bruise on the back of your right hand from the inverted hand jam on the third move."—Anonymous climber, describing how the climb "Blue Rose" got its name.

Ilchester is a west-facing 65 foot wide, 35 foot tall outcropping of rock up and left of the railroad tunnel east of Ellicott City in the Patapsco State Park. It can get extremely crowded during the weekday afternoons (most people take off on roadtrips during the weekends). It is not uncommon to find upwards of 20 people here on a late afternoon midweek. To complement the crowds, there are probably more routes squeezed into any given 5 square feet of rock here than there are at Carderock. Contrived variations rule! The occasional train emerging from the tunnel adds to the ambiance of the place.

The history of Ilchester climbing is rich and deep, and more of it has been preserved than most other places in Maryland (partly due to how tight the local climbing community is). *Beginners Corner*, *Blue Rose*, *Middle Climb*, and *Omega* were the first climbs put up here, all predating 1972. *Ninja* was also established pre-1972, and was a **major** accomplishment for its time. It still reigns as the local testpiece today. *Renaissance* appeared right about 1972. After this, though, very few new routes were established until around 1980 when Rob Savoye began infusing new energy into the crag.

Mike Carroll, Mike Endicott, Joe McManus, and the aforementioned Rob Savoye are some of the first who pioneered the major lines at Ilchester back in the '70s and early '80s (there was evidence that the area had seen climbers a few decades before them, but there was no recorded information anywhere attesting to the original ascents; just a lone, heavily rusted piton or two spoke of ascents dating back to the '40s). Joe McManus was one of the original "modern climbers" at Ilchester, and worked many of the routes before pursuing other activities. He's still out there, lurking online, but not climbing much. Mike Endicott did the first ascent of *Friction Slab* at Friction Wall, as well as a number of routes in the Rocks State Park area (e.g., *Mike's Finger Buckets*). Rob Savoye, who wrote the original guide for Maryland Heights climbing (found now only on the Web), hangs out in Colorado and can still be found plying the Internet. Mike Carroll, when not leading groups of Catonsville climbers out to Seneca, can still be found pulling down at Ilchester. Mike appeared on the scene in 1972 and was the third person to climb *Renaissance* after it was established.

Over the years the local climbers have done a lot of trail work here, and they would appreciate any extra help anyone decides to lend during future projects (be it trail work, area cleanup, etc). In the late '80s the trail was just a footpath, barely wide enough for a single person to pass. Now it is practically a highway, and used by not only climbers, but also by many hikers, horseback riders, and quite a few mountain bikers who access other trails deeper in the Park from this trailhead.

DIRECTIONS

Work your way to the Baltimore Beltway (I–695) as best as you can from wherever you are coming from.

From points north: Take I–695 around the west side of Baltimore to Exit 14 (Edmonson Avenue). This will be two exits south of I–70, less than a mile past the exit for Route 40. Turn right at the end of the off-ramp. At the third light (Rolling Road), turn left. At the next light (approximately 1/4 mile), Rolling Road pauses at a T-intersection. Turn right onto Frederick Road (144). In less than 0.1 mile, just after the small rise/hill there will be two parallel roads on the left. You want the second of this pair (Hilltop Road).

Wind your way through the residential neighborhood and into the woods (in the late '80s to early '90s these woods were littered with remnants of old refrigerators, stoves, car bodies, etc; by the mid 1990s it was cleaned up quite nicely). Continue through the woods on the twisting road until you come to a clearing with a parking area on the left (the road will turn sharply to the right and pass a house). Park here.

Follow the wide, yellow-blazed path into the woods, bearing right whenever presented with more than one option. Eventually there will be a path heading downhill to the right. There is a new sign that reads "Ilchester Rocks" that marks this turn. This dull green-blazed path will become steeper as you go downhill, and end at the top of the cliffs.

To get to the base of the rock, scrambling down around the right side is probably the easiest, though you can also scramble down and around on the left side, too.

From points west: Take I–70 towards Baltimore, but get off at Exit 87A for Route 29. Take Route 29 south for approximately 1 mile to Route 40. Take Exit 24A, which will put you on 40 East. Go 4.4 miles until you come to Rolling Road. Turn right onto Rolling Road

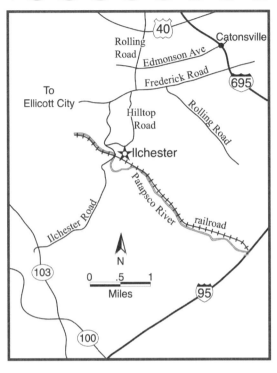

and follow that for 1 mile to Frederick Road (144). Turn right onto Frederick Road and follow the rest of the directions as if you were coming from the north.

From points south-southeast (D.C., Glen Burnie, Annapolis): Take I–95 to Exit 43B and head west on Route 100. After 1 mile head right onto Route 103 (west). Take 103 for 1.4 miles and turn right onto Ilchester Road. You will take Ilchester Road for 2.5 miles to Hilltop Road. First go 1.8 miles on Ilchester Road and come to the top of a long and **steep** (18 percent!) hill—take it easy. You'll reach the bottom after another 0.4 miles and pass under a railroad bridge. Just one quarter mile later Hilltop Road will be on your right. Take it and go 0.6 miles up the steep, narrow, and winding road (think as if you were in the mountains or something). The parking area will be on your right.

From points south (Columbia region): Take Route 29 north to Route 100. Take 100 for 2.1 miles to Exit 2 (Route 104/Route 108). Turn left and go .25 mile to a light. Turn left again and take 104 north 2.1 miles and bear right onto Route 103, go .75 mile, and turn left onto Ilchester Road. Follow the rest of the directions as if you were coming from D.C.

GEOLOGY

The rock at Ilchester is part of what is known as Mount Washington Amphibolite, which consists of plagioclase and amphibole. This rock has a crystalline texture due to metamorphic recrystallization. The skin-shredding, rough, sharp holds on the rock are due to the plagioclase mineral structure. Hope you enjoy it!

EQUIPMENT

You won't need too much in the way of equipment for most routes here (to set up top-ropes, that is). Moderately long anchors (30 to 40 foot) will suffice for most routes on the main face, left of *West Ilchester*. In the past, pre-2000, there was a circular concrete plug embedded in the rock with a couple of rusted steel rods poking up. This was the anchor point for climbs on the main part of the rock. But as erosion took its toll, this became an untenable anchor point and was ultimately removed by local climbers (when the Parks Department threatened to do it themselves). Over a year later, through the intervention of Yoda, the Dark Side was overcome and in the fall of 2001 a new beefy top system appeared at Ilchester.

To set up ropes for routes to the right of *West Ilchester* you may find it helpful to have some gear and/or longer anchors to wrap around the boulders or reach further away into the woods for the larger trees.

A few routes can be safely led here, but a number of locals who are intimately familiar with the rock and routes will solo climb here (also known as 'high ball bouldering') rather than deal with dragging a rack in from the car.

CAMPING

The nearest camping in Patapsco Valley State Park is at the Hollofield Campground on Route 40. The campground is open from the first Friday in April until the last weekend in October, and offers both electric hookup sites and tent sites. You may get more information from them by calling 410-461-5005 Monday through Friday, from 8:00 a.m. to 4:00 p.m. There is another campground closer to Ilchester in Catonsville at Hilton, but it has been closed for a couple years for refurbishing.

RESTRICTIONS AND ACCESS

There are no real restrictions or access problems. Just be out by dark, Patapsco State Park policy. Be aware, occasionally a ranger will check.

LOCAL EATS

The most variety of food will be found a few miles away on Route 40. Simply retrace your directions until you reach Rolling Road. When heading north on Rolling Road, do **not** turn right onto Edmondson Avenue. Instead, continue straight, and a couple of traffic lights later you will reach Route 40. There is a diner on the far left corner, some fast-food places in the immediate vicinity, and other restaurants up and down 40.

Barring that, instead of turning left onto Rolling Road, you can instead continue east on Route 144 into downtown Catonsville and find a small collection of restaurants.

OTHER INFO

Be warned that while I have not had this experience, there are stories of unfriendly anti-climber types who occasionally come in and sabotage the top-rope anchors (like putting a lit cup and candle under your webbing—or just dismantling the entire anchor array and throwing it down on you while you are climbing—yes, this has happened). Just keep an eye open for such antics. I won't say anything if you pitch them off the cliff. However, on the other hand, there are a lot of non-climbers who do visit these cliffs for the view. Be courteous; some of the hikers and visitors are friendly to climbers (and may offer you food, drink, or, umm, other stuff).

If you need a diversion from climbing, historical Ellicott City is just a few minutes down Frederick Road. It's a bit touristy, but quaint.

And if you've had your fill of Ilchester climbing, there are a number of other crags within a 15 minute drive. See also Friction Wall, Woodstock Rock, Alberton Rock, and Leakin Park. Not covered in this edition of the guide are other areas that are scattered about the park, such as Dam Rock (a.k.a., Blode Dam—has three routes ranging from 5.8 to 5.10: *Sansfoy*, *Sansjoy*, and *Sansloy*), and The Rock Above The Dam (sporting a pretty nasty fingertip eating overhang, plus some friction walls; this was also a popular area for some people to go, eat LSD, and melt into the rocks back in the '70s). A future edition will pull these other areas together.

The Ilchester Mountain Search And Rescue group (IMSAR) grew out of Mike Carroll's climbing classes at Catonsville. A small group of climbers (Rob, Mike, Joanna Macaluso, Ed Bollack, Rene, and Dru Marshall) got together quite regularly outside of Mike's classes, and around 1978 they began to call themselves IMSAR, a tongue in cheek joke (come on, Ilchester, a mountain?) As time went on, the IMSAR group grew to over 30 folks and became a rather large social climbing club. The IMSAR group started the Seneca Seafood Fest, as well as doing a lot of trail and erosion control work both at Seneca Rocks and in the Patapsco State Park. Their motto at the time: "somebody has to pick up all the trash." By the mid '80s many IMSAR members had moved out of state, but a number of them have kept in touch over the years. Even now, after nearly 30 years, some of the original members still get together and climb, somewhere in the world.

IMSAR was (and still is!) a great opportunity for new climbers to meet partners, and many folks later went on to become professional guides, and very competent climbers. Through the years IMSAR never lost their social focus and was responsible for some of the wildest and craziest parties seen out at Seneca (and other areas). IMSAR was also very much into exploring the surrounding region, and its members were responsible for putting up routes at such places like Woodstock, Friction Wall, Blode's Dam, and Maryland Heights, to name a few. The IMSAR group has a very rich history, and if you meet one of the older members, ask them to sit down and tell you a few tales. You'll not regret it.

The Routes

The routes are described from left to right as you face the rock. Due to the density of routes at this crag, not all of them are noted on the topo photo. Otherwise you'd be even more confused than before! Note that in 2001 a few local climbers began to try and camouflage the graffiti on the rock, so matching some of the route descriptions that used the graffiti as landmarks might be problematic. The topo photos should help, at least.

1. Renaissance (5.10a*)—16 ft. Really a "high-ball" boulder problem (i.e., normal climbers will drop a top-rope; boulderers might bring a crash pad). On the north-facing face of Ilchester outcropping, start off the ledge approximately 5 feet off ground on left. Angle up and right to the center of the face, then head more or less straight up. The left wall is off-route (i.e., stemming off of it is illegal).

2. Midnight Lightning (5.10c*)—20 ft. Almost a variant to *Renaissance* with its own variations, this route was put up by Mark Chapman and named after the famous boulder problem in Yosemite. The climb is basically a 5.10 route, but variations can go upwards of 5.12 in difficulty. Since the variations aren't always called variations, but rather referred to as **the** route, climbers have given this route a wide range of ratings over the years, ranging from 5.10a to 5.12a. Start a few feet right and a body length lower than *Renaissance*. Power through the first few moves to the overhanging wall above. Angle left then finish on *Renaissance*. If the four white graffiti diamonds are still evident, the route starts by climbing through the lower right one, and angles to the right of the upper right one before aiming left towards *Renaissance*.

3. Stone Free (V4*)—24 ft. Basically a three to four move boulder problem. Start a couple feet left of *Chicks Dig It*, move straight up to the arête in three to four moves (if the graffiti is still there, start in the "S" of "SKETCH"). Pull around the arête and "walk" off. Typically done as a boulder problem, and then rarely due to the less than ideal landing zone (e.g., the stairs). Bring a spotter. The original climbers needed to pile three stones up at the

base of the rock in order to get on the wall, but the idea was to do it **without** using the stones—hence *Stone Free*.

4. Chicks Dig It (5.12b/c*)—25 ft. Can you? Start directly below the right side of the overhanging wall split by a horizontal crack. Move up on thin holds to the right end of the horizontal crack. Once there, follow the arête to the top. This used to be approximately 5.8/5.9 until the flake halfway up sheared off.

5. Viper (5.12a)—37 ft. Don't let it bite you. A somewhat contrived route on the north wall. Start at the right edge of the north wall, immediately left around the corner from *Beginner's Corner*. Follow the arête up and left, but stay on the north face, not using holds to the right of the arête (hands on arête, feet on north wall). When you hit the horizontal crack in the overhanging headwall, traverse left approximately 5 feet or so through the conjunction of *Renaissance* and *Midnight Lightning*. When at the flake just left of the joining of these other two routes, move for a horn high and left. This route is sometimes confused as being *Midnight Lightning*. Not often climbed. Put up by local climber "Ancient Bob" in the '90s.

6. The Arête Climb (a.k.a. Alex's Arête) (5.10c)—32 ft. Climb the arête left of *Beginner's Corner* to the top. The crux is the start, but the final moves are no walk in the park, either.

7. Beginner's Corner (5.4)—33 ft. Also known as **Easy Climb**. A rather stiff start for a simple 5.4 route. It is easier to chimney off the *Mike's Move Boulder* next to the climb to get past the 5.6+ moves off the deck. Begin on the boulder at the extreme left end of the main wall, just right of *The Arête Climb*, and work up the face on good holds that are spaced rather far apart. Technique comes into play to make this an easier route. *Mike's Move Boulder* can be considered a "replacement" for the "cheater's tree" that used to grow next to the rock, immediately right of *Beginner's*. People would use the tree to "chimney" up the first few moves of this route. However, said tree is long gone.

8. Special Kay (5.11d)—44 ft. A rising traverse problem, named after a special girl. Start on *Beginner's Corner*, traverse past the crack of *Ninja*, past the low roof partway up *Blue Rose*, and onto the horizontal crack/ledge on the main face. Continue up and right, finishing at the top of *Double-O*. First climbed by "Ancient Bob." This hasn't seen a second ascent yet (as far as anyone knows).

9. Ninja (5.11d**)—35 ft. Area testpiece! Brutal; think "stiff 11d." Stealthily climb the thin face 5 feet right of the arête up to a shallow groove to a bulge above. Pull through the bulge onto easier ground. A classic line that does not see much traffic. Put up in the early '70s, this route was an incredible accomplishment for its time.

10. Captain Crunch (5.13a)—37 ft. Probably the hardest route at Ilchester. Climb the face immediately left of *Blue Rose* without using the *Blue Rose* crack (however, the lower left-facing corner at the start of *Blue Rose* is on). Follow the black streak up to the 'hang and pull. This route has maybe seen one or two repeats since Chris Schenking and Pat Eagen established it in the mid to late '90s.

11. Blue Rose (5.8+** G)—37 ft. Seriously, think 5.9 when you climb this stout route. Follow the most prominent vertical hand/finger crack at the left end of the

west-facing main wall of the Ilchester outcropping. It is a sandbag. The crux is in the first few moves, but it doesn't let up. Sink that third hand jam deep. Did I mention that at 5.8 it was a sandbag? Note that the ground at the base of the rock here was 2 feet higher about 15 years ago (making the start now that much harder). Why the name? See the quote at the beginning of the chapter. This is **the** area classic. And a testpiece. And a sandbag. Enjoy!

The next eight routes all climb the 17 foot wide stretch of rock between *Blue Rose* and the corner that forms *Middle Climb*. The two main traverses of Ilchester (see the end of this chapter) also start in this area.

12. Blue Balls (5.10b)—35 ft. Start on *Blue Rose*, but move left at the upper overhang. From there head on up to the top.

13. Cote Joe (5.9)—37 ft. Start on *Blue Rose*, but 12 feet up reach high to the right to a hold on the face. Climb the face for a ways until it gets significantly harder, then step back over onto *Blue Rose*. Yes, a contrived variant. Named after Joe Cote from New England.

14. Impossible Dream (5.11b/c)—35 ft. Not so impossible—if you're solid at 5.11! Start at the overhang 7 feet off the ground immediately (within 2 feet) right of *Blue Rose*. Climb straight up the rock, paralleling *Blue Rose* but never touching it or any of the vertical cracks to the right. Not impossible, but damned hard. People began working it in 1984, but no one succeeded until 1990.

15. 3 D Direct Variation (5.11a)—35 ft. A rather confusing name, for this "direct" route is not. Begin a few feet right of *Impossible Dream* at the base of a right-arching

corner. Work straight up through this corner/overhang to the face above. Step right and finish on *3 D*. Really a variant to *3 D*. To tone the beginning down a little, instead of pulling up through the arched overhang, follow the arch left until it meets *3 D*. Finish on *3 D*.

16. 3 D (5.10b)—35 ft. This route is sandwiched in between *3 D Direct Variation* and *High Anxiety/Middle Climb*. Starting 8 feet right of *Blue Rose*, a few feet right of *3 D Direct Variation*. Climb up to a small overhang 6 feet off the ground with undercling holds. Make a long reach to the next overhang (formed by the right-facing arch) to an undercling and step up again, avoiding the good blocks on the right. Pull through this overhang onto the face above, and continue on up, using small right-facing flakes in the upper section. So named for the faint reversed or upturned D-shaped features formed by cracks and flakes in the rock.

17. High Anxiety (5.9*)—35 ft. Start as for *3 D* (**V1**), and go straight up to the undercling/notch in the second overhang. Move 3 feet left and climb through a very small, short, shallow crack. Angle slightly right away from *Blue Rose* and climb to the top. This was originally rated 5.8, but is now more accepted as a 5.9. To keep the "spirit" of the climb, avoid using the ledge three-quarters of the way up (obviously the route is easier if you do use it). This route was first climbed in 1980 and is still fairly popular today.

V1 High Anxiety Direct (5.11a*) Use the same start as *3 D Variation*. Climb through the overhanging right-facing corner at its midpoint, angling left to join up with *High Anxiety*. Finish on *High Anxiety*.

18. West Ilchester (5.7)—37 ft. Work up the start of *Middle Climb* until about halfway through the right-facing overhang. Pull the small overhang and head straight up the face, staying between *Middle Climb* and *3 D*. Pull the final mini roof and top out. Do not use the corner or crack that forms *Middle Climb*.

19. Middle Climb (5.6* R/G)—37 ft. A very popular route. There are a number of optional starts to gain the slightly overhanging left-facing corner approximately 10 feet off the ground. One of the more popular starts (**V1**) uses the two underclings about 7 feet left of the large left-facing corner (most people have to start by stepping on the boulder there), immediately right of the overhanging right-facing corner that marks the start to *3 D*. Then work your way up along the right-rising overhangs until you reach the large left-facing corner. Follow that corner to the top. Caution is recommended as non-climbing locals have been known to pee down the top of this crack. This route is also known as *Beginner Crack*. If you lead this route, note the first third of it is pretty run-out until you gain the corner. Then you have pro everywhere.

V1: X-Start (5.8*) An alternate start to *Middle Climb*. Begin directly below the overhanging left-facing corner 10 feet above. Pull straight up and finish on *Middle Climb*. Note a couple of vague cracks 5 feet off the ground that form a loose "X," just right of the tree.

20. Central Pillar (5.8)—37 ft. Contrived, like so many routes here. Start on *Middle Climb*, but when you reach the corner, climb **only** the left-facing wall and arête that form the main corner of *Middle Climb*. Do not step left onto the main face. When the corner runs out, step right and pull through the small overhang and continue up to the top.

21. Double-O (5.7)—35 ft. This climb used to be the trademark route of the area. However, it is rarely climbed these days, mainly due to the change in erosion patterns pouring dirt down the rock at this spot over the years. Begin with a two-handed right-facing flake 7 feet off the ground, 5 feet right of the tree. Pull up and onto the face, then angle left through the dirty and sometimes wet double overhangs just right of *Central Pillar*. Note the pockets in the first overhang.

22. East Ilchester (5.10a)—35 ft. Start on *Double-O*, but instead of going up left, climb straight up through the overhang working past underclings to a desperate V-notch layback (crux). Finish by grabbing the bomber hold high up to the right.

23. Omega (5.9*)—30 ft. Begin 5 feet right of *Double-O*. Find a two-handed undergrip about 6 feet off the ground (it used to be a couple feet lower, but erosion of dirt at the base of the rock over the past 30 years has had the effect of raising it, and making the route harder—especially for shorter people). Said undergrip is part of the horizontal vein of rock that forms the footholds for *High Traverse*. Pull on this, then claw your way to the overhanging face above, traversing right to reach easier ground. Finish over the omega shaped arch to the right. One of **the** original routes here.

24. Weekday Workout (5.9)—29 ft. Start on *Omega*, and go up the shallow inside corner to easier ground above. Often overlooked in favor of other routes surrounding it.

25. Omega Direct (5.9*)—29 ft. A solid 5.9 route. Climb the right-facing corner of the omega-like arch/roof system near the right end of the main wall. Go straight up and finish on easier ground. The crux is pulling through the roof/arch.

26. U Slot (5.9)—29 ft. Begin on *Omega Direct*, but step right to climb through the highest part of the omega-like arched overhang just left of *Peace Sign Boulder*, laying back the widening notched section of the roof (starts out as a crack halfway up).

27. The B.O.B. Problem (V3/V4*)—30 ft. Stands for *Bob Ozgar's Boulder [Problem]* or *Baby, Oh Baby*. This route ascends up the overhanging left-facing corner "arête" that forms the left corner of *Peace Sign Boulder* and arcs up left to the top protruding blocks of the omega arch. Start with an awkward layback, facing downhill, on the corner arête (harder if the feet are also on the corner; easier if the feet are on the block to the left of the corner). After a few moves, reach out left to the small right-facing corner and regain a little of your balance. Begin stepping left ("legal" now to use feet on the block left of the corner) and work over to the protruding blocks at the top of the omega arch. Straddling the upper block, grip it with your thighs (baby, oh baby!) to make a quick "hands-free" move to some holds above.

28. Peace Sign Boulder (5.9)—23 ft. Climb the slab with thin holds at the left end of the rock. Named for the large, red peace sign that used to adorn the rock face (you may still be able to make out faint remnants of it even today).

29. Upper Boulder (5.9*) This boulder problem is located 10 feet above the top of the *Peace Sign Boulder* slab. Starting as far back as you can in the "cave," layback out the roof until you can pull around it to easier ground. Stout.

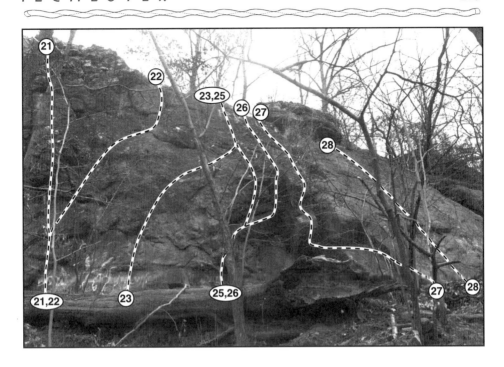

30. Beginner Slab (5.4)—22 ft. Another featured slab is 44 feet to the right of the top of the *Peace Sign Boulder* slab. Climb up this slab using numerous holds to the ledge. You could keep going up past the ledge for another 15 feet, but the climbing at that point is basically 3rd class. While it houses some fun moves, this area is rarely visited anymore.

The boulder next to *Beginner's Corner* is known as *Mike's Move Boulder*. There are a myriad of variant boulder problems that adorn this rock (including several "hands-free" problems—one of them backwards, a Bob Ozgar special). Only a few of the more obvious problems are noted here. They are noted from left to right when at the far side of the boulder from the main rock. For other problems, ask one of the regulars if they are around, or make something up. It may have already been done, but what the hey!

31. Mike's Move (5.8*) Climb up the center of the north face. Simple and straightforward, this is one of those height-dependent problems (i.e., harder for shorter people).

32. Mike's Move II (5.10*) Begin on the west side of the boulder, in the left-facing corner. Traverse left along the overhang using the horizontal ledge to the end, heel/toe-hooking as needed, until you reach the corner. Turn the corner **without** using the arête and get totally onto the *Mike's Move* face. Finish on *Mike's Move*.

33. Blood Finger (5.10*) Do the first half of *Mike's Move II*. When you hit the corner, though, begin working up the arête to the top, hands on the arête, feet on the face. Named for a crystal located partway up the arête that used to puncture a finger of the people who climbed it originally.

34. The Ilchester Boulder Problem (5.7*) Pull the overhang directly, popping onto the slab above using only three to four holds. This actually is harder for taller people. There are numerous variations to this.

35. Hands Free (unrated) Starting at the lowest point on the west end of the boulder,

step up the ramp—without using your hands! Walk up through the notch and traverse as you go. It has been done backwards and forward. A slightly scarier and more sequency variation is to step up to the notch, then work your way left over *Blood Finger*, turning and going up after a couple of moves.

There is a nice traverse, aptly named *High Traverse*, that spans the main face, beginning at the start of *Middle Climb* and ending at the far right end of *Peace Sign Boulder*. Pull up onto the face at or left of *Middle Climb*, then move right, using the horizontal "pipe" of rock for footholds, traversing through the start of *Omega Direct*, and then reversing the first half of *The B.O.B. Problem* (crux), finishing at the right end of *Peace Sign Boulder*. Be careful that a fall, especially early on, could result in a busted an ankle or two. An optional finish is to climb up the right edge of the rock on *Peace Sign Boulder*. There is also a harder, lower traverse known originally as *Finger Stinger*, now more often referred to as *Perverse Traverse*, which parallels *High Traverse* until they meet at the start of *Omega Direct*. *Perverse Traverse* originally started at *Double-O*, but the start has evolved over time further and further to the left. Some people now start at the tree, and others start at *Blue Rose*. Both *High Traverse* and *Perverse Traverse* are much harder going from right to left instead of left to right. If you're feeling hot, try doing laps of these two traverses. Paul Marshall, an old-timer, once did laps using both traverses connecting at X-Start—five times clockwise, no pauses. How many can **you** do?

FRICTION
WALL

Mike Carroll searches for the truth of 40 Weight (5.10b)

FRICTION WALL

RATINGS BREAKDOWN:

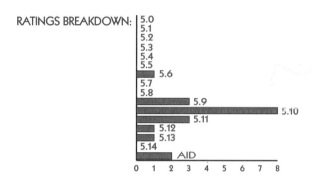

NUMBER OF CLIMBS: 18 plus a variation

SPECIAL NOTE:

"Heh! We did more by 6 a.m. than you guys did all day!"
—**National Guard dude**
"Yeah. But what we did was harder."—**No-Chalk Scott**

A couple of miles west of Ilchester, and a thousand feet east of Ellicott City, is an infrequently-visited ex-quarry that sports a dozen or so routes suited primarily for the hardman climber or the adventurous aider.

This crag does not see a lot of traffic, as in the humid days of summer, or after a good rain, the mainly north-facing rock stays damp and/or soaking wet. Combine this with how dirty one can potentially get while climbing here (it's not the cleanest rock around, and a lot of dirt comes down from the top!) plus the fact that the bulk of the routes here are 5.10 or harder, and you'll understand why you won't find many "weekend warriors" here climbing. However, despite the lack of traffic, there are still new routes going up here, as a small number of local climbers (such as John Kelbel) continue to pry out new lines from underneath the rubble and debris.

This area is also sometimes a favorite hangout/living area for local hobos. Most won't bother you, but there is the occasional one who will harass people, if only just because. Just be aware of your surroundings, and keep an eye on your gear.

LOCATION/DIRECTIONS

From Baltimore and points north: From the Baltimore Beltway (I–695), get off at Exit 13 (Md. 144/Frederick Road) and head west. After 2 miles, you will come to Hilltop Road, where you would turn if you were going to Ilchester. However, you're not. Continue west on Md. 144 for another 2.1 miles. After about 2.0 miles you will pass a Citgo station on the right; the rocks may or may not be visible (depending on the leaf coverage) across the river (and railroad tracks) on the left. Go 0.25 mile further, and just as Md. 144 turns sharply to the left to enter historic downtown Ellicott City, Oella Avenue will be on the right, just before a small bridge. Turn right onto Oella Avenue. On the right corner will also be The Trolley Stop, one of a number of local restaurants.

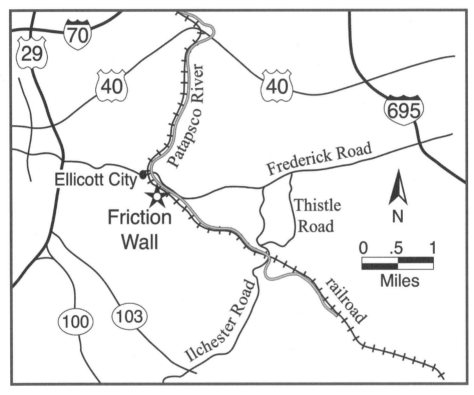

Go down Oella for all of maybe 0.1 mile, and there will be a parking area on your right. This is the **only** free parking in Ellicott City convenient for accessing FRICTION WALL. Because of this, it can be fairly crowded in the summer months and weekends. Pretty much everywhere else you have to pay (at least until 6:00 p.m., then some of it becomes free; there is another free parking area on the very far end of town, so if you're desperate....)

From points west of Baltimore: Follow I–70 east until you get to Exit 82 (Route 40). Drive east on Route 40 for 5.4 miles and turn right onto Saint John's Lane. Less than half a mile later is another light for Frederick Road. Turn left onto Frederick Road and follow it into Ellicott City; you'll reach the outskirts after 0.9 miles. Go through downtown Ellicott City, passing three lights. After the third light you will go under a railroad overpass, then over a bridge spanning the Patapsco River. Immediately after this is Oella Avenue. Turn left onto Oella Avenue, go 0.1 mile to a parking area on the right, and park.

From the Columbia region: Take Route 29 north to Route 100. Take 100 for 2.1 miles to Exit 2 (Route 104/Route 108). Turn left and go 0.25 mile to a light. Turn left again and take 104 north 2.1 miles. Bear right onto Route 103, go 0.75 mile, and turn left onto Ilchester Road. Follow this for 2.75 miles until the road splits at a Y-intersection (this is about a mile after you come down from a very steep hill). Follow the main road to the right (Thistle Road; there is no sign). Continue on this winding road for another mile until you come to 144/Frederick Road. Turn left and go 1.7 miles to Oella Avenue (there will have been an Oella Avenue earlier after about half a mile, but you don't want that!) Left onto Oella Avenue just before Ellicott City, then 0.1 miles to the parking area on the right.

From Washington, D.C. Take I–95 to Exit 43B and head west on Route 100. After 1 mile, head right onto Route 103 (west). Take 103 for 1.4 miles and turn right onto Ilchester Road. You will take Ilchester Road for 2.75 miles until it splits at a Y-intersection. Take the main, right branch (Thistle Road) and follow that winding road for another mile to 144/Frederick Road. Turn left and head toward Ellicott City. After 1.7 miles, turn right onto Oella Avenue, then after 0.1 miles turn right into the parking area.

After you've parked: Walk back down Oella to Md. 144 and head right toward downtown. Either cross the road and then cross the bridge, or cross the bridge and then cross the road. In any event you have to do both of these actions at some point. Once across the bridge you will immediately pass under the railroad tracks. Immediately after that, angle to your left and follow the brick sidewalk as it parallels Maryland Avenue (you will pass the B&O Railroad Museum—that would be the building on your left). A couple hundred feet further, when Saint Paul Street comes in from the right, Maryland Avenue will deposit you into a parking area (Lot C; metered parking until 6:00 p.m.). Continue on through the parking area, passing The Clay Station on your right (this used to be a small coffee shoppe, but now it's a "paint your own pottery" shop).

At the end of the parking area is Mulligans Hill Lane and a dirt/gravel access to the railroad tracks. You want to follow the CSX railroad tracks from this point on for about 900 feet. (Be alert for trains—these tracks are active! Don't be stupid and get hit, okay?) Just before the tracks bend to the right there will be a small, broken concrete post on your right. Enter the woods here; the rocks will be visible ahead of you and to the left. The Friction Slab itself will be very prominent toward the left as you enter the woods.

GEOLOGY

The rock of this ex-quarry was hewn from the ground for the quality Ellicott City Granite that exists here. Granite typically has great friction qualities to it. Some of the routes here have good friction (e.g., *Hidden Art*). On other routes, the friction qualities of the granite are not as evident. The "sand" and dirt you get to experience at the top of the cliffs (especially over *Hidden Art* and *Dirty Dog*) is merely granite broken down into a finer state. Still sucks to deal with, though. Take care at the top of the cliff (but enjoy the unbroken stuff in the middle).

EQUIPMENT

While all the routes in this area are top-ropeable, many of them are bolted. For most of the bolted routes, a half dozen or so quickdraws should suffice. For the top-rope routes, you'll want moderate length anchor systems. When top-roping routes on the Slab, in order to keep dirt from falling down the Slab onto you, rig your anchors from the large tree set back from the rock, but rig a directional about 4 or so feet off the ground from the smaller tree at the top edge of the Slab. That will keep your rope and anchor system from getting totally dirt encrusted, and keep the dirt from being coaxed off the top and down the face—onto where you are climbing (and in your eyes, hair, teeth, etc.).

CAMPING

While there is evidence that some of the more ragged climbers or local homeless may have once camped here in the quarry, officially there is no camping in this section of the park. See the Ilchester section for more detailed information on nearby camping.

RESTRICTIONS AND ACCESS

There are no restrictions with the climbing here. Just be aware of the CSX trains that periodically scream by (if possible try **not** to be walking on or along the tracks when this happens!)

LOCAL EATS

Food can be gotten at The Trolley Stop over near where you likely parked (moderately priced, dress appropriately; there is a bar within, also, where you can deal with your dry throat after a hard afternoon of climbing if that is your thing; they serve breakfast, lunch, and dinner—and you **can** get a beer with breakfast if you want!), plus a bar & grille place about a mile or so east on Md. 144. There are no fast-food joints in the immediate area. For that, you'll want to head over to Route 40 (see the Ilchester chapter for this information).

OTHER INFO

In the distant past, back in the early to mid '80s, the Bolt Wars were present in this quarry. One camp of climbers wanted to bolt things and did ("It's an old **quarry**, fer god-sakes!"), while the other camp came and chopped them out ("You can top-rope these routes; no reason for having freaking bolts!") By the early to mid '90s the anti-bolting sentiment relaxed somewhat, and a few high-end bolted lines were put up (the *Unknown-FW-#* climbs), as well as a line of bolts established on *40 Weight*. One of the routes even had a number of finger pockets drilled because no one could make the moves without them. Rumor has it that the pocket driller was ostracized from the local climbing community for that act and no longer climbs in Maryland—quarry or not, that was an unacceptable practice! While no new bolts have gone in since the mid '90s, someone has recently (late in 2001) chipped a couple of holds about 15 feet or so up on *40 Weight*. More than a few members of the local climbing community would like to thank you, personally, for this unwarranted and unjustified action (are you really that weak you couldn't make it up a simple 5.10 without altering the rock?)

There are a number of unclimbed lines yet to be done. All of these can be done on top-rope. No need for bolts, or chipping.

Since this **is** an old quarry, there is an abundance of loose rock around, even to this day—take care! Wearing a helmet in some areas here (or in general) might be prudent (although some of the blocks are large enough that not even a helmet would matter if the block pulled free and found your head on the way down). Erosion, especially around the top and sides of the wall, is severe. This accounts for the extremely dirty conditions on many of the routes. Take extreme care when up top setting anchors for top-roping. A lot of the ground at the top edge of the cliff is just sand, and could give way without warning (i.e., it may be prudent to anchor in while setting anchors).

Oh, and the light blue remains of the Kawasaki motorcycle? That has been sitting there forever and a day. It's a fixture; leave it be.

The Routes

Routes are described from left to right (you'd naturally be drawn to the Slab first, anyway). Access to the top used to be scrambling up and over the broken blocks beneath the large protrusion of rock to the left of the upper Slab. However, the dirt at the left end of these blocks is heavily eroded, so you may have or want to walk the long way around, on either side of the quarry. That or start leading!

All the routes on the Slab start at the lowest ramp of the Slab, slightly left on the first horizontal crack 10 feet up. *Surrealistic Pillow* moves to the left of this horizontal; *40 Weight* will move to the right up the line of bolts.

Note: from the very beginning days of climbing here, the small overlap halfway up the Slab has always been referred to as "the soffit" (referring to where the roof "overhangs" around a house). The soffit pretty much runs the width of the Slab.

1. Unnamed (5.10)—45–55 ft (depending on where you call the start). This route is rarely climbed. Scramble up the very left end of the Slab to a sizeable roof. Climb up left into the open book and take that to the top. The grade for this route was set in the early days, and has not been reconfirmed in recent years.

The next seven routes climb various lines up the Slab. There is a two-bolt anchor system at the very top of the Slab. It is a little sketchy to access from the top, so take great care setting up top-ropes from them.

2. Surrealistic Pillow (5.10b*)—68 ft. Named after a Jefferson Starship song that was running through Rob Savoye's head when he climbed this route. Start on the far left end of the horizontal crack 10 feet up, left of the bolt (**V1**). Angle up and slightly right toward the overlap to a very shallow corner ("staircase") directly below an old bolt. Step up the "staircase," passing the large roof, and gain the corner before the next roof. Follow the corner (feet on the Slab, hands on the wall) to the top, passing a second old bolt.

V1: Surrealistic Pillow Direct Start (5.10c) Start to the right of the first bolt and head straight up the face to a horizontal, intersecting with *Surrealistic Pillow* here.

3. Make Believe (5.10c)—59 ft. Climb *Surrealistic Pillow* to the first old bolt, just past the first big, flat roof. From here, transfer yourself onto the left-facing wall and climb up through the second roof, to the top. Make believe you have footholds when you need them, because they won't be there otherwise.

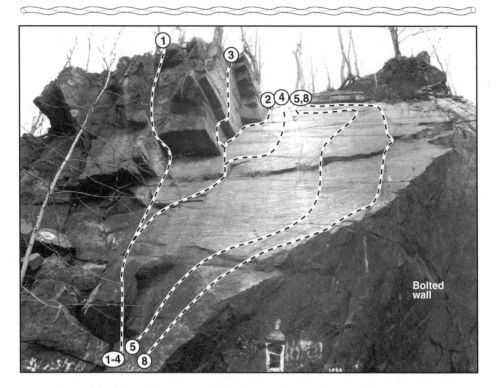

4. Friction Slab (a.k.a. **Patapsco Slab**) **(5.10d/5.11a*)**—68 ft. Climb *Surrealistic Pillow*, but at the top of the "staircase," do a slightly angled traverse until you are climbing up the face between *Surrealistic Pillow* and *40 Weight*. Aim directly for the opening above.

5. 40 Weight (a.k.a. **The Truth**) **(5.10b** PG)**—68 ft. Climb up to the horizontal and follow the bolt line up and right, staying to the right of the bolt line (you'll find the holds over there). After the fourth bolt, follow the right-rising crack up to a good horizontal seam/wannabe ledge, then traverse left to the sixth bolt (making the clip of the fifth bolt might be a bit of a reach). Go straight up from there to the two-bolt anchors. There is a nice pocket near bolt #4 for you to rest on. This line was led free with traditional gear (bashies, pitons, angles, and a single nut) in 1984 and rechristened *The Truth*. But the original name seemed to stick like glue, and remains so to this day.

6. Far From The Truth (5.10b)—68 ft. Don't go astray. Follow *40 Weight* until you reach the soffit (shallow overlap). Follow the soffit directly left to the corner, then up to the top, finishing on *Surrealistic Pillow*.

7. Above The Truth (5.10b/c)—75 ft. Climb *40 Weight* to the soffit (shallow overlap), then break right, following the soffit to a vertical crack and small right-facing corner. Continue up the crack to a number of exit options. Just a nudge harder than *40 Weight*.

8. Go West, Young Man, Go West (a.k.a. **The Arête**) **(5.9*)**—80 ft. As the name says. From the right end of the horizontal, traverse right (west) and up, following the edge of the arête with your feet (your only footholds; kinda airy) until you get to the obvious vertical crack. Climb the crack up and past the shallow overlap (the soffit) with a small right-facing corner. Continue up, but as you reach the munge, traverse left to the anchors.

Below and to the right of the main Friction Slab are four bolted routes and an aid climb.

9. Unnamed (A2)—20 ft. Starting at a thin 8 feet tall crack/detached flake system (it flexes), climb up to the point, then follow the incipient crack up to a horizontal. Traverse right to the two-bolt rap anchors.

The next four lines are sometimes referred to as the Eagan-Schenking Bolt Routes, but this is an unofficial title at best. The grades of the routes are also unconfirmed.

10. Unknown-FW-1 (5.11-ish)—25 ft. Climb up the shallowly carved face past three bolts to a two-bolt rappel anchor.

11. Unknown-FW-2 (5.13-ish)—44 ft. Climb the face with six bolts to two beefy shuts. Rap off (or step up onto a ledge and then continue up the Slab to the top, adding another 40 feet of climbing to your run).

12. Unknown-FW-3 (5.12-ish)—33 to 44 ft. (depending where you end it). Following a series of drilled three-finger pockets, climb the face past five bolts, then either step right to a two-bolt rap anchor, or stretch left and finish on the previous route.

13. Unknown-FW-4 (5.11-ish)—33 ft. Climb four bolts to a two-bolt rap anchor.

The next two routes start on the small ledge 20 feet above the ground, to the right of the previous four bolted routes. Take care at the top here as the ground is deteriorating quickly, and the granite "sand" could cause you to slip, allowing you to test gravity out the hard way.

14. Yoda's Vision (5.10b*)—56

ft. Do...or do not. There is no try. Start on the left end of the same ledge as *Hidden Art*. Climb up and slightly left to a shelf that is level with the rap bolts for *Unknown-FW-4*. May the Force be with you as you move up on mantle ledges to the face just left of *Hidden Art* and pull over onto the Friction Slab at a small notch. Climb up to the top of the Slab to finish.

15. Hidden Art (5.9*)—56 ft.

This little gem of a route was unearthed by John Kelbel early in 2001. Rappel down to a stance on the left end of the long but narrow (and in most sections, sloping) ledge 20 feet off the ground, to the right of the last bolted route below the Friction Wall itself. Following a thin finger crack, climb fun moves up the shallow, left-facing corner, passing a couple of ledges, until it ends on a ledge. Continue up and pull onto the right edge of the Friction Slab. Finish by continuing up the slab to the top. Take care that the rope should drop down a notch at the edge of the Friction Slab. The edge is sharp to the right. The first crux has a trick move on the right. The second crux is height dependent. In order to access this route, either rappel, or climb the rightmost of the 4 bolted lines and traverse over. Unfortunately right now this route is dirty. However, if it can be maintained clean, it's destined to be an area classic.

There are a handful of routes between *Hidden Art* and *Dirty Dog* that were climbed in the late '70s to early '80s, but fell into neglect and disuse, and have subsequently been forgotten. There are more potential lines between *Dirty Dog* and *What We Did Was Harder*, as well as more unclimbed rock to the right of *What We Did*, although the further right you go in the quarry, the worse the quality of the rock.

The next two routes begin at or near a northwest-facing slab halfway between the Slab and *What We Did Was Harder*. To set these up as top-ropes, anchor off of the **huge** tree at the top, and run the slings down the steep upper section, using the moderate sized trees as directionals. Allow your anchors to drape over the carpeting at the edge of the cliff (beware that the ground between the last, curved tree and the carpeting is made up of the same geologically "decomposed" granite "sand" and is eroding away; a slip here if you are not anchored in could result in your having a Real Bad Day).

16. Four Bolts (5.9)—37 ft. Halfway right down the north-facing wall is a steep northwest-facing slab with four bolts. Climb the face past the four bolts to a ledge. Most people stop at the fourth bolt and rap off, but you could turn right and continue up the upper wall if you want. These bolts were not here when Rob Savoye and others first climbed *Dirty Dog*; they are a relatively recent addition in the last 10 to 15 years or so.

17. Dirty Dog (5.6)—65 ft. The route begins in the right corner of the slabby face. Scramble up mangy ledges to reach and climb the extremely dirty corner to the right of *For Bolts*. Just before or as you get to the block roof, come left around the right-facing corner onto a ledge system. Walk left until you are directly over *For Bolts*. Then follow the left-leaning crack up to the overhangs, pulling the small roof at the chockstone block near the left end. The name comes from how dirty one tends to get when climbing here (both on this route and in general), which is why not many people climb it. This is Rob Savoye's favorite 5.6 in Maryland. Instead of stepping left at the block roof halfway up, pull it directly for a variation about 5.8 in difficulty.

The swampy area on the right end of the quarry should be avoided during the summer months, as the fetid water supports lifeforms that you would rather avoid (chiggers, anyone?)

18. What We Did Was Harder (A2+)—48 ft. On the east-facing wall on the right end of the quarry, approximately 20 feet right from the large ledgy corner, is a thin, thin crack that you can nail your way up (think RURPs and knifeblades). Start on the right-facing blocks 5 feet left of the most prominent tree next to the wall. The first ascent party had come here one day in '93 to work on this route and found a platoon of National Guard types doing rappelling practice all over the walls here (and knocking things down, sometimes even on the climbers). After the climbers finished the route and hiked out, they found the Guardsmen waiting for chow at the edge of town. The Guardsmen asked if the climbers were done already, to which the climbers said yes. One Guardsman boasted that he and his buddies had done more by 6 a.m. than the climbers had done all day. The response became the name of the route.

ALBERTON
ROCK

Anna Custo gets trim on Celluloid Heroes *(5.4)*

ALBERTON
ROCK

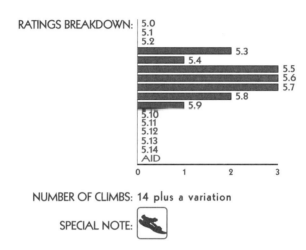

RATINGS BREAKDOWN:

NUMBER OF CLIMBS: 14 plus a variation

SPECIAL NOTE:

"Pretty easy for an overhang."—**Charles Danforth**

If your soul is up for a little adventure but time is pressing, or you cannot get very far away from Baltimore, and either you've climbed out the Ilchester/Friction Wall and/or the Woodstock Rock areas or they are too crowded for you, there is still hope: Alberton Rock! Located along the Patapsco River in Patapsco State Park on the border of Howard and Baltimore Counties, this little outcropping of rock has some infrequently traveled routes (as is evidenced by the amount of green lichen, spiderwebs, and foliage covering the rock). A leisurely 10-minute walk down the old Alberton Road (which is now the main path for hikers and bikers along this stretch of the Patapsco State Park) from your car puts you at the base of the southwest-facing rocks.

The area does not see a lot of climbing traffic, probably due to the fact that most of the routes here are only moderately difficult, and do not offer much of a challenge to the high level climber. But it is still fun climbing, and offers a different set of problems than most other areas around.

Also, being 50 feet high, these are the tallest rocks within a half hour drive of downtown Baltimore.

LOCATION/DIRECTIONS

There are a number of ways to get here. If you are coming from the Security Square Mall area (essentially from the west end of I–695, the Baltimore Beltway), head west on Security Blvd. until you come to Rolling Road (3rd light west of I–695). Turn right, heading north on Rolling Road, until you come to Dogwood Road (the next light, less than a mile up). Turn left and go 2.1 miles, reaching a parking area on the left a couple hundred feet after passing Hollofield

Road. Park here (do **not** block the gate!) Be warned that sadly, yes, thefts sometimes do occur here, so keep valuables out of sight (or better yet, take them with you!)

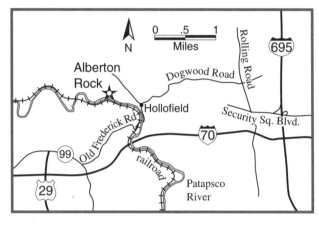

Alternatively, go south from Liberty Road on Old Court Road for 3 miles to Dogwood Road. Turn left onto Dogwood Road (turning right would put you into someone's yard) and proceed for another 3 miles. At the bottom of a severely twisting hill, park immediately on the right. If you pass Hollofield Road, you just missed it; find a way to turn around and go back.

Thirdly, from I–70, get off at the exit for Route 29 and head north to the T-intersection and stop light. Turn right onto Md. 99 and proceed down about 1 mile to a left turn onto Old Frederick Road. Follow this down into the Patapsco Valley, cross a bridge, and continue on less than half a mile to a T-intersection with Dogwood Road. Turn left onto Dogwood Road, and in less than 0.1 mile (immediately before Dogwood Road curves hard to the right as it goes up a hill) you reach the small parking area on the left.

Finally, from Woodstock, head north on Old Court Road for 3 miles and turn right onto Dogwood Road. After 3 miles, at the bottom of the twisting hill, park on the right.

If the gate is open, do **not** continue past it with your car. The local residents will very likely lock it up later, trapping you within. This is not a large parking area, so if you're coming with a group, strongly consider carpooling.

Start walking down the old roadbed (stay to the left when going through the residential area!) and enter Patapsco State Park itself. Keep going down the old roadbed until the pavement ends (at a leisurely pace this will happen about 10 to 11 minutes after you leave the parking area). The rocks will show up 30 feet later on your right. If you miss them, you were probably looking the wrong way!

GEOLOGY

Alberton Rock is an outcropping of quartz and schist known as Setters Formation, composed primarily of feldspathic mica schist and mica gneiss, with some quartzite. The starts of many routes along the RIVER WALL have sharp holds that are due to the feldspar crystals (some fairly large) imbedded in the rock. You can find evidence of mica gneiss along the base of the RIVER WALL near the center and left end. The upper portion of the rock is primarily a schist, and the layering that you see is due to weathering of the exposed schist.

EQUIPMENT

There are trees scattered atop the cliff, but some of them are a bit questionable (okay, one or two are definitely dead, so they don't count!) You can use live trees to rig your top-rope anchors for all the routes, but you'll need slings that reach upwards of 60 feet.

CAMPING

See the Ilchester section for camping information.

RESTRICTIONS AND ACCESS

No known access issues exist here.

LOCAL EATS

There is a Pizza Hut in the shopping complex at the corner of Rolling Road and Dogwood Road (head east on Dogwood Road for 2 miles to the first light). If that's not the way you want your food sliced, turning right onto Rolling, and going down approximately 1 mile to the Security Square Mall area, will yield a small assortment of fast-food and sit down restaurants. If this is not enough either, continue down Rolling Road for 1.1 miles to Route 40, where you will find an assortment of food options (particularly to the west on 40), or go north on Rolling Road for a few miles to Liberty Road, where again you will find additional restaurants to choose from. And if this isn't enough…I can't help you!

OTHER INFO

The buildings right around where you parked are part of the old town of Alberton, an old Quaker village from the 1700s. The Quakers who lived here were the first European settlers to inhabit this area. The old roadbed that you take to get to the rocks is known as Alberton Road (there is a blue street sign indicating this at the entrance to the parking area) and runs along the Patapsco River here.

WARNING: Beware of deer ticks that lurk in the area! There have been some local residents who recently picked up Lyme disease from deer ticks in these woods, **so be careful!** Wear bug repellent and check for ticks after you get home. Lyme disease… it's not a pretty thing.

The access path and the top of the rocks are choked with nettle-like vines and green-brier bushes of various types. Until these are cleared a little, they will make setting up anchors a little tricky. Some thorny bushes also exist at the base of a few routes (notably by THE GREEN WALL).

The old roadbed is the **main** hike/bike path for other users in the park, so don't spread your ropes and gear all over the path, blocking the hikers and bikers from being able to travel unimpeded. Exhibit coolness; don't be clueless! There are already enough people out there who do not particularly like climbers; there's no need to give them any real reasons to back their stance. Right?

The Routes

For ease of descriptions, the crag can be divided into 3 sections (from right to left as you face the rock): The GREEN WALL, RIVER WALL, and LEFT WALL. The tallest section of rock is the RIVER WALL, and boasts the most number of lines. There are a few routes on the LEFT WALL, but it usually is so overgrown that it is rarely climbed. The GREEN WALL has the shortest routes, practically boulder problems that go up through the light green dust-like lichen. There is a small path 30 feet right of GREEN WALL that will take you to the top of the rocks to set up anchors (some routes are easier to set than others; bring extra long runners for the harder-to-set routes). Alternatively, lead climb up one of the cleaner (heh!) routes on the RIVER WALL (beware that many of the incuts and grooves are quite shallow, though there are some great places for pro scattered around). Most of the routes on RIVER WALL are probably the best ones here. The routes are described from right to left.

THE GREEN WALL

So called because of the dusty light green lichen that covers the lower half of the rock, the GREEN WALL offers the shortest routes to climb.

The blank section of wall on the right end of this crag sports a few short boulder problems. Be sure your landing doesn't take you into the thorny bushes of wild roses!

1. Aaron's Problem (5.5)—33 ft. Starting at the base of the short, right-facing corner in the rust colored rock, approximately 5 feet left of the small trees, climb up past a quartz bulge to the thin face above. Finish on the slanted ledges and holds to the top.

2. Zeta (5.4—5.6*)—33 ft. A number of variations exist on this section of rock. Start anywhere within 3 feet of the shallow Z-crack in the center of the face 7 feet off the ground. Climb the lichen dusted light green face to a large horizontal crack, then upwards onto the slanted washboard walls above. The easiest way is not necessarily always the most obvious.

Enjoy the right-slanting holds that make the climb feel slightly more difficult than it really is. The hardest variation starts through the bulges just right of the Z-crack and ascends the thin face immediately above.

3. Fate Amenable To Change (5.6)—35 ft. Start to the right of the double-trunked tree. Climb up to and hook through the short roof 8 feet off the ground. Follow the face along the arête up and right to the top.

THE RIVER WALL

The tallest routes are here. Most routes are fairly easy to set up using the trees above (**Caution:** Note the dead trees! I shouldn't have to tell you not to use them, but I have **seen** people tie off to far shakier and looser things…).This wall is characterized by a series of large and small roofs, plus a couple of oblong "cavities" partway up at the tallest section. The lower "cavity" has a pointy rock projecting out of it; the upper "cavity" has not. Over the whole wall, watch for spiders.

4. Animal Farm (5.5)—25 ft. As per George Orwell, different levels of climbers will view this in a different light. Begin beneath the 8-inch wide crack that splits the rock on the left-facing corner of GREEN WALL, a few feet left of *Fate Amenable To Change*. Climb the pointed overhang on jugs to the jungle above.

5. Celluloid Heroes (5.4*)—25 ft. Start below the large roof system approximately 15 feet off the ground, a few feet left of *Animal Farm*, in the middle of the somewhat left-facing wall between GREEN WALL and RIVER WALL. Climb up to the roof above, and heroically haul over it on large holds. The route ends once past the main roof, with a jungle in your face. A machete is recommended for continuing up past this point. A good optional finish, on the other hand, is to traverse left onto *Limelight* and climb to the top from there.

6. Limelight (5.3*)—46 ft. Start in the shallow, broad groove just right of the blocky overhang 4 feet off the ground. Stem up the corner above to the top. This corner and the face several feet to the left (Quaker Oats) tend to stay wet longer than the rest of the rock after it has rained.

7. Quaker Oats (5.5–)—46 ft. A slightly contrived variation to *Limelight*. Climb the blocky overhang 4 feet off the ground, then follow delicately up the face just left of *Limelight*, without using holds on *Limelight*. Merge with *Dragonfly* at the second cavity in the wall.

8. Dragonfly (5.6)—46 ft. Start on the ramp left of the blocky overhang 4 feet off the ground that marks the start of *Quaker Oats*. Go up to the right end of the right downward-trending main roof. Go directly up to the first cavity with the small projecting boulder. Continue up the right side of the second cavity and to the top on easier (if sideways-sloping) terrain. So named for a large and fat brown dragonfly found hanging out on the route one day.

9. Out Of Position (5.7*)—49 ft. Really a variant on *Dai!*, this route sends you up to the roof a few feet left of *Dragonfly*. Find good finger and handholds to start working the roof, then pull it (a heelhook is ideal) on moderate to great holds (the shorter you are, the more moderate the holds are to pull the roof). Finish by working your way up *Dai!* (or use any variation you can think of above).

10. *Dai!* (5.7+*)—49 ft. As the Italians say, "do it!" Go up over moderate ground until you are approximately 10 feet to the left of the right-end terminus of the roof, beneath a small, left-facing corner/notch. Grab the great flakes and do it! (Watch the small thorn bush concealing some of those good holds.) Once above the roof, continue up on easier but non-trivial terrain, working through the upper cavity, to the top.

11. Alberton Roof (5.9–**)—41 ft. Climb up the ramp until under the intimidating 8 foot roof cut by a thin crack left of a seam, 5 feet left of *Dai!* (**V1**). Reach out right for the bucket in the stacked flakes that form the small left-facing corner and power through the roof on huge holds (be careful, the thinner flat shelf halfway through the upper part of the roof may break), gaining a large horizontal ledge. Once past the roof, climb the face above between two small trees to the top. The upper half of the route is protectable, but you cannot get protection in until you are halfway through the crux. **Classic**.

> **V1: Alberton Roof Right (5.8*)**—45 ft. A slightly easier variation to dealing directly with the intimidatingly large *Alberton Roof*. Start on *Dai!*, but traverse out left on shelves over air when you hit the roof on *Dai!*. Finish on *Alberton Roof*.

12. Moonbeam (5.7*)—41 ft. Pull the overhang right off the ground on good holds and pass a small right-facing corner at the left end of the large roof. Pull the roof directly or slip around on the left end to a large ledge below the next roof above. Pull this second roof and finish on the face above with a small, right-facing crack/flake. The hardest move is probably right off the deck.

13. Buddha Paste (5.8)—41 ft. Start at the left end of the overhang 5 feet off the ground (where the black and light brown rock meet), below the small black oak tree growing out halfway up the rock. Pull this initial overhang using some painfully sharp holds until you reach more forgiving rock (i.e., not so sharp). Climb through the notch just left of the oak tree, then work past a short left-facing corner to the top. Climbing up immediately next to the tree to pass by the notch on the right is a bit easier.

14. A Walk In The Park (5.3)—43 ft.

What you have to do to get to the rock here, and a nice, easy climb, to boot. Climb pretty much anywhere between *Buddha Paste* and the left edge of the blocky, flat arête between RIVER WALL and LEFT WALL. This is a good route for getting used to the type of rock in this area, as well as a good route for beginners to learn to deal with overhangs. You can make this a bit harder by doing variants on the wall, but there's nothing really harder than 5.4.

WOODSTOCK
ROCK

John Kelbel looks ahead to some Agitation *(5.11)*

WOODSTOCK
ROCK

RATINGS BREAKDOWN:

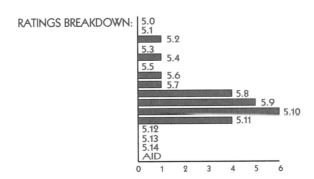

NUMBER OF CLIMBS: **19 plus variations**

SPECIAL NOTE:

"Enjoy beautiful, clean rock with good, Yosemite-like holds."—E. Hörst

"Beautiful clean rock with good, Yosemite-like holds" lie buried **somewhere** beneath all the grit, lichen, moss, spiderwebs, and dirt! This small north-facing crag is a mere 2 to 3 minute walk west along the railroad tracks out of Woodstock, Maryland, a bit more than a mile north of Route 99. It is somewhat larger than Ilchester, but doesn't see anywhere near the level of traffic that Ilchester has (you can tell after your first visit). The rock has far more roofs and overhanging problems than Ilchester, is somewhat taller than Ilchester, but due to the lower numbers of visitors, it is dirtier than Ilchester.
A few hundred more climbers coming here over the course of a month would clean it up pretty well.

While rumor sometimes held that this outcropping was only recently discovered and climbed on, pretty much all of this rock was developed in the late '70s and early '80s by Rob Savoye and Scott McClurg. However, the rag guide they put out came and went, and nothing more existed until the early '90s, when John Kelbel put out his own local photo-copied guide. Since then John has continued developing this rock, and there are a number of variations and new routes that he and others have come up with over the years. Some are repeats of older, unrecorded variations. Only a few of these numerous variations are covered here.

With some effort and cleaning, this crag could be made an afternoon "destination" place once again for the Baltimore climber. John Kelbel has been busy working on this for years—get out there and help him a little. The overhanging rock sports numerous cracks that allow for some very different techniques to be worked out on the rock that you cannot get elsewhere.

LOCATION/DIRECTIONS

From I–695: Head west on I–70 approximately 5 miles to the exit for Route 29 North. Take this exit, and immediately work into the center or left lane (as the road ends 0.1 or so miles after you get on it!) Turn left at the light onto Route 99. Go down Route 99 for 4 miles and turn right onto Woodstock Road. Head north on Woodstock Road for 1.2 miles to the bustling metropolis of downtown Woodstock. The parking area is on the left, just before the railroad tracks (if you crossed the tracks and bridge immediately beyond, you just missed it—turn around).

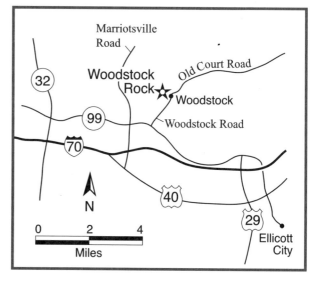

An alternate access is to keep going on I–70 to Exit 83 (approximately 8 miles or so west of I–695), Marriottsville Road, bearing right (north) at the off-ramp. Go approximately 0.75 mile to the traffic light, turn right, go down approximately 0.75 mile, then turn left onto Woodstock Road. After 1.2 miles you'll be at the parking area.

Another option is to get off of I–695 at Liberty Road, travel just shy of 2 miles west on Liberty, and turn left onto Old Court Road. Take Old Court Road south for about 6 miles to the town of Woodstock. Cross the bridge and railroad tracks, and park immediately on the right.

WARNING: there are some people less scrupulous than others who sometimes hang around the parking area, and car break-ins have been known to happen here; take all proper precautions, including keeping valuables out of sight!

Start walking west (the side of the road you are parked on) along the left side of the tracks. A few hundred feet later, when the two sets of tracks merge together at the switching station (first small building you come to on the left), look uphill to your left. You will see in the woods a substantial shadow of rock. The path rises steeply up from near the small building to the rocks. The routes are mainly top-roped, though they can be led or soloed. Who in their right mind would want to **lead** these routes, though….

GEOLOGY

Woodstock Rock is a small outcropping of Baltimore Gneiss making up the large geologic region known as the "Woodstock Dome." Baltimore Gneiss is composed primarily of biotite-quartz-feldspar gneiss and biotite-hornblende gneiss as well as some other types of gneiss complexly intermingled. This Precambrian rock offers good, sharp cracks to jam and solid holds to hang from.

EQUIPMENT

There are beefy trees all along the top of the cliff here. They're just set back a ways from the edge, is all. So you should bring some anchors— stuff in the 60-foot range should suffice for most routes here. There used to be trees closer to the edge, but they were (illegally) removed on the theory that the upper areas of the rock would remain freer from dirt and debris. If you intend on leading any of the routes here, be very knowledgeable in lead climbing techniques and pro placement. This is not a place for the novice leader. Many routes should be considered one level harder (from "G" to "PG," for example, or "PG" to "R") if you are not spot-on in your gear placements.

CAMPING

You're kidding, right? See the Ilchester section for nearby camping options.

John Kelbel psyched to Do What! *(5.10)*

RESTRICTIONS AND ACCESS

There are no known access issues with the area here. Just be careful with your car and some of the seedier locals.

LOCAL EATS

For local spirits there is a tavern, the Ye Old Woodstock Inn, located across the street from the parking area where you can get a drink (beer or whiskey) or some food (a non-climber local praised the ham & cheese sandwiches and greasy pizzas). It is usually frequented by a rather rough crowd (look, **don't** wear pink lycra if you know what's good for you!), so if you want something on the quiet side, your best option would be to head north on Old Court Road 6 miles until you come to Liberty Road. Heading either left or right on Liberty you will find a collection of fast-food and sit-down restaurants scattered about.

OTHER INFO

With the exception of The Cave, the rock tends to stay wet for a few days after a good rain. This is due to seepage from the numerous cracks in the rock. This seepage contributes directly to the holds being so covered with dirt, moss, and lichen. Add to this the seedy looking individuals sometimes found in the parking area, and you'll know why this rock does not see a lot of climber traffic.

Due to the north-facing nature of the rock, Woodstock Rock tends to be more of a late spring to early autumn climbing area. When Ilchester is baking you off the routes, why not come here? Plenty of rock to climb, in and outside of the Cave!

It has been said that if you find an unclimbed outcropping of rock somewhere in the United States, Fred Beckey probably already beat you to it. This adage holds true for the rocks in the Patapsco State Park. Except replace "Fred Beckey" with "Rob Savoye."

The Routes

The routes on the main wall are described from right to left. There are numerous two- or three-move or start/finish variations to many of these routes. Most of them have not been charted (lest this take on the look of Ilchester!) At the far right end of the main rock is a short wall that is ideally suited for bouldering.

1. Intrepid (5.10c) On the far right end of the main rock, climb the center of the face to the overhanging wall near the top (5.9 down low; one trick is a high-step and an undercling plus a crimp, although there are other ways past this). Angle up and left under the largest part of the overhang, climbing through it on horizontals a few feet right of the corner forming the main wall. Find the small right-facing flake; pull on it to reach a knob. Match hands on the knob and reach for a horizontal finger crack. Step up right and roll onto your foot. Topping out is the crux.

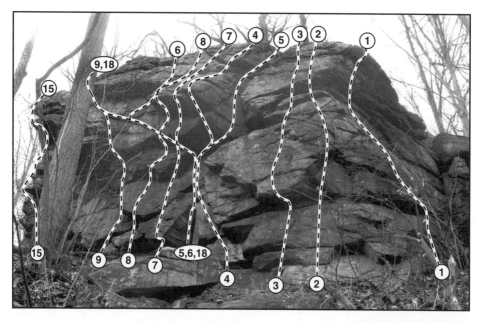

2. Quiver (5.8*) What your leg will probably do at the crux. On the right corner of the main wall, pass a ramp by climbing the shallow arête with a powerful layback in the crack to a ledge. Finish the last couple of moves through ferns on the gray face above. This could potentially be a nice climb—if it were cleaner!

3. Do Or Die (5.10c) Begin at the base of the wall a couple feet left of *Quiver*. Step up on the face below a small 2-foot overhang (**V1**). Pull through the overhang and head directly up the blank face (crux) to the ledge, then finish on the next face above. The name comes from the first ascent party(ies) who rope-soloed the route using a Gibbs Ascender as the belay. Since no one really **trusted** the Gibbs, at the crux it was either move or fall— **do or die**.

> **V1: Do Or Die Indirect (5.7)** Instead of climbing directly up the face, follow under the blocky overhanging left-facing corner until it ends, pulling over the final section of the overhanging corner onto a ledge. Traverse right a few feet and finish on *Do Or Die*.

4. Imagination (5.11b*)—37 ft. Climb the left-facing corner between *Do Or Die* and *Gratefully Dead* until you reach the ledge atop the *Do Or Die Indirect* corner overhang just below the flaring *Gratefully Dead* chimney. From the ledge, aim **far** left to the bottom outer corner of the *Agitation* roof (**V1**) and pull through it using a horizontal crack and a sloper hold higher up, finishing on large holds to the top. An alternate start is to climb the first half of *Gratefully Dead* and finish as described above.

> **V1: Imagine the Agitation (5.11a*)** Climb the first half of *Imagination*, stepping briefly on the *Do Or Die* ledge, then traverse left under the *Agitation* roof, finishing on *Agitation*. Really a one-move connection between these two routes.

5. Gratefully Dead (a.k.a. Orange Juice) (5.6* G)—37 ft. The **original** route at Woodstock! Its name was lost between generations of climbers and more recently it has been referred to as *Orange Juice*. It is pretty clean compared to most of the routes here, although seldom climbed (too easy for most who come here?). Climb through the open book with two triangular faces a few feet left of the start to *Imagination*, then aim right (**V1**) to follow through the flaring chimney to the top.

> **V1: Unnamed (5.8)** Climb partway up the flaring chimney of *Gratefully Dead* corner, then traverse out the left face, around the corner, and onto the slab above the *Agitation* roof. Finish on to the top.

6. Bloody Bucket (5.9* G)—37 ft. It used to be the main route for this area, but doesn't see as much traffic these days. Use the same start as *Gratefully Dead* (**V1**), but instead of heading to the flared corner up and right, follow the crack up to the *Agitation* roof. Continue following the rising crack up and passing left under the roof until the crack splits right. Follow the right-rising crack until above the *Agitation* roof, then top out. The name comes from the hand jam you need to do at the crux, and how the first ascent parties left blood behind on the rock there (this seems to be a common theme for a number of routes in the park). Remember: if it doesn't hurt, you're not doing it right.

> **V1: Bloody Bucket Direct (5.9+*)** A contrived variation, sure. Start at the same point as *Agitation*, but at the first small overhang/right-facing corner move left, then pull the overhang to the crux of *Bloody Bucket*. Finish on *Bloody Bucket*.

7. Agitation (5.10d* R)—37 ft. An excellent problem. Start at the lowest point of the overhang 3 feet left of *Gratefully Dead*. Pull through the overhang, then work up the face above. Move under the left side of the overhang. Step up and layback using the offwidth under the overhang (a kneebar is very helpful), then make a **l-o-n-g** reach up to the bucket in the center of the upper roof. Pull through and finish. First pulled off by John Kelbel in 1991.

8. Stoned (5.10a)—37 ft. Climb the left side of the overhang that marks the beginning of *Agitation* to the face above. Pull the tiered roof system on the left side. And finish on *Bloody Bucket*.

9. The Wimpy Whiner Way (5.9*)—40 ft. Climb the prominent overhanging left-facing corner, following the crack through a small roof. Pull the roof on handles and chick-enheads (warning: the rope has a tendency to get jammed here!) Finish by following the prominent crack up and left to the top. The climb is named both after a coworker some of the original climbers had to work with and because of a "rope trick" one had to do in order to free the jammed rope at the crux (you see, some climbers used to whine about having to jump off the rock to free the rope when it got caught in the crack at the overhang; pay attention so it doesn't happen to you!)

10. Knuckle Peeler (5.11a)—34 ft. Start 3 feet left of *The Wimpy Whiner Way*. Climb the face straight up to the flat, 5 foot roof. Find the finger crack and jam it out under the roof (you'll figure out the name at this point). Make a long reach for the horizontal crack at the end of the roof. Avoid all of the handholds on *The Wimpy Whiner Way*.

11. Do What! (5.10c* R)—33 ft. Start on a couple of short, vertical broken cracks 5 feet left of *The Wimpy Whiner Way*. Climb up until you reach the left side of the large, flat

roof above. Traverse out right along the bottom of the roof to the outside corner, swing around, and pull the roof. Trend right toward *The Wimpy Whiner Way* crack, then follow it up left to the top. A great route. However, be warned: even though protection is adequate, a lead fall at the crux **will** be severe! First led in 1999.

12. Flying Lessons (5.10b)—33 ft. Climb the large, broken crack system 9 feet left of *The Wimpy Whiner Way* to a large hole in the rock. Passing the hole, climb up and stem out the bomb bay roof above to its very end (some rock has broken off from here since the first ascents; **V1**), then follow the flared crack on the right (directly above the left side of the *Do What!* roof). Finish on easier ground. There is a small trick to getting this route.

> **V1: No Fly Zone (5.9)** Climb *Flying Lessons* past the holes and follow the squeeze chimney through the roof above on the left. Finish on easier ground. While easier than *Flying Lessons*, it still has some tricky spots. Find the right holds.

13. Mother F (5.11c)—30 ft. Following horizontal finger/hand cracks, climb the face immediately left of *Flying Lessons* to a small projecting/pointed rock/roof. Pull past this and step left. Climb through the next small overhangs and then follow the thin crack through the 3 foot overhang near the top. The climb is significantly harder than it used to be due to a lot of loose rock being removed from the upper roof over the years. Originally done as a rope-solo in the mid '80s by Rob Savoye, using a Gibbs Ascender as a belay (no, really!)

14. Dyno Man (5.8)—28 ft. Make that leap of faith! At the left end of the main wall, stand on the slabby rock sticking out of the ground and, well, dyno for a good hold at the end of the first overhang. If you don't stick the move, you're going to swing. Yard up and angle left, continuing through overhangs to the top. Dirty, mossy, licheny, but there are good holds hidden about.

15. Dyno Wimp (5.8)—28 ft. At the left end of the main wall, instead of dynoing, climb the shallow arête with slanted holds through the overhangs above to the top. The starting holds are usually exceptionally dirty and often wet.

16. Unnamed (5.4)—15 ft. Starting on a vegetated ledge, midway between *Dyno Wimp* and *The Corner*, clamber up ledges to an overhang with a small hand crack. Pull through the overhang at that point. There is a bashed-in piton by the ferns at the top of this route.

17. The Corner (5.2)—15 ft. Essentially a two-move route. Climb the large inside corner to the right of the obvious cave to a notch at the top. Short and simple, this was often used by the old-timers as a quick boulder-problem/solo to gain access to the top of the rock (instead of walking around). Topping out on this climb is a little tricky, given the amount of dirt and vegetation coming down the notch. This route isn't highly recommended, and is noted only for hysterical (or historical) purposes.

18. The Woodstock Traverse (5.9* G)—46 ft. This rising traverse of the main Woodstock face is pretty nice and fairly protectable, but top-roping is not recommended due to the span of rock it crosses. Begin on *Gratefully Dead*, then climb up and traverse left onto *Bloody Bucket*. Where *Bloody Bucket* turns sharply right, continue following the main crack up and left until you reach the end. A John Kelbel special.

19. The Cave Possibly some of the cleanest stuff here, this spot sees far more traffic than the outcropping—probably owing to the fact that this place stays dry even when it's raining hard outside (though the water will eventually seep through). *The Cave* is located on the left end of the outcropping, around the corner and up hill from the main wall. There are innumerable variations in and around the cave, but only three, Rob Savoye Specials, are noted here. All are at least 5.10 or harder. If you want something different, go and make it up!

Note: someone needlessly put a couple of bolts halfway up the face above the cave (you can top-rope or trad lead anything here; no need for bolts!) Do not trust them as they are not well placed, and the block they are in may or may not be attached to the rest of the wall—you have been warned! Additionally, if you try to lead up to them, you risk ground-fall damage until you successfully clip the bolts.

The Original Route Start 4 feet inside the right side of the cave. Step up to the ceiling and reach out to the 3-inch flake on the center of the ceiling (much of the rock here is now missing, making this significantly more challenging than when it was first done). Without feet touching the ground, hand and heelhook traverse out of the cave to the face above. This can be top-roped with the bolts above, or trees farther back (recommended).

The Standard Route Start in the center of the Cave. Reach up to the broken blocks on the ceiling and flow the main flake system out the center of the cave. Finish on *The Original Route*.

The Long Route Start at the left side of the cave where a thin finger crack is found in the ceiling. Follow the crack to the blocks where *The Standard Route* begins and finish on *The Standard Route*.

All routes finish following the flake system in the center of ceiling, out the roof and up the small left facing corner to the old piton and two bolts (no hangers) at the top. Optionally take on the main face more directly and go for the bolt in the high center of it, halfway to the top.

There are several other bouldering-sized rocks scattered along the ridge in the woods to the east (left as you face the rock) of this outcropping. All have been explored at one time or other, but are undocumented.

CARDEROCK/
GREAT FALLS

Climbers enjoying a sunny afternoon at Bonsai Wall

CARDEROCK/ GREAT FALLS

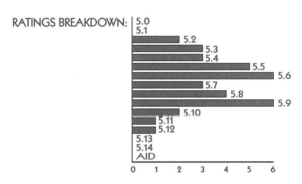

RATINGS BREAKDOWN: 5.0 / 5.1 / 5.2 / 5.3 / 5.4 / 5.5 / 5.6 / 5.7 / 5.8 / 5.9 / 5.10 / 5.11 / 5.12 / 5.13 / 5.14 / AID

NUMBER OF CLIMBS: 33 plus variations

SPECIAL NOTE:

"What does poison ivy look like?"—Deimos

"I dunno. 'Leaves of three, leave them be.'"—Indy

"They all have 'leaves of three'!"—Deimos

No book covering climbing in Central Maryland would be complete without at least mentioning the climbing at Carderock and Great Falls (Maryland). As there are already several fairly comprehensive guidebooks out on the market that cover these two areas, this book makes no pretense at replacing them. Instead herein the two areas mentioned will be covered in brief, spotlighting a few areas. For full details of Carderock and Great Falls (Maryland), I suggest picking up the other guidebooks.

Carderock. For the D.C. region climber, the very name invokes images of slick, polished rock, worn smooth over the years by thousands of climbers. Some people think this is the greatest place in the world to climb. Others will shun it like the plague. You'll have to make your own decisions in this matter. It is, though, very likely the home of the highest concentration of climbers per square foot of rock (at least on the main cliffs). Carderock also hosts climbing on the islands across and upstream from the main climbing area. However, due to access difficulties, people rarely visit these fine crags.

Great Falls has climbing not only on the Virginia side, but also on the Maryland side.

And while there are more and generally taller/steeper routes on the Virginia side, the Maryland rock should not be overlooked—especially on crowded days, as these areas see little climber traffic. Access to some of the rock is problematic and is dependent on the water level (as are some of the routes at Carderock), which probably contributes to the lower popularity levels of these routes. But for the adventurous soul (or sole) willing to get a little wet, it is possible to gain access to a number of routes here even when the Potomac River is running at moderate levels.

Carderock and Great Falls (Maryland) are actually not two unique areas but a collection of crags and outcroppings, a couple of which are well known and heavily visited, and the rest all but lost in obscurity.

LOCATION/DIRECTIONS

Carderock: From the D.C. beltway, I–495, get off at Exit 41 in Maryland and head west on Clara Barton Parkway. There will be signs at this exit for Carderock and Great Falls. Once off the beltway, take the first exit you come to (this will be for the David Taylor Naval Research Center as well as for Carderock). Turn left at the end of the off-ramp and follow the road into the park. At the T-intersection, you can either turn left or right. In order to get to the more popular climbing areas, turn right and follow this road to its end, then park. If you want to explore some of the downstream outcroppings (e.g., CAMP LEWIS) that are not oft visited, turn left and follow this road a short way to its end and park.

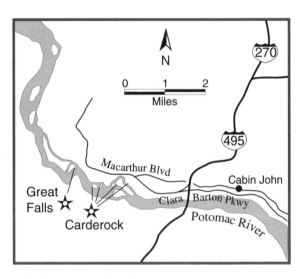

Great Falls, Maryland: Follow the directions as for Carderock above, but do not get off at the first exit. Instead continue down Clara Barton Parkway to its end at a T-intersection (you have a stop sign; please try to stop, as the other drivers will appreciate it). Turn left onto MacArthur Blvd. There are two places for you to park. For the climbing areas on the upstream side of Bear Island, go to the main Great Falls National Park area, located down a turn-off approximately 3 miles after you've turned onto MacArthur Boulevard. For climbs on the downstream end of Bear Island, or on Sherwin Island, park at the Old Angler's Inn parking area (dirt parking area on the left side of the road approximately 1 mile after you've turned onto MacArthur Boulevard), directly across from the Old Angler's Inn restaurant. You would also park here if you were accessing the island climbs around Carderock via boat. Please, do not park in the main restaurant's parking area! And yes, I know parking can get tight around here (many other people besides climbers use this lot), so plan accordingly and arrive early.

GEOLOGY

The rock at Great Falls and Carderock is primarily made up of mica schist and metagraywacke (say that three times fast), punctuated by exposures of quartz nubs (especially around Carderock). The mica schist is the silvery gray rock that contains coarse flakes of mica; the schist component contains small deposits (nubbins in this case) of quartz. The metagraywacke was once a muddy sandstone. Compressed over time, it is now the grayish rock you see around. It is made from a composite of fine grained quartz, feldspar, and mica. You may also find around small areas of amphibolite (metamorphic recrystallized rock composed of amphibole and plagioclase, which is the predominant rock type at Ilchester), granite, and lamprophyre (you'll probably identify the granite before the lamprophyre—unless you're a geologist). There is good friction at most of the rocks in the area—except for the main climbing walls at Carderock due to visitation of the countless hordes of climbers since the '40s.

EQUIPMENT

For most areas in either locale, moderate to long lengths of webbing (20 to 60 feet long) will suffice. A few routes will also take gear for anchors.

CAMPING

There is no overnight camping permitted in either Park. Or even nearby, for that matter. If you are in need of camping facilities, you might ask at Potomac Outdoors for some suggestions as to what options may be available to you.

RESTRICTIONS AND ACCESS

Other than the crowds that can dominate some areas of Carderock, the primary access issues for these two areas here are water levels. If the water's high, getting to some of the routes is problematical at best (**even wading can kill!**) and some of the routes may be half underwater anyway. The only other issue you may have to deal with is foliage (as many of these routes are not frequented very often). Be careful of poison ivy! Finally, if you are heading to the islands, you do need to secure permission to climb on Offut Island from Potomac Outdoors, Ltd. (301-320-1544). The island is privately owned and under their management (contrary to popular misconception, Potomac Outdoors does not own Offut Island). On occasion the island is closed. More often than not, though, you can secure that permission to climb there.

LOCAL EATS

There are very few food options in this area. The Old Angler's Inn restaurant, across from the dirt and gravel lot parking area for Great Falls, is the closest. However, they are rather pricey (you could buy a new rope), and you'll probably leave still hungry. Another option is to head into Cabin John. There is a small shopping center that has a Chinese restaurant (with carry-out and delivery options), a Pizza Hut (delivery), and The Market On The Boulevard (they make great sandwiches in their deli). And if you happen to be in the main section of Great Falls Park, there is a seasonal snack stand near the parking lot.

OTHER INFO

Carderock: The main cliffs (OUTLOOK ROCKS, JUNGLE CLIFFS, HADES HEIGHTS) are easy to get to. Just park and walk in a few hundred feet. Some of the other areas (JAM BOX, CAMP LEWIS) require a longer walk and bushwack along an almost nonexistent trail (assuming you find one at all). Still other areas (notably VASO ISLAND) require wading when the water is low **(note the warning about getting in the water here—even wading can kill!)** or use a raft like they did back in the '40s.

Carderock seems to be the "home" of contrived climbing (although Ilchester possibly holds the crown for having the highest density of routes per square foot of rock). If you are climbing on a given route and use an off-route hold, don't be surprised if a Carderock crag cop shouts up at you to "get back on route!" Most of the local climbers are more forgiving, though.

Soloing is a popular activity amongst a number of the local climbers here. Unfortunately a few of them have attitudes about top-ropers and "tolerate" top-roper presence (and may at the same time just solo through you while you're climbing on a top-rope—beginners beware!)

Carderock has a high concentration of easy and moderate routes for one to learn how to climb. There are a number of climbing schools that take advantage of this and bring their classes to Carderock for outdoor lessons. Due to the crowds, the presence of the climbing schools adds to the competitive atmosphere of getting to the climbs first and camping on them for the day. Some of the schools will allow you to climb on their top-ropes if asked (or

Cat Lazaroff steps up and prepares to Shoot The Rapids *(5.5)*

allow you to drop your ropes next to theirs if they aren't using theirs at that time), but others have been known to section off entire areas of the cliff (top and bottom) for themselves, denying anyone else access to the rock. This happens even if the schools aren't or won't be climbing on the rock in question for hours. Taking beginners out to "teach them the ropes" is a Good Thing. Hogging unused routes so no one else can climb on them to ensure they are available for a select few isn't.

Great Falls, Maryland: There is a Visitor's Center near the main parking area of the Park that has a wealth of information on the canals that were built here and the history of the area. You can also take a "canal ride" by signing up to get on one of the canal tour boats.

There are plenty of other things to do in the Park here. Kayaking in the Potomac River is very popular almost year round. You can hike the Billy Goat Trail, which runs along the outer edge of Bear Island (and ultimately reaches Carderock, several miles downstream from the Park), and you can bike or hike the C&O Canal Tow Path (which extends quite a distance in both directions from the Park).

And for those unenergetic yet nice days where you just want to get outside and sit, both Great Falls and Carderock have picnic areas where you can chill out.

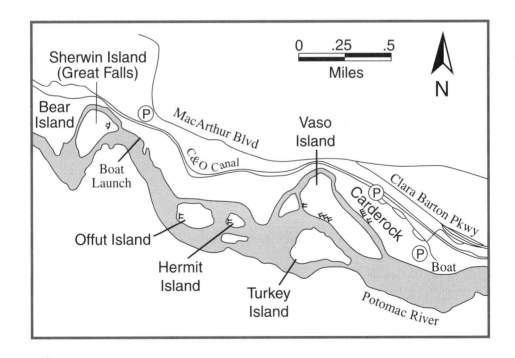

The Routes

The routes are described from left to right as you look at the cliffs, unless otherwise specified. The areas are described from upstream to downstream, starting at Great Falls.

Great Falls, Maryland

It is possible to access most of the routes herein at almost any time of the year. Only a few spots require that you somehow cross a portion of the river. If the water is down, there are ways to do this without getting wet. If the water is up…find a boat! Routes are generally described from upstream to downstream as if facing the rock.

ANGLER'S INN ROCK

This outcrop of rock is located a mere 700 feet upstream from the bridge to access the Tow Path from the Angler's Inn Parking area. There are a couple of stiff little routes on it.

CUPID'S BOWER

This southeast-facing expanse of rock is located on Sherwin Island, just upstream and across from the Angler's Inn Rocks. If solitude is what you are seeking, and you don't want to go far or have time to go far, this is the ideal place. Occasionally you may meet a group of climbers here, but more often than not you'll have the rock to yourself. If you are quiet, you'll very likely encounter wildlife wandering the island. And while you will be fairly isolated from the eyes of passersby, you can still hear hikers and tourists up on the Tow Path, and kayakers paddling about in the river. And sometimes National Airport in D.C. routes the flight paths of airlines directly overhead. You'll be alone, but you can't quite escape the sounds. The

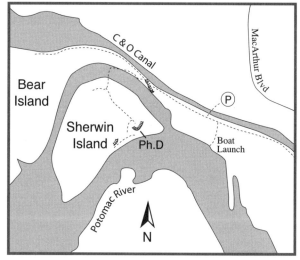

routes are described from left to right, with the prominent *Ph.D.* climb being used as a distance marker between routes. Anchors should be between 10 to 30 feet long.

To access, continue 225 feet past the ANGLER'S INN ROCK outcrop on the Tow Path to a trail leading off to the left. Follow that down to the water. If the water is low, boulder hop across to the island. If the water level is up, you may be doing some wading. In extremely high water you'll either need a boat, or more prudently pick somewhere else to climb. You'll note a broken concrete culvert and some piping at this shallow fording spot. Once on the island, follow the trail up to the right, then head left as the trail forks. Continue in the downstream direction for a couple hundred feet to the rocks at the downstream end of the island (still in the woods, not on the shoreline). If you get lost, 5 minutes of wandering around ought to bring you to the rocks. The island just isn't that big!

In addition to this main outcrop of rock, there are quite a few boulder problems scattered around the island (such as *Superman Overhang*—assuming you can find it). Explore to your heart's content.

In preparation for grad school, Fabrizia Guglielmetti tackles Ph.D. *(5.9)*

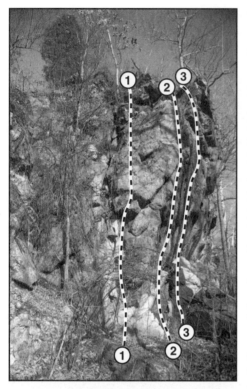

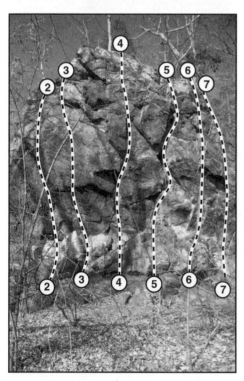

1. Elementary (5.4)—34 ft.
Beginning 29 feet left of *Ph.D.*, climb the featured face to the left and around the corner from *Vo-Tech*. It's a pretty straightforward route.

2. Vo-Tech (5.9*)—34 ft.
This climb goes up the left end of the main rock face, 23 feet left of *Ph.D.* Climb the steep wall immediately right of the arête, following flakes to the top. Using the arête drops the grade down to about 5.7 or so.

3. Waining Strength (5.12b)—33 ft.
Don't get weak! Named after climber Keith Wain, this route desperately follows the faint seam and small left-facing corners 12 feet left of *Ph.D.* through the overhanging wall to the top.

4. Post-Post Ph.D. (5.11b*)—31 ft.
This climb is located halfway between *Waining Strength* and *Ph.D.* Work the variably sized crack up a seriously steep wall (passing a small left-facing corner) until the crack ends. Continue up on larger holds.

5. Ph.D. (a.k.a. Coffin Climb) (5.9+*)—31 ft.
As with any doctoral study, this one doesn't let up until it's over, so you might as well bury yourself in it. Passing a small triangular hole at the start, power up the obvious crack in the overhanging wall through a second triangular hole halfway up to a narrow squeeze chimney (the *Coffin*). Struggle past the chimney to the ledge up top. Even the exit moves are tough. Originally this was climbed in the mid '30s and called *The Coffin Climb*, as the squeeze chimney vaguely represented a casket shape, but it was later renamed to *Ph.D.* when a local and notable climber (Harold Stimson) promised a "Doctorate of Climbing" to anyone who could get up it. The area classic.

6. Post Ph.D. Left (5.10a*)—33 ft.
And you thought your work was done when you got your doctorate! Beginning

6 feet right of *Ph.D.* scramble up the blocks until you are 8 feet off the ground and below an obvious left-facing corner halfway up the wall. Climb up to the corner, continuing up the corner itself, until you reach the upper steep wall. Pull through the overhanging wall to finish.

7. Post Ph.D. Right (5.9*)—33 ft. Sometimes you get lucky with your post-doc work. Follow a crack system 6 feet right of *Post Ph.D. Left* to a small roof. Pass the roof on the right and climb the finger crack to the top.

8. Master's (5.6*)—34 ft. You'll need to have done some studying in order to get this route. Locate the large, left-facing corner containing an offwidth crack 30 feet right of *Ph.D.* Scramble up a notch from the ground, passing to the right of a large oak tree, until you reach a ledge 12 feet off the ground. Using some creative techniques, easily work your way up the corner to the top. Classic. Oh, what creative techniques do you need to make this easy? Well, that's for you to figure out. You do want your *Master's*…don't you?

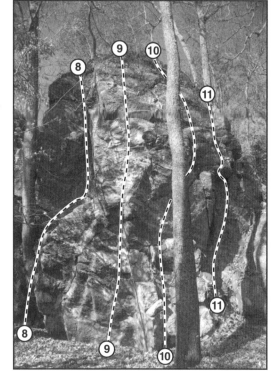

9. Alumnus (5.10b)—32 ft. Beginning 12 feet right of *Master's*, climb the short and thin bulging face to a ledge, finishing on more ledges and almost too-easy ground. More or less a boulder problem, really.

10. Secondary (5.3)—32 ft. Starting 5 feet right of *Alumnus*, scramble up to a small shelf 9 feet off the ground. Continue up the wall, climbing a short (body length) shallow corner to another small ledge. Follow the left-leaning crack past more shelves to the top.

11. Bachelor's (5.3)—32 ft. If **this** route proves too much for you, maybe some remedial training at a gym will help. Climb the system of vertical cracks 4 feet right of *Secondary* to and through a small overhang to the top.

The Islands Of Carderock

Except during times of extremely low water, the only way you can access the islands is by canoe or raft…or wading (danger!) As the islands see very little traffic (due to the logistical hurdles climbers need to surmount in order to get over there), these areas are fairly pristine…and covered with plenty of lichen! The rock quality can vary from solid to friable. The friction qualities of the rock are far higher than on the mainland, where large

numbers of climbers over the decades
have worn the mica schist down to a
smooth polish. So if you want a taste of
what climbing at Carderock was like
60-plus years ago, hit a few routes on
the islands. There are a lot of unnamed
routes in the area primarily because,
well, no one's bothered to name them
(or if they have, they've kept the route
names to themselves). However, while
much of the rock has seen climbers,
there are still first ascents hidden away
here and there (although determining
whether or not something has been
climbed before or not might be a little tricky).

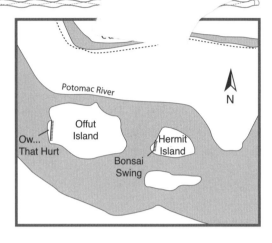

OFFUT ISLAND

This is the first island you come to after a leisurely 5 to 10 minute paddle downstream
from Sherwin Island. The climbing area is the northwest-facing buttress on the upstream
side of the island—staring you in the face as you paddle down toward the island. Most of
the climbing is off to the left section of the rock.

12. Unnamed (5.4)—approx. 30 ft. On the left side of the main wall is a right-facing
corner with a finger crack. Work up the corner and crack system to the trees and ledges
above. Plenty of holds on the main face keeps the climbing relatively easy.

13. Unnamed (unknown)—45 ft. Climb up to the left corner of the roof and work through the left-facing corner onto the face above. Continue on up to the top.

14. Ow...That Hurt Left (5.8*)—45 ft. (57 ft. if the water is very low). Climb part-way up the ramp to the roof. Find a good undercling, reach up left to a solid sidepull and haul onto the face above. Work the face to a ledge below the upper blocky overhang. Climb up through the overhang to the top.

15. Ow... That Hurt (5.6*)—45 ft. Climb the face to the right of the ramp up to the crack system to the right of the *Ow...* roof. Pull through following the crack and head up to the blocky overhang above. A few moves through that and you're done.

16. Unnamed (5.5*)—50 ft. Start at the shallow, left-facing corner slab with the large swath of dirty white quartz. Follow the corner system up and left to a right-facing corner just right of *Ow...That Hurt*. Climb up the right-facing corners to the top.

HERMIT ISLAND

This northwest-facing crag is on the upstream side of the island. Anchors can be problematic, as the trees aren't always large, there really isn't much opportunity to place gear, or the large trees are set back a ways from the edge. You'll do best to bring 40 to 60 foot anchors.

17. Unnamed (5.6+* R)—50 ft. This route ascends the pillar-like separation on the left side of the crag. Starting on the right side of the face, follow the thin crack/flake system up through black patchy rock to the top. Trend left or right as you feel for variety. All the holds are there, although sharp. The crack/flake system begs to be led, but it's not very strong to hold gear if you fall. Check out the solution pockets near the top just left of center.

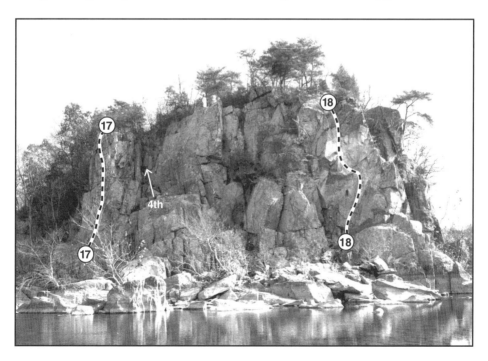

Pierre Dery steps delicately so as to not to slip and take the Bonsai Swing *(5.9)*

Hermit Ascent (4th) This alpine style scramble just right of the previous route will get you to the top of the rock. Take care going up and down here. A fall could seriously hurt.

18. Bonsai Swing (5.9*)—approx. 35 ft. There's nothing jejune about this excellent line. Located on the right end of the northwest-facing wall, it was first climbed by Pierre Dery late in 2001. Delicately work your way up the face and outside arête of the small right-facing corner until you can step left to reach the right end of the overhang. Pull around onto the thin face above the overhang and gain the beautiful perfect finger crack above a small "bonsai" bush growing out of the bottom end of the crack (try not to kill it, okay?) Follow the crack to a corner and onto a ledge. One more move puts you at the top. If the anchors were easier to rig, this would be a great and popular route.

VASO ISLAND

This island is the large one directly across from the main climbing area at Carderock. It is two islands past HERMIT ISLAND, from where you can see the extensive line of rock walls on VASO. Just paddle straight for them, negotiating and dodging rapids as you go. The first rock outcrop is BONSAI WALL, located just past Herzog Island (a small island just upstream a hundred feet from VASO). Directly across the river is TURKEY ISLAND, which has rocks of its own to climb on (beware the rapids when crossing over to it). The bulk of the climbing on VASO is located on the western/southwestern flank of the island. This was a fairly popular area in the 1940s, but the only access one had was by raft or canoe. Covered here is a sampling of areas from VASO ISLAND. Most routes noted here are from the latest generation of climbers, as the locations of the historical ones were poorly recorded (okay, they're lost). Should the locations of these historical routes (such as *Fingertip Balance Climb, The Inside Corner Climb, Arnold's Overhang*, and *Superman's Roof*) come to light once again, hopefully a future edition of a Carderock guidebook or another edition of this guide will carry that information. Until then…explore away!

BONSAI WALL

This outcrop of rock is located at the far southwest corner of this oblong shaped island, directly across from the southeast end of Herzog Island. As with most of the cliffs on the south-southwestern portion of the island, this faces west. The walls don't see a lot of direct sun in winter, but are ablaze in summer. This outcrop sports a half dozen routes of moderate difficulty. The left half of this rock is either overgrown with bushes, trees, or other flora, or is so broken up as to be 4th class at best. The routes basically begin in the center of the outcrop, at a large

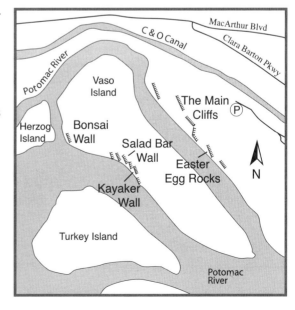

right-facing corner. For anchors here, use the cedar tree at the top, or wrap the boulder near it. There are spots for placing gear anchors as well. The rock tends to be sharp, so pad your anchors well!

19. Juniper (5.7)—45 ft. Start at the base of the large right-facing corner in the center of this outcrop of rock. Climb up the corner, pulling past a roof halfway up (**V1**) and gain a ledge that has a tree. Continue to the top.

> **V1: Juniper Right (5.8)** For fun, when you get to the roof, step right a move or two and pull the roof in the middle. Just a little more tricky than the normal way.

20. Toby's Little Tree (5.5)—45 ft. This fun little route is located to the right of *Juniper*. Starting on a small right-facing corner, climb up to the larger corner higher up and step onto a sloping ledge with a bush. Pull through the roof onto easier ground and finish to the left of the protruding block at the top. A fun route to practice hands-free climbing below the roof.

21. Natal Plum (5.8)—
45 ft. Begin 6 feet right of
Toby's, at another short right-facing corner, under the center of
the main face. Gently maneuver
up the face to the roof high
above. Pull through the roof
using strong side-pulls and finish
with easy moves.

22. Bonsai (5.5)—46 ft.
Start directly below the cedar tree
at the top of the rock, 4 feet right
of *Natal Plum*. Trim your way up
the face, passing by large quartz
nubbles to the left, to a ledge
halfway up. Continue to and
through the small overhang just right of the right-facing corner near the top, and end at the cedar tree. A bit harder than *Toby's*.

23. Chinese Elm (5.8)—46 ft. This bouldery route climbs the rightmost end of the main face, staying right of the quartz nubbles and left of the arête. Use of the arête is legal, especially for the first moves off the deck, as is one of the quartz nub side-pulls. The climbing gets easier once you pass the short face just above the ledge halfway up.

24. Bonzai (5.7)—45 ft. Yee-ha! Charge up the right-facing corner (**V1**) to the right and around the corner from *Chinese Elm* until you get to a huge sloping ledge (you could walk off here). Take a breath, turn left and climb the right-leaning cracks to better (and sharp) holds to reach the top.

> **V1: Bonzai Arête (5.9)** A little bit of Carderock Contrived Climbing here. Simply bestride the arête and ride it to the top. What else to say? Don't slip....

SALAD BAR WALL

Identifiable from the dome-like cap that sits atop the wall (some people see an arrowhead instead; just as long as you can find this rock!), this is one of the taller outcrops along the river. Located more than 800 feet downstream from BONSAI WALL, it has a few established routes on its main face, ranging from 5.4 to 5.7 or so. There isn't much up top for anchors short of slinging the dome-like cap.

NO NAME CRACK WALL

This wall is the major face 250 feet downstream from SALAD BAR WALL with a prominent crack rising up and right from near the center of the wall. There are beefy trees near the top to anchor from. You can access the top by either leading *The Crack With No Name*, or by scrambling up one of the nearby foliage choked gullies. The slabby face to the left of the crack is covered with that dusty lichen, but there are holds and a few routes to play on there.

25. The Crack With No Name (5.4* G)—

approx. 45 ft. There's only one crack on this wall; it's pretty hard to miss! Beginning at the base of a downward-flaring chimney flake system, climb past that and follow the wide layback crack-flake to the top. If you want to lead this, bring large gear!

26. Ventura Highway (5.6*)—48 ft. This route

is located on the wall approximately 50 feet right of *The Crack With No Name*. Work up the center of the face to the right of the blocky right-facing corner, following the left-facing corner/finger flake system to a stance. Finish by climbing the sweet little finger flake to a square notch at the top.

KAYAKER WALL

Downstream 520 feet from SALAD BAR is the first of two enticingly tall walls right on the water. In relatively low water level conditions, this wall has a broad rock for belaying and tying off canoes (et al.) at its base; the wall just downstream to the right does not, making belaying and rope management there a **little** tricky (boat belay—fun!—or top belay). To get to the top of either rock, bushwhack up the gully to the left of KAYAKER WALL then head right in a pleasant wooded environment.

27. Riffle (5.5)—71 ft. Starting just left of the center of the face, climb up to the shallow

right-facing corner, following until it ends at a ledge. Continue up to another ledge halfway up the rock, and climb easy terrain to the top.

28. Shoot The Rapids (5.5)—71 ft. Climb the short crack splitting the center of the face just right of *Riffle* to a small ledge. Continue up on smaller holds (many hidden under the dusty lichen), following a seam to a ledge halfway up. Keep going to the top on easy but lichen covered rock.

29. Against The Current (5.7)—75 ft. Try not to fight it. From the belay boulder, make a delicate 5.7 traverse (crux) above the water to gain the left-leaning finger crack on the right end of the wall, 12 feet right of *Shoot The Rapids*. Follow the discontinuous crack (5.6) up to a ledge with bushes and a small pine tree. Walk left to the prominent blocky corner and follow the corner up to the top. Beware that some of the rock in the upper corner is rotten and prone to breaking—it's a long drop to your belayer if you break one off!

TURKEY ISLAND

This island is located due south of VASO ISLAND, and supports a moderate amount of rock to climb on (there is climbing on both sides of the island). If you've made your way to VASO ISLAND you should be able to easily access TURKEY ISLAND. From the northwest corner of TURKEY ISLAND, the main cliffs of VASO ISLAND are easily visible.

Carderock

PARKING LOT ROCK

This boulder, which stands to the left of the trail leading to the rocks from the parking lot, offers a couple of relatively easy bouldering problems.

OUTLOOK ROCKS

This band of rock is situated right along the river, a bit upstream from the main climbing areas of JUNGLE CLIFF and HADES HEIGHTS. Except for a handful of climbs on the downstream end of the rock band, most of the routes here are not often visited. When the water level is low, there are some nice walls to play on away from the crowds.

Brian Poore works up The Crack With No Name *(5.4)*

JUNGLE CLIFF

Tucked away in the trees, this **heavily** visited stretch of rock is a bit shorter overall than HADES HEIGHTS. But just because it is shorter doesn't mean it's any less popular! Be prepared for crowds, especially after work during the summer (when the sheltering trees take the scorch out of the summer heat), and on the weekends in the fall through spring.

HADES HEIGHTS

This is the tallest of the two most popular areas of Carderock. The main wall (Nubble Face) is often used by cavers for rappel and rope ascending practice during the midweek, and solo climbers at other times. Of the areas close to the parking lot, this gets the most late afternoon sun, and is an extremely popular destination for the local after work and weekend climbing community in the early fall through late spring. But that does not mean people don't visit it during the summer. Be prepared to wait in line if you want to do routes in this area.

EASTER EGG ROCKS

If climbing with the crowds at the main cliffs is starting to be reminiscent of driving on the D.C. beltway, check out these rocks. Isolated and next to the water, and still not that far from the parking lot, this outcrop of rock offers a nice basket of routes to hop on. It's a perfect place to climb on a sunny day in the early spring. The cruxes are all within the first 15 or so feet off the ground. The main face of this rock is marked by the Scoredos' Overhang, a large, 21 foot wide, 4 foot deep (max) roof that is between 6 to 8 feet off the ground.

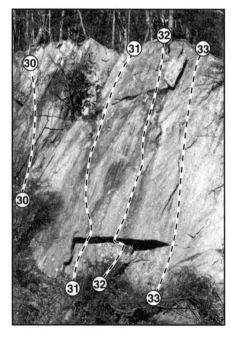

30. Pink Easter Egg (5.2)—25 ft. Climb the short and slabby corner system at the far left end of the main face to the top.

Easter Egg Escape (4th) Scramble up the corner 11 feet right of *Pink Easter Egg*. This offers a quick way out to the top of the cliff (instead of plodding up/down the path around the upstream side of the rocks). It's easier going up than down, though; take care!

31. Green Easter Egg (5.2)—45 ft. This route offers several ways to gain the top. Start at the far left end of the Scoredos' Overhang, at the right-facing corner. Climb up the corner (**V1, V2**) and main face below the roof. Pull through it, making the moves as easy as possible (it is easy to miss moves and make this harder than 5.2), to gain the face above. Follow the main crack up and left, then leap straight to the top on easy ground.

V1: Unnamed (5.3) Start on the face immediately left of the right-facing corner marking the end of the Scoredos' Overhang. Climb up, then delicately step right over the

Overhang/corner to gain the large left-rising crack. Finish as normal. This variant is easier than it first appears as soon as you work out the crossover step on small crystals and ledges to get around the Overhang.

V2: Green Easter Egg Slab (5.6–*) Start 7 feet left of the right-facing corner at the left end of the Scoredos' Overhang, next to a tree. Climb straight up the face, stepping on small nubs or frictioning as needed. Once you gain the ledges higher up, finish on easy ground.

32. Courte Echelle (5.9)—45 ft. Start to the left of the right-facing corner in the center of the Scoredos' Overhang. Climb up to and pull through the Overhang above. Then either hop left, right, or continue straight up the face to the top. For an added challenge down low, you can pull the Overhang at its widest point instead.

33. Blue Easter Egg (5.6*)—42 ft. Beginning at the right end of the Overhang (**V1**), climb up to the shallow right-facing corner. Either step left and layback up the crack, or follow the shallow corner up, paralleling the crack to your left. Higher up, follow the crack as it hops left, then hops right to the top. The crux is in the beginning, but the middle section is no slouch if you're not paying attention.

V1: Unnamed (5.5) This "variant" is really a stand-alone climb. Starting 6 feet right of the Scoredos' Overhang, climb the face past a few small inverted ledges to the nubbles higher up. Finish on this easier terrain.

JAM BOX

This outcropping of rock is visible just downstream from EASTER EGG ROCK, maybe a couple hundred feet away. It offers a small number of lines.

CAMP LEWIS

This is a long walk for a handful of short (and now heavily overgrown) climbs. Still, it's nice to escape the crowds once in a while, isn't it? Even this close to Washington, D.C. To gain access to this area, park at the far downstream parking lot (to the left as you entered the Park and hit the T-intersection) then begin walking down the Tow Path for a while. However, if you have a boat (canoe, kayak, whatever), there are better options for escaping the crowds (see The Islands of Carderock earlier).

LOCK 10 BOULDERS

Downstream from CAMP LEWIS and inside the beltway are a number of boulders scattered in the woods, hosting problems such as *V* and *Reverse V*. The numerous problems are not detailed in this guide. Stay on the mainland, though; the one island is off limits and privately owned (as are many of the islands inside the beltway). If you explore but cannot find the mainland rocks, polite inquiries to other local climbers will direct you to them. The easiest is to park at the Lock 10 parking spot, hike upstream to Lock 11, then cut in past the white building and work your way to the Potomac. Just as you can see the water's edge, turn right and start peering through the underbrush. The rocks are most easily found between late fall and early spring. In the summer, forget it (unless you already know where they are!)

SIDE PULL —

UNDER CLING —

LINE —

HAND JAM —

ANOREXIC HOLDS —

RAPPEL ~

PUMPY —

GEAR —

HEEL HOOK —

FISSURE —

HORN —

V NOTCH ~

SWING —

GROUND FALL —

FINGER LOCKS —

RIDGE LINE —

CONTRIVED ROUTE —

LEAD CLIMBING —

SOLO CLIMBING ~

Recommended Routes:
When Only The Best Will Do

"It's fun to reach down and pull on the flake, causing all your gear to fall out and your belayer to panic."—Eric Cook, describing the expanding flake on Strawberry Jam

Time is short—with so many options, where do you go? Arranged by area, below are some of the best routes (in this book) for you to enjoy. This is the ultimate Maryland tick list—have fun!

Alberton Rock
Alberton Roof 5.9–

Annapolis Rocks
Black Crack 5.9
Cynosure 5.10b/c
Faint's Roof 5.10a
Nixon's Nose A1
Ounce Of Perception 5.9
The Dragon 5.10a
Trantor 5.6

Black Rocks
No Surrender, No Retreat 5.10a

Carderock/ Hermit Island
Bonsai Swing 5.9

Friction Wall
40 Weight 5.10b

Ilchester
Blue Rose . . . . 5.8+
Ninja 5.11d

Maryland Heights
B–1 Climb 5.3
Dee's Rival 5.4

Raven Rock Hollow
Aquafina 5.4
Deer Park 5.6
No Caws For Alarm 5.7

Right Fork Rocks
Witch's Tit 5.10a
The Boulder Problem 5.10b

Rocks State Park
Breakaway Green Scar 5.10a
Breakaway Right 5.9
Smoke 'N' Ash 5.11a
Strawberry Jam 5.8
Vertical 5.6

Sugarloaf Mountain
A Flake Called Lee 5.5
Bloodguard . . . . 5.9+
Rhythm Roof 5.9
Reprise De La Bastille 5.4
Seven Wishes 5.6
Slow And Easy 5.7

The Fin
Hawkeye 5.7

White Rocks
Force Ten 5.10b/c
Hubble 5.11c/d
The Sherpa Connection 5.8

Wolf Rock
Eye Of The Mind 5.9
May The Force Be With You 5.8

Woodstock Rock
Agitation 5.10d
Bloody Buckets 5.9

Ilana's Guide To Climbing Shoes For Everybody

	Beginner	**Novice**	**Competent**	**Expert**
Who:	Your SO who thinks you're crazy but is willing to try it.	Has actually climbed on rock, knows what 'friends' are.	Knows who Derek Hersey and Christian Griffith are.	Friends are Derek Hersey and Christian Griffith.
Does:	Climbs 5.4, eyes closed, screaming.	Climbs 5.9, still screams sometimes.	Climbs 5.11, no more screams.	Solo 5.11
Shoe Fit:	Comfortable.	Snug.	Tight.	Cuts off circulation
Size:	Same as sneakers.	A size smaller.	Would fit Cinderella.	Would fit a four-year-old.
How:	Arms give out long before feet hurt.	Feels good to take them off at the end of the day.	Loosens shoes at each belay stance.	Must soak feet in hot tub at end of 1 pitch.
Quote:	"Are you sure I'm not going to kill myself?"	"I bet I'd climb 5.10 if my shoes were tighter."	"I bet I'd climb 5.12 if my shoes were tighter."	"Could you look and tell me if my feet are still there?"

—compliments of Ilana Stern, Cliff Swallow of Colorado

Bibliography: Further Reading

"Annapolis Rocks Guide." Savoye, Rob. Online web guide. Early 1990s.

Carderock Big Wall: The Ultimate Guide to Rock Climbing at Carderock. Borotkanics, Robert. Self-published. 2001.

Carderock: Past & Present, A Climbers Guide. Potomac Appalachian Trail Club Mountaineering Section. Edited by Selma I. Hanel. 1990.

Climber's Guide to Carderock. Gregory, John Forrest. S&S Printing, Inc., 1980.

Climbers' Guide to the Great Falls of the Potomac. Potomac Appalachian Trail Club Mountaineering Section. Edited by James A. Eakin. 1985.

Climbers' Guide to the Great Falls of the Potomac. Potomac Appalachian Trail Club Mountaineering Section. 2nd ed. Edited by Alex Tait. 2001.

"Climbing in the Baltimore, Maryland Area." Savoye, Rob. Online web notes. Mid 1990s.

ES 3: Caves of Maryland. Franz, Richard and Slifer, Dennis. Maryland Geological Society, 1976.

"A Guide to Rock and Ice Climbs in the Washington, DC, Area." Klapatch, Ken. Draft manuscript. Hukum & Skruum, 1990.

"Leakin Park." Kelbel, John. Self-typed guide. Early 1990s.

"Maryland Heights Guidebook." Savoye, Rob. Online web guide. Early '90s.

Maryland's Geology Schmidt, Martin F. Jr. . Tidewater Publishers, 1993.

Mountaineering: The Freedom of the Hills, 6th Ed. Graydon, Don and Hanson, Kurt, ed. The Mountaineers (self-published), 1997.

Nearby Climbing Areas, Third Edition. Canter, Rob & Kathy. 1980.

RI 27: The Geology of the Crystalline Rocks Near Baltimore and Its Bearing on the Evolution of the Eastern Maryland Piedmont. Crowley, William Patrick. Maryland Geological Society, 1976.

RI 55: Lithostratigraphy of the Western Blue Ridge Cover Rocks in Maryland. Brezinski, David K. Maryland Geological Society, 1992.

Rock Climbing: Virginia, West Virginia, and Maryland. Hörst, Eric J. A Falcon Guide. The Globe Pequot Press, 2001.

Rock 'n' Road: Rock Climbing Areas of North America. Toula, Tim. Chockstone Press (now published by The Globe Pequot Press), 1995.

"Rocks State Park, Maryland" Mistarka, Ed. Online web guide. 1996.

"Sugarloaf Mountain & Other [Central] Maryland Areas." Kochte, Mark ("Indy"). Online web guide. 1990–2002.

"Topo Guide for Frederick Watershed Area." King, George. Draft manuscript. Late 1980s.

"Woodstock Rock." Kelbel, John. Self-typed guide. Early/mid 1990s.

Routes Indexed by Area

The Fin

Weverton Overlook

White Rock

White Rocks

Wolf Rock

Woodstock Rock

Routes Indexed by Rating

5.5

5.6

5.7

5.8

5.11

5.12

5.13

Aid climbs

Bouldering

Unrated

Afterword

"The obvious usually needs to be stated at least once. "—Michael Llaneza

W hen I first undertook the project of turning the website into an actual guidebook, I had no idea what I was getting into. I knew there was a lot of climbing scattered about in Maryland, but I had **no** idea of just **how much** climbing there truly was! And in the course of writing this book, a few new, untouched areas were discovered. New routes are still going up in already well-known/well-traveled areas (e.g., *Hidden Art* and *Yoda's Vision* at FRICTION WALL, *Knuckle Peeler* at WOODSTOCK ROCK, *Bonsai Swing* on the GREAT FALLS/CARDEROCK islands). In the 60-plus years of climbers exploring in Maryland, no one had any idea of the amount of climbing that this state offers. This book gives the first view of this potential. Maryland is not tapped out. There's plenty of rock out there for all of us to share and enjoy. I hope you have as much fun exploring some of these places you've never heard of as I had when I was first visiting them. Be safe, and climb on!

Mark Kochte